TRADE UNIONS,
THE LABOUR PARTY
AND THE LAW

K. D. EWING

———

TRADE UNIONS,
THE LABOUR PARTY
AND THE LAW

A STUDY OF THE TRADE UNION ACT
1913

EDINBURGH UNIVERSITY
PRESS

© K. D. Ewing 1982
Edinburgh University Press
22 George Square, Edinburgh

Set in Linoterm Plantin by
Speedspools, Edinburgh, and
printed in Great Britain by
Redwood Burn Limited, Trowbridge.

British Library Cataloguing
   in Publication Data
Ewing, K.D.
Trade unions, the Labour Party and the law
1. Great Britain. Trade Union Act of 1913.
2. Trade-unions—Great Britain—Finance
3. Trade-unions—Great Britain—Political
I. Title
331.87′35   HD8395

ISBN 0 85224 436 3 (paperback)
      0 85224 453 3 (hardback)

The cover photograph is reproduced by
courtesy of The Scotsman Publications Ltd

CONTENTS

PREFACE

This book is a study of the Trade Union Act 1913, which is the principal source of regulation of the financial links between the trade unions and the Labour Party. The book examines the Act from three different perspectives. The first is historical, with Part One being an examination of the background to and the reasons for the enactment of the Act. Secondly, the study looks at the Act from a legal perspective, examining in Part Two problems that arise for the lawyer in its administration and adjudication. Finally, Part Three looks at wider issues and considers the effect of the Act on the relationship between unions and the party and addresses arguments for its reform. The main issue that this section of the book considers is one that is conveniently overlooked by modern critics of the present law. The fundamental question is not *how* but *why* trade union political spending should be regulated.

This book is the product of my doctoral thesis, which began life in 1976 at Trinity Hall, Cambridge, under the supervision of Dr Patrick Elias. To him I owe a great debt, particularly for his example of intellectual integrity. I would also like to thank Professor D.N. Mac-Cormick, Professor A.W. Bradley, Dr W.B. Creighton, Dr Paul O'Higgins and Professor Reuben Hasson for their encouragement at various stages in the preparation of this volume. The staff of the Certification Office were very helpful with the provision of information; trade union and Labour Party officials responded with patience and kindness to my persistent demands on their time; and the staff of Edinburgh University Press provided invaluable assistance in the later stages of production. Chapter 6 of the book appeared in the *British Journal of Industrial Relations* and is reproduced with the permission of the editor. Finally, I record my debt to Gail and Kate, who in different ways encouraged me in the writing of this work and accepted its intrusion into their lives. The book is dedicated to my mother and father.

Keith Ewing
5 September 1982

ABBREVIATIONS

ACTT	Association of Cinematograph, Television and Allied Technicians
AEU	Amalgamated Engineering Union
AFL	American Federation of Labor
ALP	Australian Labor Party
APEX	Association of Professional, Executive, Clerical and Computer Staff
ASB	Amalgamated Society of Boilermakers, Shipwrights, Blacksmiths and Structural Workers
ASLEF	Associated Society of Locomotive Engineers and Firemen
ASRS	Amalgamated Society of Railway Servants
ASSET	Association of Supervisory Staffs, Executives and Technicians
ASTMS	Association of Scientific, Technical and Managerial Staffs
ATWU	Amalgamated Textile Workers' Union
AUEFW	Amalgamated Union of Engineering and Foundry Workers
AUEW	Amalgamated Union of Engineering Workers
AUEW-TASS	Amalgamated Union of Engineering Workers (Technical, Administrative and Supervisory Section)
BALPA	British Air Line Pilots' Association
BIFU	Banking, Insurance and Finance Union
BISAKTA	British Iron, Steel and Kindred Trades' Association
CAWU	Clerical and Administrative Workers' Union
CIO	Committee for Industrial Organisation
COHSE	Confederation of Health Service Employees
COPE	Committee on Political Education
CTU	Conservative Trade Unionists
DATA	Draughtsmen's and Allied Technicians' Association
EAT	Employment Appeal Tribunal
EETPU	Electrical, Electronic, Telecommunication and Plumbing Union
EIS	Educational Institute of Scotland
EPCA	Employment Protection (Consolidation) Act 1978

ETU	Electrical Trades' Union
FBU	Fire Brigades' Union
FTAT	Furniture, Timber and Allied Trades' Union
GFTU	General Federation of Trade Unions
GMWU	General and Municipal Workers' Union
IRSF	Inland Revenue Staff Federation
ISTC	Iron and Steel Trades' Confederation
LRC	Labour Representation Committee
MFGB	Miners' Federation of Great Britain
MNAOA	Merchant Navy and Airline Officers' Association
NACODS	National Association of Colliery Overmen, Deputies and Shotfirers
NALGO	National and Local Government Officers' Association
NATSOPA	National Society of Operative Printers, Graphical and Media Personnel
NATTKE	National Association of Theatrical, Television and Kine Employees
NAUSA	National Amalgamated Union of Shop Assistants
NDP	New Democratic Party
NGA	National Graphical Association
NUAAW	National Union of Agricultural and Allied Workers
NUB	National Union of Blastfurnacemen
NUBE	National Union of Bank Employees
NUDBTW	National Union of Dyers, Bleachers and Textile Workers
NUFLAT	National Union of Footwear, Leather and Allied Trades
NUHKW	National Union of Hosiery and Knitwear Workers
NUIW	National Union of Insurance Workers
NUM	National Union of Mineworkers
NUPE	National Union of Public Employees
NUR	National Union of Railwaymen
NUS	National Union of Seamen
NUSMW	National Union of Sheet Metal Workers
NUT	National Union of Teachers
NUTGW	National Union of Tailors and Garment Workers
PLP	Parliamentary Labour Party
POEU	Post Office Engineering Union
RCA	Railway Clerks' Association
REOU	Radio and Electronic Officers' Union
RSD	Reports of Selected Disputes referred to the Chief Registrar of Friendly Societies 1938–1949
SDP	Social Democratic Party

SLADE	Society of Lithographic Artists, Designers, Engravers and Process Workers
SOGAT	Society of Graphical and Allied Trades
STUC	Scottish Trades Union Congress
SWMF	South Wales Miners' Federation
TGWU	Transport and General Workers' Union
TSSA	Transport and Salaried Staffs' Association
TUC	Trades Union Congress
TULRA	Trade Union and Labour Relations Act 1974
TWU	Tobacco Workers' Union
UAW	United Auto Workers
UCATT	Union of Construction, Allied Trades and Technicians
UPW	Union of Post Office Workers
USDAW	Union of Shop, Distributive and Allied Workers

PART ONE

THE BACKGROUND OF
THE 1913 ACT

THE EMERGENCE
OF THE LABOUR PARTY

EXCLUSION FROM POWER

In their classic work, *Industrial Democracy*, the Webbs tell us that 'an Act of Parliament has, at all times, formed one of the means by which British Trade Unionists have sought to attain their ends'.[1] In the eighteenth century, many groups of workers relied upon legislation to regulate working conditions and although working people did not at that time enjoy the franchise,[2] 'the majority of the educated and the governing classes regarded it as only reasonable that the condition of labor should be regulated by law'.[3] Yet by the early nineteenth century such tactics on the part of trade unions had all but ceased, and the period 1800 to 1867 is usually represented by historians as one dominated by a trade union movement passive in all things political. Indeed, one authority goes so far as to identify the mid 1860s as one in which trade unions were 'converted' to political action.[4] There is little evidence of the unions seeking to use legislation as a means of regulating the conditions of employment during this period, and there was apparently little trade union involvement in contemporary political movements.

There are several factors which may help to explain this lack of interest in politics. In the first place, the predominance of the doctrine of laissez-faire meant that it was no longer worthwhile for the unions to seek the regulation of their trades by legislation. Pressure for legislation involved not inconsiderable cost, and as the Webbs point out, 'it soon came to be a waste of money to organise petitions, to send up delegates and witnesses, or to pay the fees of solicitors and counsel, only to be met by a doctrinaire refusal to go into the merits of the case'.[5] Secondly, it seems that there may have been powerful institutional pressures militating against a trade union commitment to contemporary political issues. An embryonic movement was more concerned with building up membership and with techniques which had a much more direct bearing upon the improvement of working conditions. It was thought that politics would serve only to dissipate resources and generate internal dissension. Fears of this nature were confirmed by the mild flirtation of some unions with Chartism in its early stages: 'no politics' rules were introduced in many cases for the first time after 1842.[6]

Yet although there is much evidence to support the view that trade unions took little interest in politics in these years, like many other generalisations this can be overstated. A continuous thread of political involvement and aspiration can be found woven into the pattern of trade union activity, albeit not as a central part of the movement. The period saw the development of radical and at times revolutionary union methods, for although Marxist political thought did not begin to emerge until well into the latter half of the century, it is clear that the unions were inspired from time to time by less mature socialist ideas. Perhaps the best known illustration of the influence of such ideas was the Grand National Consolidated Trades' Union which unsuccessfully sought to create one mass union of which all working people would be members. The union, influenced by the thought of Robert Owen, was based upon the perceived need to destroy the economic power of the capitalist, and it considered the idea of a general strike to achieve this object.[7]

Cole has suggested that such radical action by trade unions was inevitable, arguing that where workers are voteless, working class political movements are bound to take a revolutionary form.[8] There can be, he says, no democratic working class party seeking reforms by constitutional means. Yet the unions did resort to conventional political techniques and they continued to lobby Parliament with their grievances. But, because union members did not yet enjoy the franchise, the effectiveness of trade union political action depended upon the unions finding a sympathetic member of Parliament to promote their cause or upon a benevolent government minister who was prepared to meet them and listen to their grievances. Perhaps the best known, and by all accounts the most significant, lobby conducted by the unions in this period related to their attempt to reform the master and servant laws. Workers smarted under the liability of imprisonment for breach of contract while employers were subject to the theoretical possibility of civil action. Simon records how the master and servant laws were one of the great union grievances of the period, alluding to the patent injustice of the legal provisions and also the incredible magisterial bias in the operation of the law.[9] In the years 1858–75, there was an average of 10,000 prosecutions per annum in England and Wales alone.

The movement for reform started in Glasgow in 1863 but soon embraced wider interests. Unlike earlier trade union lobbies, which tended to be organised on a sporadic and sectional basis, those organising the campaign for reform of the master and servant laws sought to build up a powerful mass movement. A national organisation was formed and individual trade unions were asked to contribute to a fund to meet the expenses of the campaign. Petitions were collected, Parliament was lobbied, and a sympathetic member of Parliament was found to introduce a Bill. The persistence of the campaign was rewarded when in 1865 the government first agreed to receive a deputation of trade union leaders to discuss the issue and then appoint a Select Committee to examine the question. The recommendations of the latter were implemented in the Master and Servant Act 1867 which although retaining a criminal sanction for breach of contract, replaced the penalty of imprisonment for the most part by fines. The worst feature of the law was thus remedied, though the Act was nevertheless a bitter blow to the trade unions which had demanded a radical reform rather than simply a relaxation of the law. Yet despite this disappointment, the Act did represent a success for the unions in the political field and the campaign had a number of important spin-offs. The first was that it acted as a catalyst for the creation of a permanent body to perform a similar lobbying function on more general issues of concern to the labour movement. Equally important, it did much to increase the confidence of the unions in parliamentary action.[10] The 1867 Act had been secured despite the mobilisation of some employers in an endeavour to maintain the status quo.[11] So there was no reason to feel now that the union case would always fail to receive a fair hearing. The spirit of optimism which the 1867 Act helped to create could only have been enhanced by the extension of the franchise to many trade unionists in the year of their limited triumph.

FRANCHISE REFORM

Extension of the franchise to the working class was crucial to the development of the trade union political programme. A trade union movement whose members were armed with the right to vote could much more readily secure concessions by political action. Lack of voting power did not mean however that trade unions were totally powerless. There was always, it seems, a sympathetic member of Parliament willing to take up the claims of labour and, as we have seen, the task was not always a futile one. Furthermore, as Pelling points out: 'It was always the case that a strong demonstration of support for a particular candidate, even by non-electors, could have some influence at the hustings, for the voting took place in public. Thus, even before 1867, if the unions chose to take a definite stand at an election there was a chance of their doing so to some purpose.'[12] But before the unions could wield effective political power, the franchise had to be extended to their members.

Yet for much of the nineteenth century trade unions were politi-

cally dormant. Musson argues that in relation to the reform movements culminating in the Representation of the People Act 1832:
'There simply is not enough evidence to be dogmatic on this point,
but such evidence as there is tends to suggest that trade societies did
not generally involve themselves in politics, though many of their
members certainly were Radicals as well as trade unionists'.[13] Similarly, the classical view of the union connection with Chartism, one of the
six demands of which was universal suffrage, is that there is 'no reason
to believe that the Trade Unions at any time became part and parcel of
the [Chartist] Movement'.[14] The Webbs reinforce this conclusion by
noting that Fergus O'Connor, the Chartist leader, complained that
union failure to subscribe to Chartist funds was 'criminal apathy'.[15]
Other writers have noted that trade unionism and Chartism drew on a
common basis of support, but accept the Webbs' argument that the
institutional relationship was never close.[16] While there is little evidence to suggest that the established position is incorrect, some
historians are beginning to urge caution, suggesting that the weak and
unorganised trades took refuge in politics during this period.[17] And
while it is thought that the strong and well organised trades generally
held aloof from politics, relying more on traditional trade union
action, it is further contended that in the case of Chartism, 'political
involvement may have become rather wider'.[18]

But the general position would seem to be that in relation to both
Chartism and the reform movement culminating in the Representation of the People Act 1832, the trade unions were diffident. The
same diffidence was evident in the 1860s when the pressure for the
second Reform Act was beginning to gather momentum. Historians
have traced the period of the early 1860s as one in which trade union
leaders, themselves actively involved in the political movements of the
time, were constantly frustrated in their efforts to lead their unions
into the political arena.[19] Indeed, there is some controversy among
historians whether there was any corporate trade union involvement
in the reform movement at all. But while most historians now accept
that there was some such involvement, there are differences of opinion
as to when and why the unions became involved. The view which
seems to command most support is that the unions became involved
only towards the end of the campaign, largely in response to a series of
events which struck at the very heart of trade unionism. In other
words, union participation in the reform campaign which culminated
in the Representation of the People Act 1867 was largely a reaction to
their own insecurity.

Despite the warmth of some middle class groups, the weight of
public opinion in the mid 1860s was hostile to trade unionism. The
British economy was suffering from a period of recession and trade

unionism provided an obvious scapegoat.[20] Union outrages in Sheffield and in other industrial centres had shocked the nation. It is not surprising then that the unions should be gripped with the fear that hostile legislation was imminent. At the same time, the status and security of the unions was being undermined by the courts in a manner which only Parliament could remedy. Trade unions had registered their rules under the Friendly Societies Act 1855 in the belief that this provided them with a summary procedure for the recovery of money misappropriated by any officer of the union. But in *Hornby* v. *Close*,[21] an action by way of the statutory procedure to recover £24 from the secretary of the Bradford branch of the United Society of Boilermakers, it was held that this procedure could not be used by the union because it was established for an illegal purpose, being in restraint of trade and against public policy. So the unions were effectively denied any redress against officials who embezzled their funds. This was a great blow to the status of the unions, now clearly legal outcasts, despite having tried so hard to be accepted by the Victorian establishment. Equally it was a threat to their security. In typically graphic fashion, the Webbs commented 'the hard-earned accumulations of the larger societies, by this time amounting to an aggregate of over a quarter of a million sterling, were at the mercy of their whole army of branch secretaries and treasurers, any one of whom might embezzle the funds with impunity'.[22]

Although the unions had been slow to commit themselves to the reform agitation, their support, once given, proved to be decisive. More than one authority has observed that the union awakening was crucial in convincing the government of the need to settle the reform question with dispatch. However, the final outcome, the Representation of the People Act 1867, was a temperate measure, for although it increased the electorate by 88 per cent, it clearly did not change the United Kingdom into a democracy overnight. It was only the borough franchise which was extended and it was not until the Representation of the People Act 1884, some eight years later, that similar measures were extended to the counties. Moreover, a property qualification was retained with the right to vote depending upon whether or not the citizen occupied, either as owner or tenant, any dwelling house within the borough, and if so whether he was liable to be assessed for the poor rate. Yet the unions had no reason to be pessimistic about the content of the Act, for as Cole has argued, it was drastic enough to change profoundly the balance of forces in Parliament and to compel both parties to frame their policies for the future with more regard to the needs of the working class. And he continued, the unions had secured for the first time a place in the electorate large enough, if they chose to make use of it, to make them a formidable parliamentary force.[23]

THE EMERGENCE OF THE TUC

So henceforward, if the unions could mobilise the working class vote, neither party could afford to ignore them. This realisation was apparent as early as 1868 when the unions began flexing their electoral muscles by impressing upon their members the importance of registering their names as electors and of voting for those candidates who would promote their interests as trade unionists.[24] However, the immediate need of the trade unions was for the development of a pressure group which could effectively organise their new political power to deal with the crisis which the movement now faced. In 1867, in response to the public hostility to trade unionism mentioned above, a Royal Commission was appointed to examine the trade union question.* It was widely anticipated that the Commission would emerge as an instrument of repression. At the same time, the courts were continuing to restrict the legal framework in which trade unions could legitimately operate. In one particularly notable case, it had been held to be illegal to participate in a picket which 'was calculated to have a deterring effect on the minds of ordinary persons, by exposing them to have their motions watched, and to encounter black looks'.[25]

The political campaign which was undertaken by the unions to deal with this crisis was conducted by a small group of London-based leaders of the so-called New Model Unions.[26] It was this group which organised as the Conference of Amalgamated Trades and which the Webbs labelled as the Junta. The Junta were assisted in their campaign by a group of middle class allies who were disciples of Comte, the French positivist. The latter group not only played a vital part in shaping the strategy which the unions adopted, they also had access to important avenues of influence. The group was represented at Westminster by Thomas Hughes and one of their number, Lushington, was engaged at the Home Office as permanent counsel to advise on the

---

* The terms of reference of the Commission were as follows: 'to inquire into and report on the Organization and Rules of Trades Unions and other Associations, whether of Workmen or Employers, and to inquire into and report on the effect produced by such Trades Unions and Associations on the Workmen and Employers respectively, and on the Relations between Workmen and Employers, and on the Trade and Industry of the Country; with power to investigate any recent acts of intimidation, outrage, or wrong alleged to have been promoted, encouraged, or connived at by such Trade Unions or other Associations, and also to suggest any improvements to be made in the law with respect to the matters aforesaid, or with respect to the relations between Workmen and their Employers, for the mutual benefit of both parties.'
(*Parliamentary Papers*, 1868-1869, vol. XXXI.)

drafting of bills. Moreover, although the government refused to nominate any trade unionists to serve on the Commission, it permitted the unions to nominate Frederick Harrison, one of the positivists, to sit on the Commission as someone likely to be sympathetic to their cause.

The first task of the Junta was to convince the Royal Commission that not all unions participated in or condoned the activities alleged to have taken place in the name of trade unionism in Sheffield and in other industrial centres. In this, the leaders of the large unions of skilled craftsmen were successful, being able to convince the Commission that their organisations were primarily national friendly societies which, far from fomenting strikes, were mainly occupied as insurance companies. Consequently, the reports of the Commission did not shed an unfavourable light upon trade unions as many people had anticipated, and their publication led to a marked change in public opinion on the trade union question.[27] The Junta's second task was to secure legislation to deal with the judicial attacks upon trade unions and their activities. It was here that Harrison played an important role. It is often recorded that he did much to persuade the Commission to modify its anti-union tone and, on succeeding, how he refused to sign the Majority Report. Instead, he and two colleagues wrote a Minority Report which 'exposed in terse paragraphs the futility of the suggestions made by the majority'.[28] Harrison's view was that restrictive legislation should be removed from industrial relations and that henceforward 'we must cease to legislate' on the trade union question.[29] He also argued that it was not enough that trade unions were simply legalised; they should retain to the full their exceptional legal privilege, namely that no action could be brought against them in a corporate capacity. Mere legalisation, he pointed out, would place an easy weapon in the hands of employers.[30]

In their campaign to project these ideas into law, the Junta were joined by the Trades Union Congress which had met for the first time in 1868 at the initiative of the Manchester and Salford Trades' Council.[31] The sponsors anticipated that this would be the first of annual congresses which would permanently represent and voice the opinions of the whole of the trades of the United Kingdom on all questions of general trade union interest. The success of this initiative can be attributed to the crisis of the 1860s which gave the final impetus to the demand for a national platform which was representative of the entire trade union movement. Trade union unity had been fostered by earlier unsuccessful attempts to establish a similar type of forum, and in the 1860s by the rapid growth of the trades councils in towns and cities throughout the country. As Musson has argued, a united platform which represented a national movement was a natural development from the local trades councils.[32] Moreover, as Musson also points out, the emergence of the TUC 'is evidence of the growing desire for some representative body to voice general trade union opinion, and of dissatisfaction with the narrow control of the Junta'.[33]

Although the Junta initially refused to participate in the affairs of the TUC, by 1871 they were actively involved in its activities. The Congress of 1871 was held in London so that members of Parliament could be lobbied to ensure that the impending trade union legislation was consistent with the demands of the unions. When the goverment published its proposals to give the trade unions legal status, but retain criminal sanctions for picketing, they met an angry response from the union leaders: 'Protest after protest was despatched to the legislators, and the Congress adjourned at half-past four each day, in order . . . that delegates might devote the evening to waiting upon Members of Parliament'.[34] Yet despite this pressure, the government would not yield to union demands and all that it was prepared to concede was the introduction of two separate bills, these becoming the Trade Union Act 1871 and the Criminal Law Amendment Act 1871. The former provided, *inter alia*, legal protection for union funds while the latter made peaceful picketing virtually impossible. But though many trade unionists felt that the Criminal Law Amendment Act 1871 was an act of betrayal by the Liberal government, the Conference of Amalgamated Trades dissolved, its members considering that with the protection of union funds now secured by the Trade Union Act 1871, they had discharged the duties for which they had organised.

The trade union mantle was now clearly in the hands of the TUC, which had grown remarkably within the space of a few years. The first Congress in 1868 was attended by only 34 delegates representing 118,367 trade unionists. But by 1873, there were 132 delegates representing no fewer than 750,000 members. Such impressive support strengthened the TUC's quickly assumed role as the spokesman for organised labour. In order to facilitate its pressure group function, Congress established a permanent Parliamentary Committee: 'to watch over all legislative measures affecting the question of labour and to initiate whenever necessary such legislative action as Congress may direct or as the exigencies of the circumstances demand'.[35] The immediate concern of the Parliamentary Committee was to secure the repeal of the Criminal Law Amendment Act 1871, although it did express an interest in other legislative proposals in the 1870s. But the need to secure legislation to deal with criminal liability for industrial action was the first priority, particularly after the decision in *R*. v. *Bunn*[36] where it was held that simply by striking, workers could be committing a criminal conspiracy and would be liable, if convicted, to imprisonment.

In seeking satisfaction on the issue of the criminal law, the Parliamentary Committee adopted all the pressure group tactics with which the movement was now familiar. Audiences with the Home Secretary were secured, members of Parliament were lobbied, and private members' bills were introduced. But the unions had to contend with a powerful lobby of employers anxious to retain the status quo and, as the Webbs point out,[37] Gladstone's Cabinet steadfastly refused, right down to its fall in 1874, even to consider the possibility of altering the Criminal Law Amendment Act 1871. So it was left to the Conservatives under Disraeli, anxious to cultivate the working class vote, to meet the union demands within a year of their assuming office after the general election of 1874. The Conspiracy and Protection of Property Act 1875 dealt with the problem raised in the case of *Bunn* by enacting in section 3 that simple conspiracy to do acts in contemplation or furtherance of a trade dispute was not a criminal offence. The same Act extended some facility for peaceful picketing (s.7), and also removed the criminal consequences of breach of contract by an employee by repealing the Master and Servant Acts (s.17(2)).

Trade union leaders could rightly feel that a great victory had been won. Within a period of ten years not only was the legal position of the unions consolidated and improved, but the TUC had arrived as a political institution which wielded political power and which could expect an audience, if not yet participation, in the corridors of power. The achievement of the unions clearly underlined the significance of electoral reform and showed that the parties would to some extent frame their policies in an attempt to secure the working man's vote. The next logical step for the unions was to use their electoral power not simply to exploit the relationship with the existing parties and their members of Parliament, but to ensure that the trade union case was heard on the floor of the House of Commons from spokesmen directly representing the trade union movement. Although the unions had thus received some form of representation at Whitehall, representation at Westminster was equally important. Not only would it enable more pressure to be brought on ministers, but it is crucial to note that at this time Parliament had not yet surrendered all its power to the Executive, though by the end of the century the process was well under way. So there was still much work to be done in the House of Commons either by mobilising resistance to government initiatives or by organising the passage of private members' bills.

THE BIRTH OF THE LABOUR PARTY[38]

The idea of direct labour representation in Parliament was projected on several occasions during the course of the nineteenth century and a number of organisations emerged to promote this cause.[39] Yet the trade unions sustained little enthusiasm in such activity. As Pelling points out, for activity of this kind to be effective, it must have strong financial backing and for much of the nineteenth century trade unions were simply unable to provide the necessary finance.[40] Moreover, it seems that the trade union leaders closely followed the Liberals on policy issues and were, in any event, deeply imbued with the laissez-faire values of Victorian capitalism. There was a marked reluctance on the part of these trade unionists to resort to legislation to fulfil trade union needs; they saw 'every demand for securing the condition of labour by legislation . . . as an invidious exception, only to be justified by the special helplessness or incompetency of the applicants'.[41] This attitude was clearly demonstrated by Henry Broadhurst, the General Secretary of the TUC from 1876 to 1889. In 1887, he addressed Congress on the question of the eight-hour day and said that unions should 'do this work for themselves and not go grovelling to the doors of Parliament like paupers seeking a weekly dole'.[42]

But this lack of enthusiasm for direct labour representation gradually dissipated as changing circumstances demanded a fresh response. These changing circumstances not only propelled the unions in the path of direct representation, but they dictated that the channels of representation should be independent of the Liberal Party, the traditional ally of the unions. An important development in this respect was the emergence of the New Unions. The late 1880s, a period of economic buoyancy, is often identified as one of proliferation of trade unions among workers hitherto unorganised. These New Unions differed from the established organisations in that they tended to have no restrictive entry qualifications and so organised the unskilled. And unlike the established unions, many were general in character and recruited workers from several different occupations. Some of the best-known tales of Labour folklore, including the strikes by Bryant and May's matchgirls and the London dockers, relate to the achievements of these unions.

But for present purposes, the significance of New Unionism was the platform which it provided for the cause of independent labour representation. Not only did many of the leaders of the New Unions sympathise with the emerging socialist ideas, but there was a marked tendency within these unions to seek legislation to regulate working conditions. While it is true that several of the unions contained members with special skills and that consequently they did have some bargaining power,[43] this tendency towards legislation was for the most part a feature of insecurity. Pelling argues that the onset of economic depression in the 1890s attracted the New Unions to:

> the value of legislation for the consolidation of their industrial demands [and] made them favourable to the Socialist demand

for an independent labour party in Parliament. The new unionists had nothing to lose and a good deal to gain by a policy of
political action such as the Socialists were advocating, involving
as it did the legislative enforcement of what they were most
anxious to win, and, having won, to preserve. It had very soon
been made clear to them that their gains by industrial action were
not easy to maintain.[44]

But it may be noted that the influence of socialism within the unions
was limited. The leaders of the established unions maintained their
links with the Liberals in the 1880s and 1890s, and the TUC had
always shunned political unity by resisting the advances regularly
made by socialist organisations. But, there was another pressure
which moved even the established unions in the direction of direct
representation in Parliament, namely the need to respond to serious
threats to their very existence as effective organisations. Once again,
as in the 1860s, the development of the unions' political arm was to a
large extent a mirror reflection of their own weakness.

The economic boom of the late 1880s soon turned to depression.
Trade unions received a hostile press and employers, strengthened by
the fall in the need for labour, were widely believed to be waging an
aggressive counter-attack against unions. One ground for this belief
was the strengthening of national employers' associations in many
industries. The best known example, the Employers' Federation of
Engineering Associations, was formed in 1896 and within a year of its
formation it had successfully resisted a six-month strike by the Amalgamated Society of Engineers, the first national strike in British
history. The impotence of the union in the face of such determined
opposition was 'a humiliating setback for a union which was still
regarded as the foremost in the country, indeed in the world'.[45] An
Employers' Parliamentary Council was also formed. The function of
this body was partly, like the TUC Parliamentary Committee, to
lobby and influence members of Parliament. But as Pelling points
out,[46] the apprehension which accompanied its formation lay in the
belief that there were so many employers in the House of Commons
that it seemed they could easily have things their own way if they were
effectively marshalled against the interests of the unions.[47]

Another threat to trade union security at this time came from the
courts. Although those engaged in industrial action were protected
from the criminal law by the Conspiracy and Protection of Property
Act 1875, they found their activities impeded, and the freedom to
strike threatened, by the development of the torts of conspiracy[48] and
inducing breach of contract.[49] Moreover, the criminal provisions
which were retained by the 1875 Act were widely construed by the
courts. By section 7 of the Conspiracy and Protection of Property Act

1875, it is a criminal offence for any person, wrongfully and without legal authority, with a view to compel any other person to abstain from doing what he has a legal right to do, to watch or beset the place where that other person resides, works, carries on business, or happens to be. As originally enacted, the section contained a proviso to the effect that attending merely to obtain or communicate information would not be deemed watching or besetting. In *J. Lyons and Sons* v. *Wilkins*,[50] it was held that a picket which was designed to persuade people not to go to work would not be treated as merely attending in order to obtain or communicate information, and was consequently unlawful by virtue of the statutory provisions. The Court of Appeal had now clearly undermined the status of peaceful picketing, a point which employers were alive to publicise with great vigour.

In the face of these threats trade unionists were beginning to lose confidence in the Liberal Party. Many trade unionists were growing impatient with the Liberals as guardians of working class interests. The Liberal Party, it seems, was too preoccupied with the Irish question with the result that its concern for social issues waned. Other trade unionists were alienated by the failure of the party to take an initiative to secure the payment of members of Parliament from public funds. But more importantly, trade unionists had great difficulty in being adopted as parliamentary candidates by local Liberal caucuses despite the growing perception of the need for direct labour representation. Pelling argues that:

> All along, there is little doubt that most of the non-Socialist trade-union leaders would have been happy to stay in the Liberal Party – which most of them had belonged to in the past – if the Liberals had made arrangements for a larger representation of the working class among their Parliamentary candidates. Again and again, it was the fault of the official Liberal Party constituency caucuses that this did not happen; and it was the behaviour of these caucuses that set many of the leaders of the workers thinking in terms of a separate party.[51]

Thus, although the first two trade union members of Parliament were elected (as Liberals) at the general election in 1874, by 1895 the number of trade unionists elected to the House of Commons under the Liberal banner had risen to only twelve.

It was against this background of insecurity and failure to penetrate the established party system that the TUC finally agreed to join with a number of socialist organisations to consider the question of independent labour representation. The TUC took the initiative in summoning a special conference to examine the issue. The conference met in 1900 and the outcome was a new political organisation, the Labour Representation Committee, which assumed the title of Labour Party in 1906. The aim of the new organisation was to establish a distinct labour group in Parliament, which was to have its own whips and which would agree upon its own policies. But inevitably, the new organisation faced a number of serious problems. The first was the need to establish itself within the labour movement. The conference which gave birth to the LRC was attended by delegates representing less than a third of the total membership of the TUC. However, further growth was stimulated by the courts. In *Taff Vale Railway Co. Ltd* v. *Amalgamated Society of Railway Servants*,[52] the House of Lords held that a trade union could be sued in damages, as a distinct legal entity, for the tortious acts of its members. In that case, the union was held to be liable for damages of £23,000 which had been incurred during a strike. With the continued development of liability in tort,[53] the freedom to strike was further shackled, if not now paralysed. The unions realised that there was a need for effective political action and the number of trade union members affiliated to the LRC increased from 353,070 in 1901 to over 950,000 in 1904. The total affiliated membership of the TUC in 1901 was 1,200,000 and in 1904 it was slightly less than 1,500,000. By 1910, the total affiliated membership of the TUC had risen to 1,647,715 and the total number of trade unionists affiliated to the Labour Party had reached 1,394,403.

A second problem which the new organisation faced was that of maintaining its independence from the Liberal Party. A number of factors militated against complete independence. One was the common ground between the two parties on major policy issues and the apparent inability of the Labour Party to produce an alternative strategy. Another factor related to the combined effect of the two general elections of 1910 and the decision in the *Osborne* case. In the election of 1910, the Liberal landslide of 1906 had been drastically pruned with the result that the government depended upon Labour support in the Commons in order to stay in office. As a result of the *Osborne* decision,[54] that trade unions could not contribute funds to the Labour Party, the party depended on the government to provide remedial legislation, and could not contemplate bringing the government down and risking the return of the Conservatives until that had been done. Thus it was not until differences of opinion between the party leaders arose towards the end of World War One that the relationship between the parties began to cool and that perceptible moves in the direction of complete independence can be traced.

In 1918, a new constitution was adopted which committed the party to socialism. By Clause 4 one of the functions of the party was: 'To secure for the producers by hand and brain the full fruits of their industry, and the most equitable distribution thereof that may be possible, upon the basis of the common ownership of the means of production'. The independent strain of the party was thus confirmed in 1918. In the election of that year, the party won fifty-seven seats which was only a slight improvement upon the pre-war total of forty-two which had been won at the second general election of 1910. Yet Labour soon became the main opposition party, outstripping the Liberals at the polls in the general election of 1922 and at every election thereafter. For two brief, if unhappy, spells in the inter-war period the Labour Party held office as a minority government and in the post-war era there have been three Labour administrations spanning seventeen years in all.

THE OSBORNE JUDGMENT

Compared with earlier ill-fated attempts at parliamentary representation, the Labour Party grew remarkably quickly from its inception
in 1900. Affiliated membership rose from 375,931 in 1901 to 921,280
in 1905 with income from affiliation fees, at 15 shillings per 1,000
members, yielding £865 in the latter year. Affiliated organisations
were also required to pay a compulsory levy to the party's parliamentary representation fund. The levy was set at 1d per member and in
1905, a year after the introduction of the compulsory levy, the income
to the fund was an impressive £4,492. Although membership of the
party was open to socialist societies, they were small in number and
the bulk of the finance was provided by the unions. Some unions met
their commitment from their general funds, though a growing number established a parliamentary representation fund, financed by a
compulsory levy of their members, to meet this expenditure. These
funds soon held considerable sums of money.

So by the time the new organisation acquired its new name in 1906,
its future seemed secure. It was beginning to build up its finances, it
had a stable membership, and it was making an impact at the polls,
with some notable successes at the general election in 1906. But
continued growth was surprisingly threatened when the legality of
trade union support of the Labour Party was called into question. As
we saw in chapter one, trade unions had financed parliamentary
representation since 1874 when two miners, namely Thomas Burt and
Alexander MacDonald, were paid by their unions while members of
the House of Commons. Thereafter several trade unions made payments to members and officials who were elected to serve in Parliament. But no one had expressed concern when that money was being
used to finance Liberals. And indeed, any official comment on the
issue seemed to assume that this was a form of action in which a trade
union might engage, without calling into question its propriety or
legal status.[1]

PORTENTS OF TROUBLE

I. A REGISTRATION PROBLEM. The first indication of trouble came
from the Chief Registrar of Friendly Societies. A system of voluntary

registration of trade unions had been established by the Trade Union Acts 1871–6 for the purposes of which a trade union was defined as: 'any combination, whether temporary or permanent, for regulating the relations between workmen and masters, or between workmen and workmen, or between masters and masters, or for imposing restrictive conditions on the conduct of any trade or business'.[2] Many unions chose to register under these Acts, gaining in consequence some minor legal advantages over unregistered unions. Initially, the Chief Registrar adopted a very informal approach to registration, pointing out in his Annual Report for 1876 that 'if a trade union provides by its rules for the matters prescribed in the . . . Act, the Registrar is bound to register the rules, however contrary to law all the other provisions may be'.[3] So a rule relating to parliamentary representation, or indeed any other subject-matter, might be accepted for registration, but this did not guarantee its legality.

But in 1904 a different policy was implemented following the appointment of a new Chief Registrar, James Stuart Sim. He was more concerned to ensure that registered rules were lawful and seemed particularly troubled by union rules which made provision for parliamentary representation. In his first annual report he said:

> As many trade unions are seeking to include in their objects such extraneous matters as the promotion of Labour Representation in Parliament and in other elected bodies I have found it necessary to point out that such matters are not within the definition of a trade union contained in section 16 of the Trade Union Act of 1876.[4]

In fact the Chief Registrar went further than point this out for in 1905 the Railway Clerks' Association had the following words deleted from its objects clause: 'to publish a service newspaper, and to secure Parliamentary and municipal representation'. Predictably, this caused a flutter in the LRC because it was an indication that the new Chief Registrar might require all unions to give up their political activities. The distress of some officials was aggravated by press coverage of the issue and by the fear that rival politicians would further publicise and exploit the failure of the unions to register their rules on labour representation.[5]

2. THE PLUMBERS' CASE. A second threat to trade union support of the LRC came from the courts. It seems that many trade union members supported one or other of the existing political parties and objected to union funds being used to support the LRC, and objected still further to being compulsorily levied for this purpose.[6] Such trade unionists found powerful allies ready to assist them.[7] In 1905 W. M. Thompson, the editor of *Reynolds News*, supported an application by

the Canning Town branch of the United Operative Plumbers' Association for an injunction to restrain the Association from (i) using
money, paid by the branch, for the purpose of parliamentary representation; (ii) levying the branch for money for parliamentary purposes; and (iii) levying the wider membership of the Association for
this purpose.[8]

This action, to be heard in Manchester County Court on 17 November 1905, also caused some alarm in the LRC. Ramsay Mac-
Donald, then Secretary, seemed particularly disturbed and began to
think of ways by which the movement could respond if the decision
went against the union. These included inserting a clause in the Trade
Disputes Bill then before Parliament (aimed at dealing with *Taff Vale*
and subsequently enacted as the Trade Disputes Act 1906) which
would make it clear that unions could levy money for political purposes; an appeal to union members to subscribe voluntarily to the
LRC; a national campaign demanding the right of workmen to
dispose of their funds as they thought necessary; and the mobilisation
of LRC members of Parliament after the forthcoming general election
to secure some provision for the payment of members by the State.[9]
MacDonald was also sufficiently concerned to arrange for £50 to be
paid by the LRC to meet the union's legal expenses and to travel to
Manchester to listen to the proceedings.[10]

MacDonald had hoped that the decision would authoritatively
determine that the unions could use their funds for political purposes.
But these hopes were dashed for it seems from the short report in *The
Times* (18 November 1905) that the case was fought on the sole ground
that the expenditure of money from the general fund for parliamentary purposes was *ultra vires* because the rules of the association did not
authorise such a payment. All other claims by the plaintiffs were
dropped a few days before the hearing, the defendants admitted that
they had no such express authorisation in their rules, and so conceded
that they had acted *ultra vires*. An injunction was accordingly granted
on a narrow point and could simply be avoided by the union, and
other unions, taking steps to ensure that their rules did give them
power to make political payments. So the crucial questions of whether
trade unions were permitted by statute to make such payments, or
whether they could impose a compulsory levy on their members for
political action, remained open.

MacDonald was clearly displeased that the opportunity to settle the
issue had been wasted. He also seemed unhappy that the 'lines of
action had been practically fixed before the Labour Representation
Committee was consulted'.[11] Apparently, the rules of the association
contained a statement that they could affiliate with trades councils, the
TUC and 'such like institutions'. MacDonald had wished that the

case be fought on the basis that these powers would by implication have enabled the association to affiliate with the LRC, an omission which he considered all the more regrettable in view of Judge Parry's observation in the case that the expression in parenthesis, in his opinion, included not only the LRC, but Parliament itself.[12] Yet despite the limited value of the case, MacDonald felt sufficiently confident to issue a circular to bodies affiliated to the LRC drawing their attention to the fact that 'the Labour Representation Committee is a perfectly legal organisation so far as Trade Unions are concerned, and may be supported from their funds'.[13]

3. RESOLVING THE REGISTRATION PROBLEM. Of the two challenges to the use of union funds in support of the LRC, the threat posed by the Plumbers' case was clearly the most significant. The Chief Registrar could have made life inconvenient for unions, but the refusal to register political fund rules would not in itself have prevented such expenditure. Unions could have removed themselves from the register if the advantages of parliamentary representation were seen to outweigh the advantages of registration. However, notwithstanding the merits of political action, this is not a step which would be taken lightly, for several unions would have been reluctant to give up the advantages and sense of security which registration provided.[14]

However, de-registration proved unnecessary for subsequent developments reveal that the Chief Registrar had been misunderstood, though it is not clear who was to blame for the misunderstanding. In the Report of the Labour Party executive to the 1906 Conference, it is stated that the Chief Registrar's change of policy 'was generally assumed at the time to be antagonistic to us, but . . . as a matter of fact had no bearing upon our position'.[15] In fact the Chief Registrar had since clarified that although parliamentary representation could not be registered as an object of trade unionism, there was nothing 'to prevent a trade union from employing its funds in any way the members think fit, and therefore it is competent for the union to subscribe for any such purpose'.[16] The Chief Registrar was prepared to permit unions to promote parliamentary representation not as an object, but as a method of pursuing the statutory objects and early in 1906 MacDonald consulted with him in order to produce a satisfactory model rule which would enable the unions to engage in such action. The rule was then circulated to all affiliated organisations.[17]

But despite the apparent settlement of the registration problem, the matter did not rest. Questions were raised in Parliament[18] and the issue was debated at the Labour Party conference in 1906.[19] The Chief Registrar's new position caused unsettlement in the minds of trade unionists, some of whom now thought that trade union political activity was unlawful. This misconception was induced in part by the Chief Registrar who required parliamentary representation to be removed from the objects clause of some unions without explaining that such activity could be adopted as a method of trade unionism. The unsettlement in the minds of trade unionists was compounded by the belief that the Chief Registrar was not always consistent in the application of his new policy and by the claim of some unions that they had successfully registered parliamentary representation as an object of the union. It is thus not surprising that despite assurances and an explanation of the position by MacDonald, the Conference should endorse the following resolution:

> In view of the continued adverse decisions of the Law Courts affecting Trade Unions, and the recent action of the Chief Registrar in relation to rules affecting Labour Representation, this conference hereby instructs its Labour M.P.s to draft and introduce into the House of Commons, as early as possible, a Trade Union Amendment and Consolidation Bill, defining the position of Trade Unions in the clearest possible terms.[20]

But the Labour hierarchy no longer appeared very interested in this issue. As far as they were concerned, the matter seemed sufficiently settled and secured.

THE CRISIS ABATES

Further evidence that there was no legal constraint on the use of trade union funds was provided by the Opinion of counsel.[21] Several unions were advised that although they could only raise a parliamentary levy if they had power in their rules to do so, parliamentary action was nevertheless a legitimate means of promoting trade union objects. This advice was confirmed in *Steele* v. *SWMF*,[22] the first decision of the High Court in which the legality of trade union political expenditure was tested.

Rather curiously, in view of the activities of the Chief Registrar since 1904, the rules of the Federation provided by rule 3(12) that one of its objects was: 'To provide funds wherewith to pay the expenses of returning and maintaining representatives to Parliament and other public councils and boards, and to request them to press forward by every legitimate means all proposals conducive to the general welfare of the members of the federation.' In order to promote this object, the executive council of the Federation proposed to establish a Parliamentary Representation Fund which would be maintained by a compulsory levy of the membership. The proposal was supported by the majority of members voting in a ballot and was subsequently approved by a resolution at the Federation's annual general meeting.

Steele had always opposed the proposal, and in 1906, after he had paid the levy for four years, he brought an action against the Federation and some of its officers. He sought, *inter alia*, an injunction to restrain the Federation from levying money under rule 3(12); a declaration that rule 3(12) was illegal; and an injunction to restrain the Federation from misapplying its funds in returning representatives to, or maintaining them in Parliament.

The case presented by counsel on behalf of Steele on this issue lay mainly on the construction of s.16 of the 1876 Act. It was contended that this section limited the lawful objects of trade unions and that since no reference was made there to parliamentary representation, unions could not freely engage in such activity. This interpretation of the statutory definition was rejected. The view taken by both the judges was that the statutory definition was not exhaustive of the lawful activities of trade unions and that unions could have other objects besides those expressly mentioned in the Act. Phillimore J. said: 's.16 is not a limiting section at all. It says that any association which has any of the objects specified in the section as one of its objects is ipso facto a trade union, but there is nothing in it to prevent such a body from having a great number of additional objects besides.'[23] Darling J. expressed himself in similar terms.[24] But he added a second ground for his decision, holding that even if s.16 was exhaustive of the lawful objects of trade unions then parliamentary action would still be lawful on the ground that: 'one of the ways of regulating the relations between workmen and masters . . . is to get laws passed by Parliament for their regulation, and that one of the first steps towards getting those laws passed would be to send a representative to Parliament to promote a Bill for that purpose'.[25]

THE BOLT FROM THE BLUE

So trade union political spending was justified in the *Steele* case on two different grounds. Nevertheless, that decision was followed by similar litigation, *Osborne* v. *Amalgamated Society of Railway Servants*,[26] the eventual outcome of which was to have far-reaching consequences – 'second only to the Taff Vale decision'[27] – upon the trade union movement. The objects of the Amalgamated Society of Railway Servants included the securing of parliamentary representation, and a parliamentary fund, maintained by a compulsory levy, was established to support this object. But unlike SWMF, the Society was affiliated to the Labour Party, and before any prospective candidate would be accepted as a potential parliamentary representative of the union, he was required to sign and accept the conditions of the party and undertake to be subject to its whip. W. V. Osborne, a member and branch secretary of ASRS, came to court seeking a declaration that the parliamentary fund rules were invalid, and an injunction to restrain the Society and its trustees from levying and distributing money for political purposes.

The case was heard at first instance by Neville J.[28] and it was conceded immediately by counsel for Osborne that following the *Steele* decision it could not be argued that it was *ultra vires* the Society to secure parliamentary representation to promote its interests. But attempts were made to distinguish *Steele* by stressing that, although parliamentary representation may be within the power of the Society, 'that representation must be intended entirely to protect and advance the Society's interest'. By contributing to the funds of the Labour Party, this requirement was being frustrated. First, the aim of the Labour Party was not to protect the interests of trade unions. Its aim was to bring about socialism and this, it was said, would be destructive of trade unions. And secondly, even if the Society did have representatives in Parliament, these members would be subject to the Labour Party whip, and might be unable to vote in favour of a Bill for the benefit of their own union, if the Labour Party decided not to give it their support. But Neville J. rejected these arguments and said that since it was lawful for unions to select their own candidate for Parliament, it was up to them to consider whether it was in their best interests that the candidates should go to Parliament as independent members, or as supporters of one of the existing parties, or as supporters of a new party which would devote itself to the furthering of the interests of the class to which the members of the union belonged. In any event, he said, 'the wisdom or the folly of the course adopted is not a matter with which a court of justice can deal: that must be left to the consideration of the majority of the members themselves'.[29]

This decision was reversed in the Court of Appeal where it was now accepted that the statutory definition of a trade union was a limiting and restrictive definition.[30] The court could not agree with the view that 'any combination that has among its objects the regulation of such matters as are referred to in the statutory definition is *ipso facto* a trade union'.[31] Consequently, it was not competent for a trade union 'to add to its objects something so wholly distinct from the objects contemplated by the Trade Union Acts as a provision to finance parliamentary representation'.[32] The court unanimously held that the Trade Union Act 1871 gave legal recognition to organisations of a well-known type 'formed for objects and purposes which were well recognised'.[33] The idea of securing parliamentary representation was not, at that time, generally perceived as one of those objects, and although trade union objects had changed, there was no reason to think that Parliament had altered its conception of a trade union. In reaching this conclusion the court was obviously concerned to protect the freedom of Osborne and his fellow dissidents. The Master of the Rolls was of the opinion that since trade unions comprised members of every shade of political opinion, Parliament could not have intended to enable a majority of members to compel a minority to support by their subscriptions political opinions that they abhorred. The nature of the compulsion was the fear 'not only of being expelled from the union, and thus losing all chance of benefit, but also the risk, and in some cases the very serious risk, of not being able to find employment in their trade in consequence of the refusal of trade union members to work with non-union members'.[34]

The decision of the Court of Appeal was upheld by the House of Lords. However, their Lordships were divided as to the effect of the Acts of 1871 and 1876 on trade union activities. Only the Earl of Halsbury, Lord Macnaghten and Lord Atkinson took the view that the legislation limited the lawful powers of trade unions. In their view the Acts of 1871 and 1876 gave trade unions a new legal status, creating a species of quasi-corporation, 'resembling much more closely railway companies incorporated by statute than voluntary associations of individuals merely bound together by contract'.[35] Consequently trade unions, like statutory corporations, were subject to the *ultra vires* rule as it had been developed in *Ashbury Railway Carriage and Iron Co.* v. *Riche*,[36] *Att.-Gen.* v. *Great Eastern Railway*,[37] and *Baroness Wenlock* v. *River Dee Co.*[38] In the latter case, Lord Watson had said:

> Whenever a corporation is created by Act of Parliament with reference to the purposes of the Act, and solely with a view to carrying these purposes into execution, I am of opinion not only that the objects which the corporation may legitimately pursue must be ascertained from the Act itself, but that the powers which the corporation may lawfully use in furtherance of these objects must either be expressly conferred or derived by reasonable implication from its provisions.[39]

In the *Osborne* case, the Lords noted that the Acts of 1871 and 1876 had not expressly given trade unions the power to levy money for political purposes, and the majority held that such power could not be derived by 'reasonable'[40] or 'fair'[41] implication from the Acts. In his speech Lord Macnaghten said:

> It can hardly be contended that a political organisation is not a thing very different from a combination for trade purposes. There is nothing in any of the Trade Union Acts from which it can be reasonably inferred that trade unions, as defined by Parliament, were ever meant to have the power of collecting and administering funds for political purposes.[42]

So the majority held that it was *ultra vires* the Acts of 1871 and 1876 for the union to levy money for political purposes. Lord James of Hereford dissented on this point while Lord Shaw of Dunfermline reserved his judgment, but strongly hinted that he disagreed with the majority when he said that he was not convinced that the payment of members of Parliament was so foreign or subversive to the objects of a union as to make such activity unlawful. However, both of their Lordships dismissed the appeal, but on a different ground. Lord James held that the rule of ASRS was *ultra vires* a trade union because it required the elected representatives of the union to forego their own judgment on all matters and to vote as required by the Labour Party. Lord Shaw dismissed the appeal on similar grounds, but provided a more detailed argument for so doing. The key to his decision was his assumption that Parliament should be not only free in its election, but also in its advice to the king.[43] While he thought that there was nothing wrong in principle with outside bodies making payments to members of Parliament, the courts would be unsympathetic to any obligations which attached to these payments.[44] Thus, any coercion, constraint, or money payment to vote at the request of some outside body imperilled, if it did not destroy, Parliament's freedom.[45]

Consequently, it was felt by Lord Shaw that the rules of ASRS were contrary to public policy and were illegal. It was unlawful to insist that all union candidates were to be responsible to the union, and that they should sign the Labour Party pledge (which required that they accept the conditions of the party) and be subject to its whip. The first requirement, that of responsibility to the union, was potentially dangerous to parliamentary government. If unions could make such demands on members of Parliament then there would be nothing to prevent 'organisations or trusts of men using capital funds to procure the subjection of members of Parliament to their commands'.[46] The second condition involved a requirement on the part of the members of Parliament to abide by the decisions of the PLP. It followed from this that 'Unless a member becomes bound to the society and to the Labour Party by these conditions, and shapes his parliamentary action in conformity therewith, and with the decisions of the parliamentary party, he has broken his bargain'.[47] Echoing Burkean conceptions of the role and function of the member of Parliament, it was thought that such subjection was incompatible with both the spirit of the constitution and with the independence and freedom which lay at the base of representative government in the United Kingdom.

A MISCARRIAGE OF JUSTICE

In characteristically emotive terms, the Webbs described the *Osborne* judgment as a miscarriage of justice.[48] This is a conclusion with which it is difficult to take issue for there is little that can be said in support of the decision. It is true that it did seem consistent to some extent with the Realist theories of personality which were then popular, being supported by such influential writers as Maitland[49] and Dicey,[50] and subsequently by Geldart[51] and Laski.[52] Maitland had argued that 'if a group behaves as a corporation, the courts are well-nigh compelled to treat it as such', and he questioned whether 'a permanently organised group, for example a trade union, which has property held for it by trustees, should be suffered to escape liability for what would generally be called "its" unlawful acts and commands by the technical plea that "it" has no existence in the eye of the law'.[53] Similarly, Geldart was to argue that 'we cannot evade the legal question by treating legal personality as something which has no relation to the personality which is not a matter of law but of fact'.[54] But although the *Osborne* decision, by treating trade unions as quasi-corporations, satisfied this claim of the Realists, it was nevertheless consistent with only one thread of the Realist argument. Some of the Realist authors advanced the further argument that the State should not fetter the free development of the group. It was this feature of Realism which Maitland expressed when, in criticising the decision of the House of Lords in the famous Free Church case, he said that he could not think that 'it was a brilliant day in our legal annals when the affairs of the Free Church of Scotland were brought before the House of Lords, and the dead hand fell with a resounding slap upon the living body'.[55] Only Lord Shaw adopted the full force of the Realist approach when in reserving his judgment on the position adopted by the majority, he echoed Maitland by saying: 'I have some hesitation in so construing language of statutory recognition as a definition imposing such hard and fast restrictive limits as would cramp the development and energies and destroy the natural movements of the living organism'.[56]

But not only did the decision seem out of touch with contemporary ideas, it was also inconsistent with judicial developments since the enactment of the Trade Union Acts 1871–6. For example, in *Aitken* v. *Associated Carpenters and Joiners of Scotland*,[57] L.P. Inglis said:

> But no change was introduced into the constitution of these societies. They remain voluntary associations of which the law can take no special cognisance as collective bodies, and it is provided by the 5th section of the Act that the Acts relating to Friendly Societies and Industrial and Provident Societies, and the Companies Acts of 1862 and 1867, shall have no application to trades unions, the object apparently being to make careful provision that they should not have any corporate existence or capacity whatsoever.

Similarly, in *Linaker* v. *Pilcher*[58] the trustees of ASRS were sued for a libel which appeared in the *Railway Review*, a newspaper of which the union was both proprietor and publisher. It was submitted on behalf of the union that it could not be sued because in owning and trading in a newspaper, it had acted *ultra vires*. This was based on the argument that the statutory definition in s.16 of the 1876 Act cut down the rights and powers of trade unions and that unions could only lawfully engage in the activities which were expressly mentioned in that section. But this argument was curtly dismissed by Mathew J. who replied that the Act had no such operation and that the statutory definition was not intended to be a definitive statement of trade union rights and powers.

The only decision which in any sense seriously challenges the traditional view of the judges is *Taff Vale Railway Co. Ltd* v. *ASRS*[59] where it was held that trade unions could be sued for the tortious acts of their members. In that case Lord Brampton said that the effect of registration of a trade union under the Trade Union Act 1871 was to create a 'corporate body' which was a distinct 'legal entity', although 'not perhaps in the strict sense a corporation'.[60] But Lord Brampton's treatment of trade unions as species of corporation was exceptional. All that was decided in that case was that it was implicit in the 1871 Act that trade unions could be sued in their registered name. *Taff Vale* certainly did not decide that trade unions could be sued in their registered names because they were corporate bodies and indeed both Lords Macnaghten and Lindley expressly denied that trade unions were corporations, a point which Lord Lindley repeated in *Yorkshire Miners' Association* v. *Howden*.[61] Equally important is the fact that there is no indication in *Taff Vale* that trade unions operated under any statutory constraint. In fact the very opposite is implicit in the following dictum of Lord Macnaghten:

> Parliament has legalised trade unions, whether registered or not; if registered, they enjoy certain advantages. The respondent society is a registered trade union. Subject to such control as an annual general meeting can exercise, the government of the society is in the hands of its executive committee, a small body with vast powers, including an unlimited power of disposition over the funds of the union, except so far as it may be interfered with by the annual general meeting, or restricted by the operation of the society's rules.[62]

There is no reason whatsoever to believe that these views were mistaken and that Parliament either intended to impose any form of corporate status on trade unions or that it otherwise intended to limit their powers. Indeed, a review of the legislative history suggests that any such notions are wholly untenable. Thus, at common law, trade unions were simply unincorporated voluntary associations and there is no indication in the Reports of the Royal Commission on the

Organisation and Rules of Trade Unions,[63] the forerunner to the 1871 Act, that this status should be in any way altered. Similarly, there was no indication in the Reports of the Commission that henceforward the lawful objects of trade unions should be limited to the type of activity referred to in s.16 of the 1876 Act. The Majority Report of the Commission identified trade and benefit objects as being the 'general' objects of trade unions but did not recommend that trade unions should be limited to such activity.[64] Similarly, the Minority Report referred to the fact that 'some of the richer unions have other funds, and expend their resources on sundry other purposes, such as reading-rooms, libraries, donations, and charitable subscriptions – as, for instance, the contributions of the shipbuilders to the Patriotic and other public funds',[65] but made no recommendation that such expenditure should cease. On the contrary, the minority addressed itself to 'the very serious question' whether 'legislation of a far more comprehensive character is not needed to place trade unions on a full legal footing: whether, in fact, a complete statute should not be enacted, analogous to the provisions of the Friendly Societies Acts and the Joint Stock Companies Acts, and the like, by means of which uniform rules would be framed for the formation, management and dissolution of these associations'. It concluded that the time was not yet ripe for such a statute and added: 'We think the right course is that they should be left to that spontaneous activity which produced them, and that the State cannot with policy interfere to give them a permanent or systematic character'.[66]

The parliamentary debates leading to the enactment of the Trade Union Act 1871 lend further weight to the view that in enacting this measure Parliament did not intend to constrain the activities of trade unions. During the Second Reading debate in the House of Commons views were expressed to the effect that the sole purpose of the Act was to assimilate trade unions to clubs by releasing the former from the legal straitjacket created by *Hornby* v. *Close*[67] that trade unions were unlawful because they were in restraint of trade. The debates provide no ground for the belief that Parliament intended to alter the status of trade unions or limit their powers. Nor is there any reason to believe that Parliament assumed any such intention in 1876. A convincing indication of this came in the *Osborne* case itself, when Lord James of Hereford, who as Sir Henry James M.P. had been actively involved in the enactment of the 1876 Act, said that 'the Legislation only intended to require certain qualifications to exist before an entity could become a trade union'.[68] In other words, the legal definition was descriptive, not restrictive. In fact, it is remarkable that the House of Lords should have supported any other conclusion for as Sydney Webb later pointed out,[69] it is very difficult to imply a limiting intention to Parliament at a time when two of its members were financed by trade unions. If Parliament had intended to take steps which would have had potentially drastic consequences for two of its members,[70] then it is reasonable to presume that it would have done so clearly, unequivocally, and after full discussion.

But even without this background knowledge, the form of the Act makes the conclusion of the Lords difficult to justify. Thus, as Lord MacDermott argued in *Bonsor* v. *Musicians' Union*,[71] it seems unlikely that a statute which demanded trustees for an association could impliedly confer quasi-corporate capacities. In any event, if Parliament had intended to introduce such a radical change to the legal status of trade unions, it would be reasonable to insist that it would have done so by express words. As Lord MacDermott also recognised in the *Bonsor* case:

> Parliament has made no effort to incorporate the registered trade union. In the latter half of the last century incorporation was the recognised and usual way of conferring upon an association of persons the status of a distinct legal entity, and it is clear that the draftsman of the Act of 1871 had the Companies Act of 1862 before him. Yet there is not a word about the members becoming, on registration, a body corporate.[72]

So far as the lawful purposes of trade unions are concerned, the Act equally suggests that there was no limiting intention. As we have seen, the 1876 Act defined a trade union as 'any combination, whether temporary or permanent, for regulating the relations between workmen and masters, or between workmen and workmen, or between masters and masters, or for imposing restrictive conditions on the conduct of any trade or business'.[73] It may be thought that the presence of the word 'any' indicates that by this definition Parliament had recognised that trade unions embraced a variety of objects. The statutory definition was merely identifying certain fundamental features of trade unionism. The same point is implied by the Trade Union Act 1871, Schedule 1, paragraph 2. The rules of registered trade unions were required to provide for 'the whole of the objects for which the trade union is to be established'. This would appear to envisage that trade unions were to be permitted some discretion in determining what their objects should be. And by using the word 'whole', it seems unlikely that this discretion was intended to be limited to the three statutory objects.

THE CONSTITUTIONAL QUESTION

So there is no reason to believe that the majority had accurately gauged the purpose of the Acts of 1871–6. However, there was a second ground for the decision, namely that the union imposed

unconstitutional demands on elected representatives. This ground for
the decision was clearly influenced by the traditional British model of
parliamentary democracy which rejects in any shape or form the idea
that the individual member of Parliament is the delegate of any
external agency. Government is a matter of reason and judgment and
the member must not surrender his judgment or conscience to the
demands of his electorate, or even more clearly to the instructions of
an outside pressure group. Yet although the decision of the minority
reflects traditional political philosophy, it is nevertheless open to
criticism on a number of grounds, but particularly because it failed to
reflect the dynamic nature of these values. Lord Shaw's objections
were twofold: the first was that union candidates were to be responsible to the union and the second was that elected representatives were
required to accept the Labour whip. In a parliamentary democracy
the first condition would clearly be intolerable if it meant that the
member of Parliament was to act at the bidding of his union. The
member is a representative of his electors, not of interest groups
which canvass his support or to which he has any personal loyalty. But
on examination it is difficult to believe that this is what was intended
by the union rule. It simply stated that there was a responsibility of
candidates to the union, without specifying what that meant. It certainly did not say that members of Parliament would be responsible to
the union, a conclusion which in any event was precluded by Lord
Shaw's interpretation of the Labour Party constitution which required the member of Parliament to obey the majority decision of the
PLP:

> Take the testing instance: should his [the M.P.'s] view as to right
> and wrong on a public issue as to the true line of service to the
> realm, as to the real interests of the constituency which has
> elected him, or even the society which pays him, differ from the
> decision of the parliamentary party and the maintenance by it of
> its policy, he has come under a contract to place his vote and
> action into subjection not to his own convictions, but to their
> decisions.[74]

Equally questionable was Lord Shaw's attack on the requirement
that ASRS members of Parliament must accept the conditions of the
Labour Party and accept its whip in order to receive support from the
union. This was no less than a full frontal assault on party government.
Although many people, lawyers amongst them, may genuinely believe
that the party system is objectionable, it is unlikely that that could be
maintained as a matter of law. The legal norms applied must be based
upon an assessment of the values and culture of a dynamic political
system. And in 1910 when Lord Shaw was writing, it is clear that
there were in this country all the trappings of a coherent party system

in a modern mass democracy. By that time there is little doubt that the House of Commons was controlled by the Executive and that party discipline in the House was at a premium. This development had been encouraged by the extension of the franchise, and with it the development of extra-parliamentary party organisations to mobilise the large army of voters. In order to be successful, the candidate now required to be adopted by the local party, and political historians seem to be reasonably confident that by 1910, and for some time before then, the party label was much more important than any personal attribute of the candidate.[75] Indeed such was the level of maturity of the party system at that time that Ostrogorski, that most influential critic of party government, could lament that 'unqualified adhesion to the official creed of the party [had] become the supreme political virtue which singled a man out for the confidence of his fellow citizens'.[76]

It is clear then that party government was a political fact long before the Labour Party arrived on the scene. It is also clear that within this framework of party government, Labour members of Parliament appeared to be no more controlled in their parliamentary activities than were the members of other parties. Indeed by 1910, the right to dissent from the party line was formally expressed in the Standing Orders of the Parliamentary Labour Party.[77] The policy of the party was, in the words of Keir Hardie, 'unity in things essential and in all things liberty'.[78] Philip Snowden also emphasised that he had not been hidebound by the pledge, observing that it had never been an embarrassment to his independent judgment, and that 'there was a good deal more liberty given to Members than might have been assumed from the rigid conditions laid down in the constitution of the party'.[79] Unlike the present conscience clause of the party, the corresponding provision operating in 1910 was loosely drawn and appeared to enable the member not only to abstain if he could not conscientiously accept a majority decision on any issue, but also to vote against the party line.[80] It is perhaps unfortunate that these points do not appear to have been brought to the attention of Lord Shaw, though in the circumstances it is difficult to believe that they would have made any material difference even if they had been. But they do tend to show that Labour members of Parliament did not in fact operate under any 'subjection', 'coercion', or 'constraint'.

Yet although the minority decision is equally open to criticism, it nevertheless caused fewer problems for the unions. It would be a simple task to release the formal pressures on candidates and members of Parliament and to allow other pressures and assumptions to dictate allegiance to the party. Immediately after the decision, the Labour Party dropped the pledge which members of the parliamentary party were required to sign.[81] But it is doubtful if this would have been enough to satisfy Lord Shaw. What he objected to was not only the pledge, but also the other means by which the union sought to exert control over sponsored members of Parliament. So if the union continued to require its members of Parliament to accept the Labour whip or otherwise sought to control them, it would still fall foul of the law as interpreted by Lord Shaw. However there are very few unions which are now likely to encounter any difficulty on these points. It is true that a small number, including NUFLAT, NUR, NUTGW and TWU have rules which require sponsored members of Parliament to retain the Labour whip as a condition of sponsorship and that such rules are presumably unlawful. But these rules are exceptional and most unions seem content to impose similar conditions by less formal means. So despite Lord Shaw's vain claim that his decision raised questions of general and permanent importance they were not difficult questions for the unions to answer. In contrast the majority position could be alleviated only by the judges redefining its boundaries or limiting its scope, failing which legislation would be essential.

DETERMINING THE FRONTIERS OF THE OSBORNE JUDGMENT

The *Osborne* judgment clearly proscribed a wide range of political expenditure by trade unions, including expenditure on parliamentary representation through the medium of the Labour Party, and possibly also gratuitous donations to political parties. However, the *Osborne* case was uncertain on two counts. The first is that it is unclear whether the decision applied to all forms of trade union political expenditure, and the second is whether it applied to all trade unions. These questions were considered and answered by the courts in the large number of cases which immediately followed *Osborne*.

1. THE FORMS OF POLITICAL ACTION. Apart from financing or maintaining close ties with a political party, there are a number of ways by which trade union political needs may find expression. One question which arose after *Osborne* is whether trade unions could become involved in pressure group campaigns to deal with changes in the existing law or to rally opposition to a Bill before Parliament. If the answer to this question was in the negative, then even the future of the TUC would have been at risk. For, as we have seen, the TUC emerged as the other political expression of the trade unions, actively lobbying on behalf of the Labour movement at both Westminster and Whitehall. But although the House of Lords gave no guidance as to whether such activity would be lawful, it may well be that the courts in this country would have permitted some forms of such activity. This is supported by the Scottish decision in *Blackburn* v. *Stewart*[82] where a

THE OSBORNE JUDGMENT 33

dispute arose when a Bill had been introduced in Parliament to amalgamate two railway companies. The directors of one of the companies resolved to petition against the amalgamation, and authorised funds to be uplifted to defray the expense. The question before the court was whether such expenditure of company funds was competent. In replying in the affirmative, L. J. C. Hope said:

> I am very clearly of opinion that a railway company has the power to employ the funds of the company in resisting any bill in Parliament . . . which clearly tends to destroy the value of their stock, or to declare that they shall no longer be a company under their original statutes, but be sunk and amalgamated with another on terms which they consider most injurious to themselves.[83]

Further support for the view that certain forms of pressure group activity was lawful was provided by the Supreme Court of New South Wales in *Allen* v. *Gorten*,[84] where Harvey J. held that such activity would be lawful provided there was a direct connection between the campaign and the statutory objects of the union. In that case, however, a payment of £100 to an anti-conscription campaign was held *ultra vires* on the ground that this was not a matter which directly affected trade unions as such but was a political matter which affected all the lieges of the Crown in exactly the same way.

A second question is whether after *Osborne* there were any forms of parliamentary representation that trade unions could lawfully secure. Both Lords Shaw and James would have permitted such representation, provided no improper constraints were imposed on the member of Parliament. And although the Earl of Halsbury seemed uncompromising, Lords Macnaghten and Atkinson may have left some room for manoeuvre. It is arguable that their decisions were based on the belief that the union had gone too far and that it had in fact converted itself into a political organisation. This is particularly evident in Lord Atkinson's speech, and it is notable that he qualified some of his remarks by considering whether 'parliamentary representation in the manner in this case contended for' was lawful.[85] So it may well be that a union could continue to pay a modest retainer to a member of Parliament who as 'parliamentary consultant' looked after its interests in Parliament. It could hardly be said that the union had converted itself into a political organisation by incurring such a modest expense. A more difficult and controversial question is whether after *Osborne* there were any circumstances in which a trade union could sponsor parliamentary candidates and thereby continue direct representation. As we have seen, much of the analysis in the *Osborne* case was predicated upon the rule of the ASRS that the union would pursue parliamentary representation through the medium of the

Labour Party. But what if a trade union candidate fought an election on a distinctly trade union platform and presented only trade union issues? While such a possibility might appear far-fetched, it is not beyond the realms of possibility that the miners' unions in particular could have profitably embarked upon such a course. In engaging in such activity would a union have converted itself into a political organisation, or could this limited form of political representation be seen to be an extension of the trade purposes of the union?

On the whole, the courts tended to overlook such subtleties in subsequent cases and it was soon made clear that the effect of the *Osborne* judgment was to render unlawful all forms of parliamentary and municipal representation by the unions.[86] Injunctions were granted to aggrieved trade unionists in order to restrain a host of unions from making payments 'to the Labour Party or to any other bodies or persons for the purpose of securing or maintaining Parliamentary representation'. All methods of parliamentary representation were held to be unlawful, regardless of whether such activity involved any connection with a political party and regardless of whether it was clearly undertaken in order to pursue statutory objects. The first point was confirmed in a number of cases in which the courts restrained the direct expenditure of unions on parliamentary representation where the party political interest of the union was not obviously apparent. In *Buck* v. *Typographical Association*,[87] an injunction was granted to restrain the association operating a fund for the purpose of paying 'the necessary expenses incurred in running one candidate for the House of Commons; to pay such Parliamentary representative (if elected) a sufficient sum for maintenance and travelling expenses . . . and to assist branches who may obtain election to any public body'. The second point was underlined by decisions such as that in *Johnstone* v. *Associated Ironmoulders of Scotland*[88] where the rules to which Lord Skerrington took objection provided quite simply that as it is important, for the protection of our trade interest, that we should have representation in the House of Commons, the Executive Council shall take such steps as may be deemed necessary to give effect to the principle of Labour Representation'.

However, it may be noted that this interpretation of the *Osborne* judgment was not universally accepted. There were a few exceptions, even if they were but straws in the wind, to the large number of cases which did underline the orthodox view. One such exception was the case of *Wight* v. *Buckland*[89] where the plaintiff was a member of the Dundee branch of the Postmen's Federation. The Federation's rules provided that every branch should pay annually to the central fund two shillings and sixpence per member in affiliation fees. One shilling of this affiliation fee was to be set aside for parliamentary purposes. In

1909, the expenditure of the federation included the payment of a parliamentary secretary's salary, affiliation fees paid to the Labour Party, and payments amounting to over £1,000 in respect of the election expenses of the Labour candidate for Dundee. The plaintiff sought to restrain the Federation from contributing to a) the Labour Party, b) parliamentary election expenses or c) any purpose whatever connected with or in furtherance of securing parliamentary represent-ation. Counsel for the Federation took objection to c). Warrington J. sustained the objection and granted an injunction restraining the Federation 'from contributing, whether by way of contribution to the Labour Party or otherwise, to the support of the candidature for Parliament, or the maintenance as a Member of Parliament of any person who, as a condition of such support or maintenance, pledged himself to perform his duties as a Member of Parliament under the direction of a particular person or body of persons'.

2. TO WHICH TRADE UNIONS? The second major question which arose after the *Osborne* judgment was whether it applied to all trade unions, or only to those unions whose affairs were regulated by the 1871–6 Acts. In his speech, Lord Atkinson was clearly influenced by the fact that the union was registered, saying that

> it is clear, in my view, that they are, when registered, quasi-corporations, resembling much more closely railway companies incorporated by statute than voluntary associations of individuals merely bound together by contract or agreement, express or implied. And it is plain that, as soon as this character was given to them, and the rights and privileges they now enjoy were con-ferred upon them, it became a matter of necessity to define the purposes and objects to which they were at liberty to devote the funds raised from their members by enforced contributions.[90]

Similarly, the Earl of Halsbury was influenced by the fact that the union owed its legal status to the Act of 1871 and for that reason was restricted to the purposes outlined therein. He said that the 1871 Act did not legalise 'a combination' for anything but only for the statutory purposes. Lord Macnaghten was influenced by both of these con-siderations. Thus he said that the union was one which owed its constitution and status to an Act of Parliament which defined its lawful objects and powers.[91] Although this would have been a suffi-cient basis for the development of his argument, he also said, after discussing the *ultra vires* rule:

> This principle (ultra vires) is not confined to corporations created by special Acts of Parliament. It applies, I think, with equal force in every case where a society or association formed for purposes recognised and defined by an Act of Parliament places

itself under the Act, and by so doing obtains some statutory immunity or privilege. . . . The society with which this case is concerned is a trade union registered under the Act of 1871. That Act defines in language amended by the Act of 1876 the purposes of trade unions, and purports to confer certain privileges on unions registered under its provisions.[92]

But what if a trade union was neither registered nor unlawful at common law? It would seem to follow that in such circumstances *Osborne* would have no application. So those unions that were lawful at common law could avoid the constraints imposed by the decision by the simple expedient of de-registration. And in this context it is not insignificant that two years after the *Osborne* judgment, Lord Macnaghten should recognise in *Russell* v. *Amalgamated Society of Carpenters and Joiners*,[93] in litigation on a different point: 'There have been many and probably there may be still some trade unions lawful in every point of view, and not depending for their legality or for their immunity on the Act of 1871'. But perhaps unsurprisingly, the courts refused to permit *Osborne* to be circumvented in this way. The leading case on the point is *Wilson* v. *Scottish Typographical Association*.[94] STA was an unregistered union which in 1907 had adopted new rules to extend its objects to include the promotion of labour representation in Parliament. A parliamentary fund was established from which it was intended that the election and maintenance expenses of a member of Parliament would be paid. The pursuer objected to this alteration of the objects of the union and successfully obtained a declarator that the rule-change was unlawful and an interdict to restrain expenditure in pursuance of the rule. But on the crucial question of whether *Osborne* applied to unregistered unions, Lord Skerrington replied in the negative, saying that it 'has no application to a society which has no statutory constitution, and which is merely a voluntary association, such as an unregistered trade union'.[95]

However, in the Inner House, Lord Skerrington's decision on this point was reversed, with Lord Dundas holding that such an interpretation of *Osborne* was both narrow and inadequate.[96] In his view, the *Osborne* decision involved wider grounds which were applicable to unregistered as well as registered trade unions. But these grounds could only have been twofold. The first was the constitutional question, but there was no examination in *Wilson* of whether STA members of Parliament would be subject to improper pressures. The second was that the union was unlawful at common law and so relied for its legal status on the 1871 Act. Again there was no examination of this point, and even if there had been such an examination showing the union to be unlawful at common law, this would not have been conclusive in view of the fact that only two of the five Lords of Appeal were influenced by this in *Osborne*. That decision was only a compelling authority where both strands of the majority reasoning were present. In this case neither strand existed and the decision must therefore be considered doubtful, a point which was subsequently confirmed by the High Court of Australia when in *Williams* v. *Hursey*[97] it refused to follow *Wilson*. The only ground on which the decision can be supported is for the reason advanced by Lord Guthrie, namely that the parliamentary representation rule was unlawful because the Association's rules contained no power of alteration. But regardless of its merits, the decision closed an important loophole which might have permitted some unions to evade the *Osborne* judgment. If unions were to retain their political interest and commitment, it was clear that legislation was now essential to enable that interest and commitment to be expressed in a realistic and effective manner.

THE TRADE UNION ACT 1913

Predictably, the Labour Party reacted with great anger to the *Osborne* judgment, and with not inconsiderable anxiety as injunction after injunction began to control the political spending of a growing number of unions.[1] Resolutions calling for a reform of the law were passed at the annual conferences of the Labour Party, the TUC, individual trade unions, and at conferences of the Joint Board, which was a body composed of representatives of the party, the TUC and the GFTU. The Labour Party was acutely aware of the fact that eventually it would be choked by the efforts to cut off its supply of income. Within a year of the judgment being delivered, no fewer that twenty-five unions found their political activities restrained by injunction, and this number continued to rise. The unions were equally aware that the judicial activity had struck a heavy blow 'at the freedom enjoyed by trade unions to adopt from time to time such up-to-date methods of defence as changing industrial conditions seem to force upon them'. It was stated time and again that political action was necessary if the unions were to fulfil properly their duty of regulating relations between masters and workmen. For it was argued that while much could be done by collective bargaining, there were nevertheless some issues of interest to the unions – from general economic reforms to the regulation of health and safety in the mines – which could only be realistically promoted by legislation. The blow was felt all the harder in view of the feeling that unions alone of interest groups were denied the opportunity of parliamentary representation.

But apart from its effect on parliamentary representation and the development of the Labour Party, the *Osborne* judgment troubled the unions on a number of other grounds. First, they were concerned by what they understood to be the chaotic and uncertain state of the law which *Osborne* had created. Not only was there great uncertainty about the scope of trade union powers generally, but it had been suggested by lawyers that any political work in which the unions might engage, whether it be by means of the TUC Parliamentary Committee, trades councils, or even deputations to ministers, could be unlawful. Secondly, they were troubled by the apparent willingness of the judges to uphold the rights of Osborne and his dissident minority in preference to the interests of the majority in the unions. One spokesman at a special Labour Party conference to discuss the case commented that he would not have quarrelled with the decision so much if the judges, in declaring that the minority should be protected, had been content to say that if the individual had an objection he might have a refund of his political levy. But he took very great exception when a small minority was 'declared to be the master of the situation'. Ramsay MacDonald expressed similar sentiments at a subsequent meeting of the Joint Board when he said: 'No member of a Trade Union . . . ought to be able to establish, in a court of law or outside a court of law a system of individual right which paralysed the activity of the union to which he belonged'. A third reason for union concern at the *Osborne* judgment was the feeling that it was part of a more general attack on the freedoms of trade unionists. Trade unions were not only prevented from seeking redress by parliamentary means, but it appeared that the government was determined to respond more firmly to industrial action, with troops being used in South Wales to deal with strikes. At a Joint Board meeting in 1910, a representative of the Amalgamated Society of Engineers complained:

> Look at the position today – and the Trade Unionist would have to take serious cognisance of how he stands. If he came out on strike in South Wales, and if he began to put his position forcibly, a kindly State Department sent a telegram of sympathy and the Hussars. If he went to the House of Commons prepared to argue the matter out calmly and quietly . . . he was sent to the Law Lords and declared to be an exile and outlaw.

THE GOVERNMENT RESPONSE

The initial response of the spokesmen of the labour movement was to demand a complete reversal of *Osborne*. Nothing less was to be entertained. But until the necessary legislation was introduced the unions restrained by injunction were encouraged to defy the law in order to collect money for political purposes. Labour leaders proclaimed their willingness to face the risk of imprisonment, rather than face the probability of the falling to pieces of the great organisation they had built up.[2] But despite the subsequent assertion by Ramsay MacDonald that the legal developments had been met by 'a form of passive resistance which is far larger than any form of passive resistance that ever we have known in this country',[3] there seems to be little evidence that any of the unions against whom injunctions were granted had accepted the advice of their political allies. As Gwyn incisively remarked, 'defiance of the law expressed itself more in speech than action, and there were no Labour martyrs as a result of the Law Lords' decision'.[4] Much more common were funds such as those of the Amalgamated Society of Railway Servants, the Typographical Association, the Amalgamated Society of Engineers, and the miners' unions, which were maintained, if not at a very high level, by voluntary subscriptions.[5]

In raising money in this way the unions came into contact with the law yet again. The practice of voluntary contributions seems to have been accepted by the courts, though it is difficult to reconcile any form of political spending with *Osborne*. However, the courts insisted that the levies should be voluntary and that no sanctions should be applied to those who refused to contribute. And in determining whether contributions were voluntary, rigorous demands were imposed on the unions. The most significant litigation in this context was *Wilson* v. *Amalgamated Society of Engineers*,[6] the decision in which anticipated a heated political controversy. The union responded to the *Osborne* judgment by informing members that if they objected to paying the political levy they must give written notice to their branch secretary. In other words, they had to contract out of the obligation to make the payment, with the union arguing that this was quite voluntary on the part of those members who paid the levy. But the court thought otherwise, Parker J. holding that it was reasonably clear that the way the union 'levied those subscriptions in fact made them levies of a compulsory rather than a voluntary nature'. Unless the members chose to object in a particular manner, he continued, they were charged with the levy without further or in fact any consent on their behalf. That was 'really a compulsory levy, whatever may be said to the contrary'.

While some unions were thus endeavouring to raise money by voluntary subscriptions, the party and the TUC Parliamentary Committee were seeking an amendment to the law. Many traditional pressure group methods were employed: the matter was raised in an adjournment debate,[7] private members' bills were drafted, and ministers, including the Prime Minister, were lobbied.[8] These tactics were to yield some results, for ministers were on the whole sympathetic to the claim for legislation to deal with *Osborne*. But the reason why a Liberal government should have been so willing to respond to the needs of the Labour Party are far from clear. The Liberal landslide victory of 1906 had been erased by general elections in 1910 and the government now relied on the support of the 40 or so Labour members of Parliament on many issues. There is some controversy as to whether legislation to deal with *Osborne* was a price paid by the government for that support.[9] Although this seems a reasonable inference, there is nothing to confirm it in much of the contemporary documents and it was equally true that 'the Labour party was obliged to sustain the Liberal party in power at all costs'.[10] So the dependence was mutual. Withdrawal of Labour support from the government would have led to the collapse of the government and yet another general election, of which there had already been two in 1910. The party had no desire to fight another election which might lead to the return of the Conservatives. If that happened, legislation to deal with *Osborne* and the other measures for which Labour was campaigning would be unlikely.[11]

So it seems that there was no obvious haste for a government response. Yet only one Cabinet minister, Sir William Robson, the Attorney-General, appeared to urge delay in dealing with the question, drawing attention to the fact that the Labour Party was now determined to put up a candidate in all constituencies if it could afford to do so, and that by reversing *Osborne* they would open up the great war chest of union funds to the party.[12] In other words, the Labour Party would be competing for Liberal voters and it was not in the interests of the government to ensure that Labour did so from a position of financial strength. Yet his colleagues seem to have been more concerned with the injustice of the *Osborne* decision and a few permitted this to cloud their judgment on the wider political implications. Thus Sydney Buxton, the President of the Board of Trade, argued in favour of legislation on the ground that any restriction on the political activities of trade unions would seriously weaken the position of the unions, particularly at a time of strong combination of capital. Similarly, Herbert Samuel, Postmaster-General, submitted that if large numbers of the working classes desired to be represented in Parliament by members who were not attached to any of the older parties, it was wrong that legal or economic barriers should be erected to prevent them. He continued by predicting that if *Osborne* was not reversed, new working class organisations would evolve for the purposes of parliamentary representation and 'they would lack such steadying influences as many of the Trade Unions are now able to exercise on the labour movement. Existing for one purpose only, they would probably tend to emphasise their raison d'être, to increase the separation between Labour and Liberalism, and continually to become more socialistic.' So while Robson anticipated a future in which Labour and Liberals would be in open competition, Samuel it seems expected the spirit of co-operation between the parties to survive.

But although most ministers supported the need for legislation, it seems that only the Lord Chancellor would have supported an almost complete reversal of *Osborne*. His only qualification was that members who had joined before the union had adopted political objects should be exempt from paying the political levy. But this right should not be extended to any other members for he failed to see 'what considerations of morals or policy ought to prevent Trade Unions from making it a condition of membership that members shall subscribe for political purposes, always supposing that they become members with knowledge of the terms upon which they had joined'. He continued by saying that if the member did not like the politics of the union, he was free to leave, just as he could do if there was any other issue of policy with which he disagreed. No one had a right of exemption in relation to any other form of union activity and there was no reason in principle why it should be introduced here. But the Lord Chancellor was on his own for apparently without exception other ministers took the view that there should be a much wider right of exemption which should be applicable to all members. The Chancellor of the Duchy of Lancaster argued that any other proposal would 'sap all civil and political liberty' of the working class if people were compelled to support members of Parliament with whom they had no sympathy on vital issues altogether outside the field of labour. The Secretary of State for War and the Postmaster General also supported a wide right of exemption as did the President of the Board of Trade who added only that the exempt member should be required to pay a sum in lieu of the political levy to some other fund of the union.

The government's intention to legislate along the lines suggested by the majority of ministers was announced in the House of Commons by the Prime Minister on 22 November 1910.[13] A Bill to this effect was introduced on 24 May 1911 and provided that unions could engage in political objects if a number of safeguards were first complied with. Political objects were defined with some precision as relating to such matters as the election and maintenance of members of Parliament, and the registration of electors, the government thereby rejecting one suggestion made in Cabinet, namely that the objects should not be defined, or should only be defined in loose terms as relating to 'parliamentary and municipal action and representation and kindred objects'.[14] The Bill then proposed that a union wishing to engage in the political objects must first seek the approval of its members in a ballot for that purpose. A simple majority of those in favour would suffice, the government having rejected yet another suggestion in Cabinet that political objects could be established only with the support of two-thirds of the members of the union voting in the ballot.[15] With member support, the union could then adopt rules to establish a separate political fund to finance their political expenditure. The rules would be required to provide that union members were not to be required to contribute to the fund and were not to be penalised for refusing to do so.

In commending the individual rights provisions to the House of Commons, the Home Secretary, Winston Churchill, argued that it was important that the conscientious convictions of workmen should be respected.[16] And although critics might reply that the workman could protect his conscience by leaving his union, Churchill claimed that because of the operation of the closed shop, this was impossible in many cases: 'In a great many trades . . . to leave the union would involve leaving the only means by which [the worker] could earn his living'.[17] But Churchill's appeal fell on deaf ears so far as the Labour Party was concerned. The party supported the Bill at Second Reading but made it clear that it would have to be materially amended during its further stages in order to be satisfactory. Neither the Labour Party nor the unions were prepared to accept the minority right provisions, and at a Joint Board meeting in June 1911 the party was instructed not to support the Third Reading of the Bill unless these provisions were removed. As a result of this opposition, and perhaps also in response to the pressure on parliamentary time, the Bill was withdrawn, though the Prime Minister promised that another Bill would be introduced later. In the meantime the government not only faced repeated demands from both unions and party for a complete reversal of *Osborne*, but also threats of the kind implicit in the following remark made to the Prime Minister by a member of a trade union deputation which met him on 15 February 1912:

> I submit that freedom to develop along natural lines within the objects assigned to Trade Unions is essential to their effectiveness; that a refusal of this freedom will inevitably mean, as has already been the case to a large extent, that the unions will be forced to revert to less peaceable methods of securing industrial reforms. In that connection, I would remind you that since the last deputation on this subject waited upon you there has been dramatic evidence of a great unrest in the Labour world, and that this movement has assumed such proportions as to demand and receive considerable attention from Parliament. I am quite certain that recent industrial disputes have been embittered by a feeling on the part of the workers that they have been treated unfairly in the law courts.[18]

Yet despite this pressure the government's second Bill was much the same as the first, to the annoyance of the unions who deeply resented the interference with their autonomy in matters of self government. Pressure for a complete reversal of *Osborne* again concentrated on efforts in Parliament and Labour members took every opportunity to expose the injustice of the government's proposals. First, it was pointed out that the unions were only asking for the same system of government and the right of administrative action as were enjoyed by the member of the Co-operative Society, by the shareholder of a company, and the citizen of a city. In any one of these instances, it was claimed, the majority rules.[19] Labour spokesmen appeared to be genuinely astonished by the proposed framework which enabled all members of a union to participate in the ballot to adopt parliamentary objects but which then permitted members who did not agree with the decision, to opt out of the collective obligation. The role of such people within the movement, it was suggested, was to express their opinion and carry on a propaganda to turn the minority into a majority.[20] It was also pointed out that the principle of majority rule operated in all other areas of union activity, that members had no general right to pick and choose what activity they would support, and no attempt was made to protect the individual's conscience in these fields.[21] There was no reason in principle, it was argued, why the same should not apply here. Indeed, any other approach would be unreasonable and inequitable because it would encourage free riders, these members who took the benefits of parliamentary action without accepting responsibility for its cost. As J. R. Clynes argued:

> We are told that men have consciences. I have yet to find the man who has a conscientious objection to receiving any of the benefits which our political activities secure to him. If a man receives these benefits arising from the political activities of trade unions, on what principle can you say that these men shall escape paying for them?[22]

But the nearest Labour members came to securing any success was in Standing Committee when an amendment by MacDonald designed fully to restore the pre-Osborne position was defeated by only 19 votes to 17.[23] Both government and Parliament were thus unmoved by the Labour arguments, and the party had to admit defeat and accept the offer of qualified reversal of *Osborne*. It is true that there was no immediate financial need propelling the party in this direction for despite *Osborne* and the series of other injunctions, party finances were still relatively healthy. The largest single item of expenditure was the salaries of members of Parliament. In 1911 the party had forty members who were each paid £200 per annum from the Parliamentary Representation Fund Account. This fund was also used to pay election expenses, yet at the end of 1910, a year of two general elections, the balance stood at £8,411. However, income to the fund was beginning to fall, with only £7,093 being contributed in 1911, a sum which would have been insufficient to meet ear-marked expenses. In 1911 a system of State payment of members of Parliament was introduced by the government with the deliberate aim of helping the Labour Party. Consequently, the Parliamentary Representation Fund was wound up, no longer having a purpose to serve, with the balance being transferred to the general fund. Thereafter, the party anticipated that it would need an income of £5,000 per annum to meet its running costs. In order to achieve this, the method of raising money was altered with each affiliated organisation now being required to pay 1d per affiliated member. In 1912 this system of fund raising yielded almost £4,000 which was added to the balance in the general fund, which at the beginning of 1912 stood at £14,188. So the party was not without funds. In fact, such were the state of party finances, that in 1912 the party could feel sufficiently generous to invest £6,000 in Labour Newspapers Ltd![24]

Yet the party's future was hardly a secure one. Income would slowly drain as more injunctions disabled more unions from affiliating to the party. The party's reserves would thus slowly evaporate as they were called upon to meet the annual income deficit. And the relative security of the party could have been of little comfort to the leaders of several powerful unions who because of injunctions against their unions were denied any effective influence in its affairs. With an air of resignation the government's proposals were accepted, on the ground that they permitted 'Trade Unions to engage in political action under conditions which, though unfair, can nevertheless be made immediately operative'.[25] It may also be the case that the unions were moved by the anti-union activities of employers which had been undertaken with the support of some Conservative members of Parliament. Employers actively sought sweeping amendments to the Trade Disputes Act 1906 and with this end in view they had lobbied the Prime Minister and had secured the introduction of several private members' bills in both Houses of Parliament. Roberts has argued: 'Many of those who previously would have accepted nothing less than a full restoration of freedom to undertake political activities were now prepared to put up with the limitations which the Government Bill imposed, for it at least gave the trade union movement the chance to use its financial resources to fight the Conservatives in the political field'.[26]

THE CONSERVATIVE RESISTANCE

The Conservatives had two major criticisms of the government's proposals. The first was that political funds would be immune from legal action by virtue of the Trade Disputes Act 1906, s.4 which provided that an action in tort against any trade union was not to be entertained by any court. The second criticism of the government's proposals related to the provisions which dealt with the position of the dissenter. If the Labour spokesmen were convinced that the provisions for the protection of the dissenter were an unjustified intrusion into the domestic affairs of trade unions, the Conservative and Unionist opposition spokesmen were equally convinced that the proposed protection was inadequate. The following account is based mainly on reports of parliamentary proceedings where the Conservative case was presented by a group of 'young titled Members' led by Viscount Wolmer.

The *Daily Citizen* took great delight in taunting this group of Conservative back-benchers as anti-Trade Unionists whose impassioned speeches on behalf of union minorities carried make believe rather far. It is unclear how widespread this opposition was, though it may be noted that the Second Reading of the first government Bill was carried by 226 votes to 49 and the second by 232 to 132.

1. THE LIABILITY OF UNION FUNDS. The Conservatives sought to qualify s.4 of the 1906 Act so that it would not apply to any action in respect of a tortious act committed in furtherance of a political object. An amendment to the government's Bill was introduced both in Standing Committee and on Report in an attempt to give effect to this proposal.[27] In supporting the amendment, Conservative spokesmen were alert to emphasise its limited application. Thus: 'All this Clause asks is that where a trade union outside its ordinary trade activities, in the course of a political action should, in its corporate capacity, commit a libel, the political funds of that trade union should be responsible for that libel'. Some concern was expressed about the fact that if the Bill passed without such an amendment, no remedy would be available if this new power of the unions was abused in any way. Such concern was not alleviated by statements that a remedy would lie against trade union officials and members in an individual capacity. As one Conservative spokesman argued: 'The remedy against those individuals in this matter is practically futile. The individuals who have been put forward are men of straw.' Objections were also made that trade unions were the only bodies with an immunity in respect of such activity.

The Attorney-General was unmoved by these objections and pointed out that Parliament had passed section 4 of the 1906 Act without qualification at a time when 'it was thought by all lawyers – certainly by the vast majority of lawyers – that trade unions were entitled to indulge in the political activities'. The government Bill was merely reverting to that position. He also claimed that there was an enormous amount of exaggeration as to the effect of s.4 for although a remedy would not lie against a trade union for torts committed in furtherance of political activities, such a remedy would lie against the individual who was responsible. In such circumstances an injunction could be obtained, which, he claimed, was often all that was really wanted. And in this respect trade unions were no different from other political organisations. It was pointed out that if a member of the Tariff Reform League, the Cobden Club or any political party committed a libel, only the individual would be liable and not the organisation of which he was a member. The amendment was negatived without a division in Standing Committee and was heavily defeated on Report.

2. PROTECTING THE DISSENTER. To many Conservative members of Parliament the need for a comprehensive framework to protect the individual appeared to be obvious. In the words of F.E. Smith, 'intimidation [was] simply rampant in trade unions in these matters'.[28] Similar views were expressed by other Conservative spokesmen. Thus: 'As a matter of fact, everyone here who has experience of trade unions knows that the system of intimidation, terrorism and tyranny that is exercised against these few members who dare to exercise their conscience is too much for the ordinary working man to bear'.[29] It was also alleged that unless the proposed legislation was comprehensive in its efforts to protect the individual, the result would be that 'members of trade unions working side by side with men who would not contribute would make their life in that trade union impossible'[30] and that consequently the conservative and conscientious working man would be compelled to 'give his money in the form of subscriptions to the objects of socialism which he properly and conscientiously loathes'.[31] These fears spawned a number of proposals designed to improve those provisions of the Bill which related to the rights of minorities.

The Ballot. One cause of Conservative anxiety was the fact that the Liberal proposals would permit a trade union to engage in politics if a majority voting in a ballot for this purpose approved such a scheme. This meant, it was argued, that 'an extraordinary small minority of the total members of a union may legalise the practice of exhorting political contributions from all the members'. Consequently, an amendment was introduced both in Committee and on Report which would require a majority of members of the union to vote in the ballot and to approve the proposed activity of the union.[32] It was argued that the Act would, in effect, require a form of contribution 'which will be practically compulsory' and therefore it was essential that 'If people are to contribute to the return of Members of Parliament with whom they are not in agreement, then I think it is very necessary we should at least ascertain there is a majority of the members of the trade unions who have taken the trouble to vote one way or the other on this all-important subject'. However, these amendments were also rejected because they would effectively disable trade unions from engaging in political activity. It seems that then, as now, apathy in elections and ballots was a considerable problem in trade unions and it would have been almost impossible for unions to get a majority of their members to vote, far less vote in favour of the proposal. This is a problem which was confirmed by the small turnout on ballots which were held under the Trade Union Act 1913. However, in rejecting these amendments the Attorney-General made the startling deduction that 'as a rule men who do not vote refrain from doing so because they are satisfied with what the Executive proposes'. The logical consequence of such reasoning is that trade unions would be permitted to engage in political action unless a majority of the members of the union voted against the Executive proposal in a ballot. The Attorney-General was on surer ground when he met Conservative points by insisting that the Bill prevented compulsion, not only by enabling all members to vote in the ballot, but also by allowing them to contract out of the obligation to pay the political levy even if they were in the minority in the ballot or even if they failed to vote in the ballot.

Contracting-In. The Opposition sought to ensure a greater degree of minority protection by other means. Thus, rather than permit the individual to claim exemption by contracting out, they sought to substitute a scheme of contracting in by which only those who positively assented to paying the contribution would in fact do so. Viscount Wolmer thought that this proposal was 'thoroughly consistent with the whole principle upon which the Bill is founded', namely that while unions were to be permitted to engage in politics, there was to be no pressure put upon any member who disagreed with the policy of the Labour Party to contribute his money to the funds of that party. Wolmer saw as a defect in the Liberal proposals the fact that although provision was made for a secret ballot this guarantee was undermined by the requirement that dissenters must thereafter declare themselves if they wished to claim exemption. He alleged that in previous years men who had dared to make formal application for exemption from paying to the political funds of their unions had been victimised. Presumably, he thought that such practices would continue in the future and he argued that the amendment which he proposed would go a long way towards removing this danger. By simply remaining silent, the dissenter 'would not be exposing himself to the same obloquy as he would if he had to go forward and take the same steps which Mr. Osborne had to take'.[33]

Amendments to this effect were defeated both in Committee[34] and on Report.[35] Indeed, it seems that Viscount Wolmer was fortunate in being permitted to air his views in Committee for 'the Chairman gave a strong hint that [the] amendment ought not to have been brought forward, inasmuch as while it was not formally out of order it proposed in effect the reversal of almost everything done by the Committee hitherto'. However both in Committee and on Report, the Attorney-General and Ramsay MacDonald spoke firmly against the proposal. It was argued that the amendment would destroy the Bill and fundamentally alter the principle upon which it was founded. In MacDonald's view, the whole policy of the Bill was to make the carrying out of political objects one of the ordinary functions of the unions once the ballots had been taken. The Bill was not designed to enable individuals to spend money to help the Labour Party; it was to permit trade unions in their corporate capacity to engage in political activity as a means of promoting the interests of their members. The Attorney-General made similar points and also drew attention to the fact that by adopting the measures of minority protection which the Bill included, the government was already imposing duties on trade unions which no other organisation had to endure.

Remedies for Victimisation. One of the most contentious aspects of both government Bills was that although some provision had been made in an attempt to protect the individual non-contributor from discrimination, no method of pursuing these rights was provided. Consequently, it was insisted that the proposals would be inadequate to guarantee individual protection until provision was made 'to enable a man who has refused to pay the Parliamentary levy and who has subsequently been ejected from his union, to call upon the officials to shew cause why they have ejected him from that union'.[36] It was argued that that was an absolutely essential feature of the Bill before it could be made to be workable. The government had proposed that the individual should pursue his rights through the normal judicial channels. But the Opposition was quick to realise that the position was complicated by the Trade Union Act 1871, s.4, which prohibited, *inter alia*, 'any court' from entertaining 'any legal proceedings instituted with the object of directly enforcing . . . Any agreement for the application of the funds of a trade union . . . To provide benefits to members'. The government consistently took the view that this was not necessarily a bar to legal proceedings and during the Second Reading debate of the second Bill, the Attorney-General said: 'as the law stands, a trade union cannot be sued for the payment of benefits to its members, and equally a trade union cannot sue a member for refusing to pay his contributions to the union. But I am by no means prepared to say that there could not be an application for an injunction to restrain a union from excluding a member from benefit.'[37]

These assurances did little to allay Conservative anxieties and the matter was pursued in Committee where an amendment was introduced to make political fund rules enforceable in the courts.[38] This proposal was firmly opposed by the Attorney-General who said that he would sooner lose the Bill than agree to it. MacDonald also spoke strongly against the measure, saying:

> There are, as we well know, active organisations at work upon which employers place solicitors and others, who are watching every move of Trade Unions in the hope of tripping them up and smashing them. We are quite aware that if this amendment becomes law we shall have a continued series of law cases brought into court, not on their merits, but with the object of smashing

the unions by ruining them financially.

Although the amendment was defeated, Conservatives remained unhappy and complained that the rules would be useless unless they could be enforced. However, the Attorney-General's observations during the Second Reading debate made some impact on Labour Party members who were anxious to keep these matters out of the courts at all costs fearful of giving 'occupation to lawyers', to the distraction of matters of real concern. Consequently an amendment was introduced on Report by Mr George Wardle after consultation with the Attorney-General whereby any complaint of irregularity arising under the Bill would be made not in the courts but to the Chief Registrar of Friendly Societies.[39] But regardless of the reason for the amendment, it was warmly welcomed by the Conservatives. Thus Wolmer enthused: 'This amendment alters the Bill in a very important respect. It practically means that all the safeguards of the Bill, on which the Government have laid the greatest possible stress, have some reality about them, instead of being, as they were in our opinion before that, a fraud and a sham.'[40] This was a remarkable concession by a backbencher who had done much to obstruct the Bill's passage and who had earlier launched sweeping amendments to its terms. Nevertheless, the Bill was given an unopposed Third Reading and received the Royal Assent on 7 March 1913.

A Fragile Settlement

Such was the satisfaction of the Opposition in having secured this amendment, and with the provisions of the Act generally, that it might have been thought that any subsequent activity on their part to rewrite the 1913 Act would have been unlikely. Even the Leader of the Opposition said: '. . . in view of the fact that Amendments on Report stage had been made in the Bill, which have, in my opinion, gone a long way to make the protection real to enable the minority to protect itself, I do not intend to vote against the Third Reading'.[41] Much more likely would have been persistent effort from the Labour benches to remove the provision designed to protect the individual. However, events proved otherwise, and it took but ten years for a powerful move to reform the 1913 Act to develop within the Conservative Party.

By the early 1920s, opposition to the 1913 solution in the Conservative Party had become deep rooted. To a large extent this was a simple indulgence of traditional 'union bashing' and was inspired in some quarters by a desire to cripple the Labour Party. As one Conservative minister recognised in a Cabinet Memorandum:

The real point which we have to decide is this. Do we wish to attack Trade Unions as such or do we not? . . . the major part of the outcry against the political levy is not motivated by a burning indignation for the trade unionist, who is forced to subscribe to the furtherance of political principles which he abhors. It is based on a desire to hit the Socialist party through their pocket . . . What I submit is that at least we should not delude ourselves as to our intentions.[42]

However, the trade unions provided some valuable ammunition to their critics who readily identified a number of abuses, some real and some imagined, in the administration of trade union political funds. These abuses provided a pretext for the attack.

There was evidence that some trade unionists simply found it impossible to obtain exemption. This was particularly true in the years immediately following the enactment of the 1913 Act when a number of unions, not all of them small unions, paid affiliation fees and other political expenses from their general funds without complying with the terms of the 1913 Act. The party advised against this course because it exposed these unions to legal liability at the hands of dissenting members, yet also took the view that this was the business of each particular union and that it had no right or desire to interfere.[43] But even in these cases where the union had complied with the legal formalities, there were suspicions that in several unions members were not permitted to claim exemption. For example, the entire membership, 12,853, of the Plasterers' Union paid the political levy, as did the entire membership of the General Union of Textile Workers. Yet when the members of these unions were balloted, 657 and 2,037 respectively voted against the creation of a political fund. Contemporary commentators rightly doubted whether all these people were paying the levy voluntarily.[44]

There were also allegations that unions were dilatory and obstructive in enabling their members to exercise their statutory rights. A practice adopted by some unions was to continue to collect the same contribution from exempt members and to pay a refund at the end of the year, calling a special parade for this purpose. There were further allegations that exempt members were victimised by reason of their exemption and on one occasion it was even alleged that 'Intimidation goes so far on washing day for instance, that women are interfered with'![45] Whether or not this is true, it is clear that some unions required exempt members to pay a higher general contribution in lieu of their political levy, so that in effect they paid more for their general benefits than members who were not exempt. In other unions, effect was given to the exemption of members, but money was then transferred from the general fund to the political fund so that the income of the latter read as if all, or nearly all members paid the levy. For example, the practice of NUR was to allocate 10 per cent of total contributions to the political fund. In 1920 the union had 457,836 members of whom its returns identified 246,337 as contributing to the political fund. The total income of the union was £443,605 of which £42,661 was transferred to the political fund. So although only slightly more than 50 per cent of the members were contributors, a sum representing the payment of the levy by almost the whole membership was transferred to the political fund.[46]

These issues were exploited by some sections of the press in the early 1920s, and by the *Morning Post* in particular. They also stimulated the interest of members of the Conservative Party who were exerting pressure on Conservative Central Office to take steps to deal with the question. Resolutions in favour of reform were passed at the Annual Conference of the party in 1921, 1922 and 1923 and at numerous Provisional Division Meetings. There was also a keen interest expressed in Parliament by Conservative backbenchers, with Bills being introduced to substitute contracting out by contracting in in every session between 1922 and 1925. The first of these, sponsored by Colonel Meysey-Thompson, was given a Second Reading and completed a stormy and disorderly Committee stage, only to stumble because of the intervention of the general election in 1922. However, while the Bill was on its way through Parliament, both its sponsors and Conservative Central Office received together some 800 resolutions of support from various sources.[47] And such was the strength of parliamentary support for the measure that when it became apparent that the first Bill would fail because of the forthcoming general election, 258 members of Parliament signed a petition to Lloyd George and Austin Chamberlain, asking that facilities be given to enable the final stages of the Bill to be completed before the dissolution of Parliament.[48]

Notwithstanding this apparent ground-swell of support, the Lloyd George Cabinet was opposed to taking any steps to reform the 1913 Act. In 1922, in relation to the Meysey-Thompson Bill, the Minister of Labour, T. J. MacNamara, advised against any action, although he accepted that there might be some cases of people paying the political levy against their will and also that the principle of contracting in instead of contracting out was not unfair. However, to introduce legislation to make such provision would, he thought, be inappropriate for two reasons. The first was that the trade union movement was in 'very low water', with members being forced by economic depression 'to accept serious wage reductions without even a show of effective resistance'. To legislate in these conditions would be distorted to appear as an act of persecution. Secondly, the minister argued:

In recent months there has been a distinct drift in opinion among the mass of the trade unions away from fanciful political objectives to a serious consideration of the economic situation at home and abroad, and a consequent strengthening of the position of more responsible leaders. The extremists are, however, not yet settled; and they would quote the Bill as further evidence of the lack of impartiality on the part of the Government and they would use it as a means for rallying members (already disturbed by the wage reductions) to a policy of direct action.[49]

In the following year, MacNamara's successor, Sir Montague Barlow, also advised against legislation and the Conservative Cabinet was in any event reluctant to take any other course. A number of delaying tactics were suggested, including the appointment of a Commission or a Select Committee to investigate the question.[50] The Cabinet eventually decided in 1923 that it was too preoccupied with other questions to take the matter up but that it might do so later when it had less on its hands, in which case there would be full consultation with union leaders 'to try to get an arrangement that would seem fair to reasonable members of Trade Unions'.[51] A statement to this effect was made by the Chancellor of the Exchequer in the House of Commons on 19 April 1923.[52] But the government does not appear to have taken any action before its defeat at the general election in 1923. It is thus hardly surprising that the Conservative leadership continued to be pursued by aggressive backbenchers following the re-election of a Conservative government in 1924. That election, which took place after the fall of the first Labour government, gave the Conservatives an enormous majority, with 419 seats compared with the 117 and 40 won by Labour and Liberals respectively. Yet Baldwin's Cabinet stood firm against any reform of the 1913 Act and following the introduction of yet another private members' Bill in 1925, the Cabinet agreed that the Prime Minister should intervene at an early stage in the debate to impress upon the House that one of the main principles of the government's policy was to promote industrial peace. He was to make it clear that the government considered the 1913 Act to be unjust and wrong but that it would not bring its great majority to bear in support of a measure which would inevitably arouse acute controversy and bitterness. The Prime Minister would thus call upon the government's supporters in Parliament to sacrifice the Bill in the national interest.[53]

As agreed, the Prime Minister intervened during the Second Reading of the Trade Union Political Fund Bill on 6 March 1925.[54] But although Conservatives responded to his appeal, one backbencher said ominously that they could not let the matter rest for long. In fact, the campaign was rewarded within a space of two years when the 1913 Act was reformed by the Trade Disputes and Trade Unions Act 1927. This Act was introduced by a Conservative government bent on recrimination after the ill-fated General Strike of May 1926. The Act dealt with a number of issues. Section 1 took away the immunities for acts done in contemplation or furtherance of a trade dispute in the case of sympathy strikes which were designed to coerce the government, directly or indirectly; section 2 prohibited unions from expelling members who failed to take part in a strike declared illegal by section 1; section 3 introduced new constraints on the right to picket; section 4 altered the provisions relating to political funds, and in particular introduced a system of contracting in; section 5 effectively prohibited civil service unions from affiliating to the TUC and the Labour Party; and finally, section 6 made it unlawful for a local or public authority to require union membership as a condition of employment.

Rather curiously perhaps, s.4 did not figure in the government's initial plans. Even after the General Strike, the Cabinet was deeply divided on the desirability of legislating on this question. The Minister of Labour (by this time Steel-Maitland)[55] and the Attorney-General[56] opposed such a change in the law, with the former arguing firmly that it would be resented strongly by a large number of trade unionists who were not members of the Labour Party. And, significantly, he also argued that 'Outside the mining districts and apart from special cases, there was practically no sign that Trade Unionists were intimidated if they contracted out'.[57] But other members of the Cabinet took a different view, with the Lord Chancellor and the Chancellor of the Exchequer in particular arguing for some reform of the 1913 Act.[58] The latter contended that the political levy was a real and dangerous abuse and thought that it was incumbent upon the government to 'liberate working men from the unfair and humiliating position of being compelled under threat of ruin and starvation to subscribe to the propagation of political principles which they detest'. Interestingly, he coupled his suggestion with a proposal that all parliamentary candidates who polled a requisite number of votes should receive an Exchequer grant of £300 towards their expenses. This was intended to free the party from the charge that they sought to obstruct the entry of working men to Parliament. He thus recommended his policy as one of 'fair play to the workman whatever his opinions, cheaper elections for all Parties, [and] freedom of members and candidates from undue reliance on Party funds'.

In the early Cabinet skirmishes, it seems that the opponents of reform won the day. The first report of the Cabinet Legislation Committee (28 June 1926) outlining the possible forms which trade union legislation could take expressly stated that it did not consider it to be convenient to deal with the question of the political levy. The Committee was more concerned with effective measures to control industrial action and considered at length, but rejected, compulsory strike ballots supervised by the State, and recommended that it should be a criminal offence for local authority employees to break their contract of employment, a recommendation which was eventually accepted and contained in s.6 of the Act.[59] However, the Cabinet was under some pressure to deal with this question. The second report of the Cabinet Legislation Committee (2 August 1926) included the Report of an Inquiry by the Labour Advisory Sub-Committee of the National Union of Conservative and Unionist Associations.[60] This showed a large measure of support in the constituencies for the introduction of measures to deal with the 1913 Act, and the author of the report, H. E. Blain, concluded: 'The General Strike, by throwing into relief the irregularities which are associated with Trade Union administration today, has given the Conservative Party an opportunity which may never occur again to place the Trade Unions of the country once and for all upon a sound foundation'. The Cabinet had also canvassed the views of employers' organisations as to the form which the trade union legislation should take in the aftermath of the General Strike. By mid October the Committee was in receipt of three memoranda from the Enginering Employers' Federation, the National Union of Manufacturers, and the National Confederation of Employers' Organisations, all of which recommended the introduction of a system of contracting in.[61]

Following the receipt of this advice, the third report of the Legislation Committee (3 December 1926) stated that a majority of the members favoured the introduction of a system of contracting in.[62] This decision was taken despite the strongest possible reservations being expressed by the Minister of Labour. In a memorandum circulated in advance of the third meeting of the Committee, he argued:

They [trade unionists] will believe and be right in believing that political speakers, who are so solicitous for the non-labour trade unionist who has to contract out of the political levy, are less concerned with the principle of freedom of thought than with the income which the Labour Party draws from the Unions. They will say and be right in saying that most of the members who take up the cause of the trade unionist victimised in the General Strike are grasping a plausible pretext for attacking the autonomy of the union. If this be so, the alteration of the law concerning the political levy will be a boomerang that will inflict more hurt on the attackers than the object of attack. Further, by our action, we shall consolidate the Trade Unions and the Labour Party and play directly into the hands of the Extremists.

Trade Union organisation and administration is in need of reform. Reform from within is the only proper course in some respects. In others it is not and would also be a long business. In my view the policy of the Conservative party towards trade union-

ism should be in substance, and not merely in profession, constructive and not vindictive. It should be made capable of being
appreciated by the rank and file, not perhaps at first blush but at
any rate on reflection, as designed to help the unions to build
themselves up and to improve their internal administration.
Some element of coercion, or of apparent coercion, is inevitable
in any legislative proposals, but it ought to be as small as possible,
and it ought to be presented with as much regard as possible to
their deep-seated, if unreasonable, susceptibilities.[63]

But notwithstanding these arguments, which were also circulated to
other ministers, the Cabinet endorsed the Committee's new recommendation in December 1926 and the process of preparing the Bill for
introduction to Parliament was completed by the 30 March 1927.[64]
Given the pressure to which the government was exposed, from backbenchers, from the party and from employers, it is hardly surprising
that the Cabinet 'hawks' should have succeeded in the end.

THE OPERATION OF THE 1927 ACT

Section 4 of the 1927 Act endorsed many of the proposals which had
been pressed by backbenchers. Apart from introducing a system of
contracting in, it required unions to collect the political contribution
by means of a separate and distinct levy and prohibited them from
transferring any assets, other than the money raised by the political
levy, to their political funds.[65] The latter measure seems designed to
stop unions financing political activities by loans from their general
funds. However, the government did not adopt all the backbench
proposals. The Meysey-Thompson Bill, for example, provided that a
trade union could only adopt political objects if the ballot proposing
this step attracted a turnout of at least 50 per cent of the members of
the union. The Bill further proposed that there should be a majority of
at least 20 per cent of those voting in favour of the motion. These ideas
had been presented in order to respond to the fact that in many unions
political funds had been adopted following the vote in the ballot of a
small majority of the proportion of the total membership of the union.

But while the government resisted the temptation to embrace all the
proposals contained in the earlier Bills, at the same time it introduced
a further constraint on union political action. By section 5 of the 1927
Act, civil service unions were denied the opportunity of affiliating to
the Labour Party (and indeed to the TUC). This provision emanated
from the Treasury and seems to have been a direct consequence of the
General Strike. The Cabinet accepted 'the serious danger to the public
interest arising out of the entanglement of Civil Service Associations
with outside industrial and political bodies',[66] and the measure was
commended to the House of Commons on the ground that: 'Whatever

party is in power, the State should have the loyal and undivided service of those who have entered the Civil Service. They expect and receive from the State great benefits. They have a security of tenure.'[67] The proposal was warmly received by Conservative backbenchers who claimed that some civil service union officials had been involved in the General Strike, actively engaged in fomenting rebellion against the State. The liberation of civil servants from outside 'revolutionary associations', it was claimed, could only be to the benefit of civil servants and to the advantage of the State.[68] But predictably this measure was denounced by the Labour Party as a monstrous effort to sever one section of workers from another. It was claimed that the members of these unions had served every government without discrimination and that they had not entered into the General Strike nor had they been invited to do so.[69] For their part, the unions concerned saw this as an effort to destroy them or at the very least an attempt to deny them the strength and security which they had gained from association with other bodies.[70]

Labour hostility to the contracting in provisions was well-rehearsed with the party being required to resist the Conservative pressure that had been building up since the early years of the decade. Contracting in, it was claimed, would seriously undermine the political work of the unions for no good reason. The 1913 Act had been unanimously approved by the House of Commons and there had been nothing in the interim to justify any change. Indeed, the fact that the Chief Registrar had received only 66 complaints under the Act was proof that it was working well. But even if the allegations of intimidation were accurate, that still did not justify the change proposed. It simply meant that there was a need to tighten up the safeguards for the individual. Labour spokesmen argued that it was unfair to compel the unions to go through with ballots and then completely frustrate the ballot by saying that any contribution must depend on the initiative of the individual member: government by majority rule meant that it was the minority who should claim exemption and not the majority who should claim the privilege of paying the levy.[71] Labour opposition and hostility to this change in the law was all the greater in view of the widespread belief that the concern for individual liberty was simply an excuse for the introduction of a measure deliberately designed to cripple the party financially.[72]

The change to contracting in was potentially very serious. The majority of trade unionists who had previously paid the political levy because they were too apathetic to do otherwise, were now the apathetic majority whom the unions had to persuade actively to contract in. In so doing, unions adopted a number of tactics. But few were quite so cavalier as some of the constituent unions of MFGB which seemed to follow the terms of the new Act in a very perfunctory manner indeed. The constituent unions of the Federation paid a levy for each contributing member to the political fund of the Federation. In practice, the Federation permitted its component unions to remit a sum for this purpose which was based on an estimated number of contributions. In his Report for 1936 the Chief Registrar includes details of an inquiry by him into the affairs of the Federation which established that some component unions did not collect a separate political contribution and paid the political levy to the Federation from their general funds. Although other unions did collect a separate levy, they put all their contribution income into a single fund, kept no records of the number of members who had contracted in, and thus paid levies to the Federation on the basis of a number of members which bore no relationship to the numbers who had expressed a willingness to pay. In other words, money was simply lifted from the general funds to pay for a notional figure determined by the leadership. The Chief Registrar found it necessary to draw the attention of six component unions to the fact that the statute required the political contribution to be levied separately and the unions agreed to make appropriate arrangements. The unions also undertook to keep proper records of the members who had contracted in so that their returns included only the actual contributions collected.

In a number of other unions less extreme measures were adopted in an attempt to ensure that members paid the levy. First, some unions remodelled their membership application form. The one used by TGWU was criticised by the Chief Registrar on the ground that it contained only one space for the member's signature, namely immediately below the political fund contribution notice which in turn appeared at the bottom of the form, immediately below the biographical details of the applicant. As the Chief Registrar pointed out, most applicants would naturally sign the form in the only space provided and would not perceive that they were contracting in, particularly as the practice in many cases seemed to be that the form was completed by the steward who simply asked the applicant to sign on the dotted line at the bottom.[73] In such circumstances it is true that if the Act were followed, the unsuspecting member would quickly realise that he was paying the levy and could equally as quickly give notification that he was no longer willing to contribute. The Act provided, by s.4(2), that political contributions were to be 'levied and made separately' so that members would be aware of what they were doing on the payment of each contribution. But the procedure in fact became not unlike a system of contracting out and exemption would not take effect until the following January. In any event not all unions faithfully followed this provision. The Chief Registrar construed it as requiring the member's contribution card to show the amount of the political levy in a separate column. Yet as late as 1939 RCA received a letter from the Chief Registrar whose attention had been drawn to the fact that the Association's cards had no such column.[74]

A second response to the Act was to encourage local officials to take positive steps to maintain the number who paid the levy. In both TGWU and RCA, for example, branches were instructed to regard it as part of normal organising activity to strive for 100 per cent contracting in. Members of RCA who failed to contract in were sent special letters, and by 1942 it seems that stewards were successfully persuading new members to contract in as a matter of course. Such persuasion was not unlawful so long as it was properly made and did not involve pressure of any kind.[75] The third response to the Act was perhaps the most controversial. In some unions a practice was adopted whereby all members would pay the same overall contribution. Those who did not contract in would have the total paid directly to the general fund while those who had contracted in would have a portion paid to each fund. In other unions contracted in members would pay slightly more than non-contracted in members but not a higher amount equivalent to the amount credited to the political fund. In effect then some contracted in members were given a total or partial set off from their general dues. However, this practice was quickly declared to be unlawful as being in breach of the political fund rules. It will be recalled that exempt members were not to be discriminated against by reason of some disability or disadvantage because of their exemption. The Chief Registrar held that the practice in question had precisely this effect because it required the exempt member to pay a higher general contribution than the member who had contracted in.[76] Yet notwithstanding a formal decision of the Chief Registrar on this point in 1928 the practice seemed to continue, and in 1936 and again in 1938 the Chief Registrar advised the Durham Miners' Association and the National Union of Dyers, Bleachers and Textile Workers that by employing it, they were acting in breach of the political fund rules.[77]

So a number of devices were used by the unions in an attempt to induce members to contract in. But they were not universally applied and where they were adopted, their success varied. The Act affected different unions in different ways, and for the purposes of exposition it is useful to identify four categories of union.[78] The first were those which simply gave up collecting money for political purposes. One example of this was the Scottish Horse and Motormen's Association which in 1926 had a membership of 10,000 of whom some 80 per cent paid the political levy. At its conference in 1927 it was unanimously agreed to 'delete the political rule' and political contributions were not collected until the fund was re-established in the 1930s. In the meantime the balance of £625 in the political fund was used to meet normal political expenses until it dwindled to a mere £18. A second group of unions were those whose political income fell dramatically as a result of the 1927 Act. The fortunes of two different unions are traced in table 1.

Table 1. Trade union political funds and the 1927 Act

Trade Union	Income from contributions (£)				
	1926	1927	1928	1929	1930
ISTC	—	3,304	797	1,611	—
NAUSA	1,771	1,698	194	183	159

SOURCE: The Income and Expenditure Accounts of the respective unions.

In neither of these cases was there any material change in membership in the years in question, nor does it appear that the levy was increased in either union. The levels of contracting in of ISTC members settled at about 33 per cent of the membership while the income of NAUSA gradually picked up to about £1,000 per annum.

A third group of unions were those which were able to obtain initially a high level of contracting in, but which were unable to sustain this level thereafter. NUR, for example, claimed that in 1928, 92 per cent of its members were contracted in. But this fell to 77 per cent in 1934, 69 per cent in 1937, and 57 per cent in 1943. Similarly TGWU maintained that 75 per cent of its members had contracted in immediately after the enactment of the 1927 Act. But again this had fallen to 62 per cent in 1932, and may have fallen still further in later years. At the biennial delegate conference of the union in 1937 the general secretary drew attention to the 'great disparity' existing between the general membership of the union and those paying the political levy. And in 1939 delegates were urged to secure a substantial improvement of the numbers contributing to the political fund. The fourth and final group of unions were those which were marginally affected by the Act. It seems unlikely that this would be a significantly large group. Yet RCA was able to keep numbers up: in 1935, 82 per cent of the members had contracted in, and this was to rise every year thereafter, reaching a remarkable 87 per cent in 1944. But this may have been exceptional and seems to have been due to a determined effort at all levels of the Association to keep the political membership high. The endeavours of RCA were all the more impressive for the fact that the political levy for much of this period seemed to be higher than that charged in other unions. The RCA levy for much of the period was three farthings per week, compared with one farthing in TGWU; and a halfpenny in ISTC and NUR.

Yet despite the impressive efforts of RCA, the number of contributors to trade union political funds generally fell quite significantly as a result of the 1927 Act. The obvious immediate consequence of this was a fall in the number of trade unionists affiliated to the party, a pattern which is traced in table 2.

Table 2. Trade union affiliations 1925–45

	No. affiliated to	
Year	Labour Party	TUC
1925	3,337,635	4,350,982
1926	3,352,347	4,365,619
1927	3,238,939	4,163,994
1928	2,025,139	3,874,842
1929	2,044,279	3,673,144
1930	2,011,484	3,744,320
1931	2,024,216	3,719,401
1932	1,906,269	3,613,273
1933	1,899,007	3,367,911
1934	1,857,524	3,294,581
1935	1,912,924	3,388,810
1936	1,968,538	3,614,551
1937	2,037,071	4,008,647
1938	2,158,076	4,460,617
1939	2,214,070	4,669,186
1940	2,226,575	4,866,711
1941	2,230,728	5,079,094
1942	2,206,209	5,432,644
1943	2,237,307	6,024,411
1944	2,375,381	6,642,317
1945	2,510,369	6,575,654

SOURCE: Labour Party Report 1978 and TUC Report 1978

Although it gives only a rough guide, table 2 indicates that the number of trade unionists affiliated to the party fell from more than 75 to 48 per cent between 1925 and 1938. There can be little doubt that this is due to a very large extent, if not exclusively, to the change introduced by the 1927 Act. Financially, this was potentially disastrous for the party. Yet remarkably, the change in the law did not seriously impede its fortunes. It is true that between 1926 and 1929 the income of the party fell by about one-third, with income from affiliated trade unions falling from £40,000 to £25,000. However, a special levy was imposed on affiliated unions in order to raise £15,000 between 1929 and 1932. This was immensely successful, with over £15,000 being collected in this way. Secondly, affiliation fees were raised in 1931 from 3d to 4d per member. This had the effect of increasing the income from affiliated trade unions to £32,500 in 1932. Although this was still significantly short of the level of 1927, table 2 shows that there would almost certainly have been a reduction anyway as a result of the fall in the number of trade union members generally. By 1943 the levy had risen to 5d per member and the party treasurer reported to the conference in that year that party finances were not unsatisfactory. Income from affiliated trade unions in that year was £45,601, and in 1945 this was to rise to £50,000 out of a head office income for general purposes of £83,000. And it is to be remembered that while labouring under the 1927 Act, the party won its most famous ever victory at the general election in 1945, polling just under 12 million votes and winning 393 seats. It did so with the help of donations to its general election fund of £34,000 and £95,000 in 1944 and 1945 respectively. Most if not all of this money came from trade unions.

But this success is clouded by three important qualifications. First, while the Labour Party was scrambling in the early 1930s to collect £32,500 from affiliated trade unions as its main source of income, the Conservative Party was spending what was in contrast fantastic sums of money. Routine expenditure by Conservative Central Office in 1929 amounted to £234,875 while an additional £290,475 was spent on the general election that year. At the 1935 election, the Conservatives spent some £300,000 on propaganda alone, a sum equivalent to over £5 million in 1982 values. This compares with the £45,000 and £25,000 which the Labour Party spent at these elections. Secondly, the amount of money made available by the unions in 1945 may have been due to a very large extent to the fact that the 1945 election was the first for ten years. Political life was disrupted by the Second World War and party politics were suspended by a truce between the parties. Union political funds were thus able to accumulate, and there must consequently be serious doubts whether the unions could have raised this money if one or more elections had taken place since 1935. Finally, the effect of the 1927 Act further distorted the financial imbalance between the parties by seriously limiting the Labour Party's potential for growth. Income from affiliated trade unions was reduced by a possible 25 per cent and as table 2 shows, this figure was to increase, though it is difficult to say whether it would have risen as high as it did but for the war. Presumably, one effect of war was that in many workshops there were fewer collecting stewards, each with less time to spend on their union duties. It is also unclear whether Labour Party income would have been significantly higher if contracting out had continued after 1927. It is quite possible that the party would not have raised its affiliation fee quite so steadily if there had been no need to compensate for a drop in the level of trade unionists who were prepared to pay the political levy. However, the point about the 1927 Act is that it hindered expansion and growth, and significantly affected the income potential of the party by leading to a reduction in the numbers paying the political levy. The affiliation fees, and consequently political levies, were increased in the 1930s partly to compensate for loss, and not solely in response to expanding needs and commitments. It is an open question whether the Treasurer of the party could have been so sanguine in 1943 if the war had not brought about a lull in the activities of political parties.

RESTORING THE 1913 ACT

So the 1927 Act failed to inflict any great damage on the Labour Party. Nevertheless, it was deeply and profoundly resented by the movement, to an extent that is impossible to convey but readily apparent from contemporary documents. The Act induced a remarkable feeling of injustice, and resolutions condemning it were passed annually at the TUC conference and almost as frequently at the Labour Party conference. Strong and emotive language was used in criticism of the Act. At the 1929 TUC conference one delegate spoke of it as 'one of the most repressive Acts passed by a reactionary Government during the last 300 years'.[79] The hostility towards s.4 tended to be submerged in more general attacks on the Act as a whole. However, some union leaders made it clear that they deplored the measure as a dishonourable attempt by the Baldwin government to use the opportunity of an industrial dispute to take political advantage of the unions.[80]

The first opportunity to restore the 1913 solution came rather sooner than expected, with the return of a Labour government at the general election in 1929. However, the chances of this government securing any effective alteration of the 1927 Act were always limited for it was in a minority, with only 288 seats, compared with 260 and 59 won by the Conservatives and Liberals respectively. So the success of the government Bill depended on Liberal support and as a price for that support, the Liberals had originally demanded a reform of electoral law, with the introduction of some form of proportional representation.[81] But by the time the government Bill to reform the 1927

Act had reached Standing Committee 'the Liberals had entirely altered what was understood to be their previous attitude', and were now
demanding further limitations on the freedom to strike by making it
illegal to strike in any essential service or to take any action which had
an object other than or in addition to the furtherance of a trade dispute. A Liberal amendment to this effect was pressed to a division and
the government was defeated. However, these provisions were totally
unacceptable,[82] the TUC taking the view that the unions would thus
be placed in an even worse position than they were already.[83] So rather
than endure the enactment of this measure and rather than face further humiliating defeats, the Bill was withdrawn.

A second opportunity for reform did not arise for another ten years.
In 1931 the Labour Party split with Ramsay MacDonald and several
colleagues accepting the invitation to form a National Government to
deal with the economic crisis. At the general election in 1931 Labour
without MacDonald won only 46 seats despite polling some 6 million
votes. And although its fortunes revived a little at the general election
in 1935, it won only 154 seats at that election. But thereafter, interest
in reforming the 1927 Act seemed to revive. It is true that in the early
1930s resolutions were passed at the conferences of both the TUC and
the Labour Party calling for a repeal of the Act. But little seems to
have been done in consequence of these resolutions and they simply
served as a public reminder of union resentment. However in 1936,
the question of dealing with the 1927 Act was considered by the
National Council of Labour where it was agreed that the law should be
restored to its pre-1927 position and that steps should be taken to draft
a bill in readiness of such an opportunity.[84] Crucially, this meant and
it was so expressed, that the Labour leaders now accepted contracting
out rather than a system of compulsory political levies. The view was
taken that contracting out had worked well and should be restored. In
1937 the General Council began to make contacts with government
departments to review the question of the 1927 Act and in 1939 the
Prime Minister, Chamberlain, agreed to meet representatives of the
TUC General Council to discuss the issue.[85] He was informed of the
keen resentment felt by the unions towards the Act and was urged to
allow time for its repeal in order to remove the stigma on the unions
during the war. However, the Prime Minister was unable to accede to
this request, stating that the amending legislation would be highly
controversial and would be impracticable in wartime.[86] A similar
position was adopted by Churchill, who could not even be persuaded
to repeal sections 5 and 6 of the 1927 Act.[87] The TUC regarded these
as being non-controversial but at the same time as the greatest threat
to union activities, and it had maintained a persistent campaign
throughout the war for their repeal.

So it was left to the post-war Labour government to deal with the 1927 Act. In view of the intensity of the war-time pressure by the TUC for reform, it is hardly surprising that one of the first measures of the new government was to restore British labour law to a position as if the 1927 Act had never been passed. The 1927 Act had been a live and controversial issue in TUC relationships with war-time ministers, and the new government needed little prodding from the unions to remind it of their bitterness. But the government realised that its proposals would be very controversial and it was in fact exposed to much criticism in Parliament. Conservative and Liberal members argued that contracting in was the best way of protecting the minority and had not damaged the Labour Party. Trade union members, it was claimed, should subscribe to political funds because they feel that the Labour Party is worthy of support, not because they were compelled to do so by the contracting out clause. And trade unionists would be intimidated, not by the risk of violence, but by threats and pressure exerted by collecting stewards. One member recalled being visited by many miners and their wives as a result of intimidation experienced when they had tried to contract out before 1927. Other Opposition members of Parliament claimed that it was no good saying that these people could also complain to the Chief Registrar because the ordinary man in the workshop knew nothing about him or his jurisdiction. Still others referred to the significance of the closed shop and argued that its existence swayed the balance in favour of contracting in for the greater the degree of compulsion to join trade unions, the greater was the wrong of denying complete liberty to their members.[88]

Yet although controversial, the repeal of the 1927 Act and the restoration of contracting out was uneventful. The government was in a hurry and had a large enough majority to guarantee success. Nevertheless, there are several points to note about the Trade Disputes and Trade Unions Act 1946. An interesting procedural feature was the fact that the Chief Registrar was extensively consulted by parliamentary counsel during the drafting of the Bill and was further consulted on the significance and propriety of amendments proposed in Committee by both Labour and Conservative members of Parliament.[89] More significantly perhaps was his memorandum prepared for the Cabinet in which he discussed the merits of the government proposals and argued in their support, pointing out that the system under the 1927 Act whereby the unions had to ballot their members and then only collect from those who had contracted in, was without parallel. And he continued by anticipating many of the points made by the Opposition during the parliamentary debates, arguing first that contracting in was no safeguard against intimidation 'because under another system the union knows the names of members who do and do not contribute'. Secondly, he claimed that in any event the 1913 Act expressly protected members from intimidation by enacting that they could not be forced out of the union for refusing to pay the levy. And thirdly, he suggested that the reason why fewer members pay under contracting in than contracting out was due to various reasons other than fear but thought that inertia was a possible reason for non-contributing in many cases.[90] Although the Chief Registrar said nothing which was new, the consultation provides a valuable insight into his role as adjudicator and administrator, though given the commitment to repeal, it seems unlikely that any contrary advice from him on the major policy question would have had any effect.

The process of enactment is also important for underlining the fact that the Labour Party was not in any difficult financial position in 1945. In order to restore contracting out after the passing of the Trade Disputes and Trade Unions Act 1946, individual unions would obviously be required to change their rules to give effect to the new legal regime. Under the government's Bill of 1931, the change could be made simply by the executive body of the union. But in 1945 there was strong pressure in Cabinet to the effect that the change should only be made with the approval of a general meeting or of the members of the union in a ballot. If the latter proposal had been adopted contracting in would remain in force until a ballot of the members had established otherwise. The unions were only saved from this after the Chief Registrar had advised first that the holding of a special general meeting in the case of the larger unions involved considerable expense which they should not be required to incur without any good reason, and secondly that the amendment of the rules was usually little more than a formality. Equally interesting is the fact that despite its large majority after the 1945 election the party did not exploit its advantage by abolishing the right of exemption altogether, though some backbenchers were critical of its failure to do so.[91] It is true that the labour movement had accepted contracting out as a reasonable compromise in 1936. It is also true that the government had a heavy legislative programme and was looking for as little trouble as possible with the 1946 Act. But the restoring of contracting out was hardly the work of an impoverished party. Nor was the refusal by the government to accept an amendment which stopped short of such an extreme position but proposed that a union could transfer money from its general fund to its political fund. This would have permitted unions to resort to their general funds for political purposes in exceptional or pressing circumstances.

PART TWO

THE 1913 ACT IN OPERATION

TRADE UNION POLITICAL OBJECTS

The right of trade unions to spend money on political action was restored by the Trade Union Act 1913. The *ultra vires* impediment created in Osborne's case was removed by s.1 which provided that 'The fact that a combination has under its constitution objects or powers other than statutory objects within the meaning of this Act shall not prevent the combination being a trade union for the purposes of the Trade Union Acts 1871 to 1876, so long as the combination is a trade union as defined by this Act'.[1] However, the Act, by s.3, imposed restraints upon union involvement in certain activities, namely the expenditure of money either directly or in conjunction with any other trade union, association, or body, or otherwise indirectly, in the furtherance of the following political objects:

a) on the payment of any expenses incurred either directly or indirectly by a candidate or prospective candidate for election to Parliament or to any public office, before, during, or after the election in connection with his candidature or election; or

b) on the holding of any meeting or the distribution of any literature or documents in support of any such candidate or prospective candidate; or

c) on the maintenance of any person who is a member of Parliament or who holds a public office; or

d) in connection with the registration of electors or the selection of a candidate for Parliament or any public office; or

e) on the holding of political meetings of any kind, or on the distribution of political literature or political documents of any kind, unless the main purpose of the meetings or of the distribution of the literature or documents is the furtherance of statutory objects within the meaning of this Act.[2]

The term public office in paragraph c) is defined as meaning membership of any county, county borough, district, or parish council, or board of guardians, or of any public body which has power to raise money by means of a rate.

The restraints which the Act imposed on union expenditure in furtherance of these objects were threefold. First, the members of the union must approve the adoption of these objects in a ballot held for

that purpose. Secondly, the union must then adopt political fund
rules which provide that any payments made in furtherance of the
regulated objects are to be financed by a separate political fund to
which any member has a right not to contribute. Finally, any member
who exercises his right not to contribute is not to be discriminated
against for so doing, and contribution to the political fund is not to be
made a condition of admission to the union. If a member is aggrieved
by a breach of any of these rules, he may complain to the Certification
Officer who, if he considers that a breach has been committed, may
make such order for remedying the breach as he thinks just in the
circumstances.[3] Thus if a union with political fund rules is using its
general fund to finance regulated activity, then a member may complain to the Certification Officer that there has been a breach of these
rules. If, however, a union with no political fund rules uses its funds to
finance regulated political activity, an aggrieved member must bring
an action in the High Court, or the Court of Session for a breach of the
terms of the Act. The jurisdiction of the Certification Officer extends
only to a breach of political fund rules.

THE SCOPE OF THE 1913 ACT

The definition of a trade union for the purpose of the 1913 Act was
amended by the Trade Union and Labour Relations Act 1974.[4] A
trade union is now defined as being an organisation, whether permanent or temporary which either:

> a) consists wholly or mainly of workers and is an organisation
> whose principal purposes include the regulation of relations be-
> tween workers and employers; or,
> b) consists wholly or mainly of constituent or affiliated organis-
> ations which fulfil the conditions in a), or representatives of such
> constituent or affiliated organisations, and in either case is an
> organisation whose principal purposes include the regulation of
> relations between employers and workers, or include the regula-
> tion of relations between its constituent or affiliated organisations.

1. TRADE UNIONS AND PROFESSIONAL ASSOCIATIONS. The
present definition of a trade union is much wider than that adopted in
1913. One of the most significant differences which the present law
introduces is that a trade union is now defined as meaning any organisation whose principal purposes include the regulation of relations,
whereas the 1913 definition applied to any combination whose principal purposes under its constitution were the regulation of relations. So
far as trade union political expenditure is concerned, the change is not
insignificant for it removes one source of friction to which the 1913
definition gave rise, namely that several organisations sought to deny

that they were trade unions within the terms of the 1913 Act so that they could thereby engage in political action without the need to establish a separate political fund. The approach of these organisations caused some resentment and gave rise to a feeling that the law was not being applied equally to all unions.[5] NUT in particular was singled out for criticism, for although it sponsored parliamentary candidates of all three major parties, it did so from its general funds, contending that it was not a trade union, a contention which, in evidence to the Donovan Royal Commission, DATA claimed was not worthy of serious argument.[6]

It was not only other trade unions which questioned the activities of NUT. When the Chief Registrar was examined by the Donovan Commission, he was questioned on this issue and he disclosed that in the early 1960s a member of NUT had complained to him that the union was engaging in political expenditure without satisfying the legal requirements imposed by the 1913 Act. The Chief Registrar considered the complaint but took no action because NUT was not a trade union within the terms of the Act, but was 'really a professional organisation'. In reaching this conclusion the Chief Registrar examined the objects clause in the union's constitution together with its accounts of the previous year and concluded that the principal objects under its constitution were not statutory objects. When pressed that NUT was regarded by many people as being a trade union, the Chief Registrar replied:

> That is the impression. When you look at its objects clause you find it is to improve the standard of teachers, improve educational facilities, and it is very difficult to say that it is a union within the meaning of Section 2(2) [sic] of the 1913 Act, because you have got to be satisfied that the principal objects are statutory objects – and principal presumably means roughly 50 per cent or more of its objects are statutory objects; and looking at their rules, which we looked at with a certain amount of care, we did not think you could really say it was a trade union within the objects clause.[7]

Although the approach of the Chief Registrar which is outlined in the above passage reflects a perfectly legitimate interpretation of the 1913 Act, it is nevertheless true that the Act could have been construed in a rather less formal manner in order to respond to popular notions of the identity of bodies like NUT. The Chief Registrar's approach seems to have been to construe principal purposes as meaning that he must examine what were the majority of the purposes of the union. An alternative approach would be to examine not simply the constitution but those purposes in which in practice the union was principally engaged. In other words, the principal purposes of the organisation under its constitution could be those constitutional purposes in which the organisation is mainly engaged. So if the energies of NUT were channelled mainly in the direction of collective bargaining then it would have been a trade union, regardless of the fact that it was engaged in a host of other activities of a 'professional' nature, though it is difficult to believe that such activity would be wholly unconnected with job regulation.[8] As we have seen, however, this issue is now of historical interest for the 1974 Act will make it very difficult for any organisation which is ostensibly a trade union to establish otherwise. The principal purposes of an organisation need now only include the regulation of relations between employers and workers and it would now be possible to consider the practice of the organisation as well as the four corners of the objects clause of its constitution to determine what are the principal purposes. It may be noted that NUT claims to have changed its policy following the passing of the 1974 Act and does not now sponsor members of Parliament.

2. THE TUC AND THE 1913 ACT. Under the 1913 Act, as originally enacted, there was some difficulty in restraining political expenditure by bodies such as the TUC and the STUC. The 1913 definition of a trade union probably excluded such bodies on the ground that whatever were their principal purposes, they were almost certainly not the regulation of relations between workers and employers. The only other way by which an aggrieved individual could seek to control this expenditure was by proceeding against affiliated organisations so that they could be required to pay a portion of their affiliation fees from their respective political funds. However, an attempt along these lines failed in *Forster and National Amalgamated Union of Shop Assistants, Warehousemen and Clerks*[9] where the complainant objected *inter alia*, that at the 1924 general election, the TUC had applied funds to support a Labour candidate and had distributed literature encouraging trade unionists to vote Labour. In rejecting the complaint that the union had indirectly devoted its funds to finance political objects, the Chief Registrar held that in affiliating to the TUC the union had not acted in furtherance of its political objects because when these affiliation fees were paid, it was not known that there would be a general election or that the TUC would spend money on the campaign. The Chief Registrar was also influenced by the fact that in any event, only an 'infinitesimal portion' of the affiliation fees had been used in furtherance of political objects and it seems that he would have been prepared to dismiss the complaint on this ground alone.

Such difficulties appear to have been removed by the 1974 definition. The TUC and the STUC are now clearly covered by the 1913 Act: they are organisations which consist of affiliated trade unions and their principal purposes include the regulation of relations between constituent organisations. So in the event of any unlawful political spending by these bodies, it would almost certainly be open to an affiliated union to take legal action to restrain such expenditure. It also appears to be possible for an individual with sufficient personal interest to at least obtain a declaration that any such expenditure is unlawful.[10] However, so far as the TUC is concerned, this change in the law is unlikely to make much difference in practice for it does not now undertake any expenditure for the direct benefit of the Labour Party, though it has done so in the past.[11] The TUC maintains a position of relative political neutrality, not only because it must be involved in discussions with governments of any political complexion, but also because it speaks on behalf of a growing number of trade unions which eschew any connection with the Labour Party. But it is interesting to note that this position of relative political neutrality is not adopted quite so strictly by the STUC which although it does not donate money to the Labour Party, nevertheless incurs some expenditure in support of the party. In the Annual Report of the STUC for 1974 it was reported:

> The General Council decided that they should clearly identify Congress with support for the return of a Labour Government. A series of press statements and three leaflets were published, two of the leaflets concentrating on the Government's Counter Inflation strategy and supporting the return of a Labour Government. The third leaflet referred specifically to the need to nationalise offshore oil operations and also to the S.N.P.'s efforts to suggest that they alone spoke for Scotland.[12]

3. EMPLOYERS' ASSOCIATIONS. The 1913 definition of a trade union applied to 'any combination' whose principal purposes were those laid down in s.1 of the Act. The term 'any combination' meant that employers' associations were within the statutory definition of a trade union,[13] and many employers' associations established political funds, perhaps the most active of these being the National Farmers' Union which has supported Conservative candidates at general elections, particularly in the 1920s.[14] Although the 1974 definition applies only to trade unions, Schedule 3 of that Act further amended the 1913 Act by providing that it is to continue to apply to unincorporated employers' associations as it applies to trade unions. However, there does not seem to be any serious commitment by employers' associations to the pursuit of political objects. For example, the National Federation of Retail Newsagents has not collected money for its political fund for about thirty years and the fund is moribund, with a minute balance. The continuing application of the 1913 Act to em-

ployers' associations thus seems to be for purely cosmetic reasons, in an endeavour to foster the spirit that the law applies fairly and equitably to both sides of industry. But that spirit would be better promoted if similar restraints were to be extended to regulate the political expenditure of limited liability companies, which unlike donations from employers' associations, constitutes a substantial source of Conservative Party income.

EXPENDITURE IN FURTHERANCE OF THE POLITICAL OBJECTS

The largest single item of trade union political expenditure is the cost of affiliating to the Labour Party. In 1979 the total amount received by the party from the unions in affiliation fees was £1,842,383. Yet while the payment of affiliation fees constitutes the bulk of trade union political spending, this is an item which is not specifically referred to in the Act, though it is in the political fund rules of a small number of unions which include UCATT, ISTC, and NUR. But there is little doubt that such expenditure is in any event covered by the rules as being a payment in conjunction with another body in the furtherance of the political objects[15] on the ground that the only realistic way of promoting the political objects is to maintain a national political party. Nevertheless it was argued by the Society of Conservative Lawyers in their evidence to the Donovan Royal Commission that the Act should be amended to specify clearly that it applies to payments to political parties.[16] But this recommendation was rejected as being unnecessary because the language of the Act was sufficiently wide to include such payments, and because the Chief Registrar had never heard it responsibly suggested that such fees could be paid from general funds.[17] More recently, it was readily assumed by Woolf J. in *Parkin* v. *ASTMS*[18] that 'by donating money to a political party you [are] making a payment for one of the objects specified in section 3 of the Act of 1913'.

But although affiliation fees are relatively uncontroversial, much more difficulty was caused by an attempt to provide the Labour Party with new premises. In order to help the party develop property in Walworth Road, London, a consortium of trade unions agreed to take the property on a 999 year lease, develop it, and then 'grant a reasonable commercial lease on investment terms to the Labour party to secure their occupation'. Most, though not all, of the unions which subscribed to this project did so from their general funds. In *Richards* v. *NUM*[19] one of the grounds of the complaint was that in subscribing £75,000 to this project from its general fund, the union had acted in breach of its political fund rules because the expenditure was one which had been made in furtherance of the political objects. But in presenting his case, Richards faced three weighty submissions from counsel for the union. First, it was argued that there had been no expenditure by the union, but an investment of money, and that there was an essential difference both in terms of language and common sense between an investment and the expenditure of money. Secondly, it was contended that the union had no intention of pursuing the political objects. It was argued that in determining whether expenditure had been in furtherance of these objects, reference should be made to *Express Newspapers Ltd* v. *McShane*[20] where in construing the word 'furtherance' in the term 'an act done in contemplation or furtherance of a trade dispute' in TULRA s.29, the House of Lords held that it had a subjective meaning in the sense that regard must be had to the intention of the actor. In this case there had been no intention to further political objects. But thirdly, even if there had been, counsel submitted that this had not been achieved, because the investment or payment was too remote or indirect. It was simply an investment in property, albeit the Labour Party building, not an expenditure in furtherance of the political objects.

Although these arguments combined to produce a powerful case, they were all rejected by the Certification Officer. He dismissed the first on the ground that the Act and the rules apply to all outgoings of money from the union including investments. The second argument was dismissed on the ground that it was not appropriate to apply the subjective meaning of furtherance to the 1913 Act. The Certification Officer took the view that the sole question was whether there had been an expenditure on a listed object and that the purpose of making the payment was irrelevant. He continued by saying:

> the expression 'payments in the furtherance' in [the 1913 Act] is more capable of bearing an objective construction than 'an act done by a person in contemplation or furtherance of a trade dispute'. There is, I consider, a substantial difference between 'action' in furtherance of a trade dispute when 'action' is without limitation and therefore covers any kind of act and 'payments in the furtherance' of specific and detailed matters where a payment falling even marginally outside those matters is not covered. My view therefore remains that Parliament did not intend that the issue on complaints of this sort should turn only on the intention of the union in accordance with a subjective interpretation of the words 'in the furtherance'. If it had, there would be little point in the detailed description of the political objects that appears in the list in s.3(3) . . . because the intention could only be determined by an assessment of whether the union had a general political intention and not by reference to the detail of the listed political objects.[21]

But the Certification Officer added that even if he was mistaken in his view about the application of *McShane* to the 1913 Act, he would have been prepared to dismiss the argument on the additional ground that the evidence showed that there was some intention to help the Labour Party. Under the subjective test in *McShane*, it was enough that furtherance of a trade dispute was merely one of the purposes of the act and not its sole purpose. So if *McShane* applied, NUM action was caught by it anyway. In rejecting the third submission, the Certification Officer was faced by the obstacle of the *Forster* complaint where it was held that there is no payment in furtherance of the political objects if the union, when it makes a payment to an intermediary, is unaware that the latter is likely to make a payment on the political objects. But this was easily dealt with because in this case, unlike *Forster*, the union knew from the start that the money raised by trustees for the Consortium would be used to finance the Labour Party. So the Certification Officer was firmly of the view that there had been a payment made indirectly in furtherance of the political objects, a conclusion which he reinforced by the further observation that 'where a payment is made upon something which will in fact be used in carrying on the activities mentioned in the political objects, and the union knows this when it makes the payment, there is a payment in the furtherance of the political objects'.[22]

Although counsel provided grounds to decide the case in favour of the union, the Certification Officer refrained from doing so. And there can be little doubt that the decision was correct. It is difficult to see how he could have decided otherwise without flouting the principles underlying the 1913 Act. If a union cannot make payments or grants to a political party other than from its political fund, on what reasonable ground can it be argued that it may use its general fund to supply that party with premises? To have adopted either the first or the third submissions for the union would have been to engage in an unjustifiably formal approach to construction and would have strained credibility rather far, particularly in a scheme which was originally intended to avoid the pitfalls of legalism. Nevertheless, the decision caused some disquiet among trade union leaders who were concerned that if all unions were required to meet the development costs of the new premises from their political funds, the unions would be left with insufficient resources to help the party fight any forthcoming election.[23] But it is difficult to see why the decision should be so disastrous in electoral terms, even if orders were made against all the unions which met this expenditure from their general fund, a contingency which is highly unlikely to arise. The cost of the development of the Walworth Road project has been estimated at between £1.3 million and £1.6 million. Yet at the end of 1979 (after a general election) the total amount of money in the political funds of 71 trade unions was £4,239,000.[24] Even if over £1 million is deducted from this total, which presumably will increase anyway before the next election, there will still be a substantial sum of money left. To put the matter in clearer perspective, although NUM was asked to transfer over £75,000 from its political fund, the balance of that fund at the end of 1979 stood at £820,000.[25] Thus, while this decision may make some impact on the level of union expenditure at any subsequent general election, there is no reason why the party should be denied the substantial financial backing which it needs.

THE POLITICAL OBJECTS

A striking feature of the 1913 Act is that the political objects to which it applies have never been altered to take account of changing political conditions. The result is that the Act is beginning to look rather dated. In the first place, it applies only to representation in Parliament and on public bodies which are financed by means of a rate. This excludes the European Parliament and as the law stands at present there is no reason why unions should not use their general funds to finance such expenditure. Indeed, as we will see, it is arguable that trade unions are under a legal obligation not to use the political funds to finance such expenditure.[26] Secondly, the Act still applies to expenditure in connection with representation on boards of guardians. Yet the registration of electors has been the responsibility of the State since 1918 and is not an item on which unions are now likely to incur any expense. Similarly, boards of guardians ceased to function with the abolition of the poor law after the Second World War. So the political objects which the 1913 Act continues to regulate in practice are the expenditure of money in furtherance of the selection of candidates for public office; the election of such candidates; the maintenance of members of Parliament or holders of other public offices; and the holding of political meetings and the distribution of political literature. It is to a consideration of these objects that we now turn. It may be noted that the analysis will be concerned mainly with parliamentary expenditure, though the Act does also apply to local government representation.

1. SELECTION OF MEMBERS OF PARLIAMENT. This object would apply to any grant made to Constituency Labour Parties in connection with the selection or re-selection of a candidate for the constituency. It would also include any expenditure incurred by the union in selecting candidates whom it wished to sponsor. Rush has identified three principal methods adopted by unions in the selection of their candidates: some unions simply sponsor any member who is nominated by a Constituency Labour Party; others have formal parliamentary

panels to which members may be elected by the union membership; while still others resort to examination and interviews to select suitable candidates.[27] Although it is only the last method of selection which is likely to cause the unions to incur any appreciable expenditure, Rush was able to detect only four unions which resorted to it.[28] Of these, AUEW has devised the most elaborate procedure, having organised a week-long school for selection purposes, in relation to one of which it has been observed: 'a total of 80 nominees were examined by the executive over the space of a whole week. First, nominees were interviewed by three members of the executive. Then they had to address an audience for ten minutes; participate in a discussion on a set subject led by an AUEW MP; be interviewed by two industrial correspondents . . . and write an essay under examination conditions.'[29] Yet even this will account for a minor proportion of a union's political spending, and in practice few unions record any expenditure on this object.

2. ELECTION EXPENSES. Trade union expenditure at a general election is incurred mainly in the form of direct grants to the Labour Party. For the purposes of exposition it is helpful to identify the two different circumstances in which the unions generally make these grants. The first is to the Constituency Labour Parties to help pay for the election expenses of trade union sponsored parliamentary candidates; and the second is by making substantial donations to the party nationally in order to help with the general election campaign. Details of donations by individual unions during the 1979 general election are provided in table 3.

There is little doubt that the first of these items of expenditure must be met by political funds: such payments are clearly covered by s.3(3)(a), as being the indirect expenditure of money to cover the election expenses of parliamentary candidates. The second item of expenditure is not so straightforward, in view of the fact that the Act and the rules do not specifically refer to expenditure of this kind. However it would be remarkable if the expenditure was not covered for it would be hardly consistent with the policy of the Act that a union was required to use its political fund to support a candidate at an election, but not the party which he represented. It seems, however, that like affiliation fees these expenses can be brought within the framework of the Act on the basis that they are made indirectly in furtherance of the union's political objects. Thus, the payments to the Labour Party would further the unions political objects insofar as it would enable the party to (i) engage in expenditure within s.3(3)(a); (ii) hold meetings and distribute literature in support of candidates within s.3(3)(b); and (iii) hold political meetings or distribute political literature within s.3(3)(e) insofar as the meetings held or literature distributed in an election campaign are not covered by s.3(3)(b).

Table 3. Estimated major contributions to the
Labour Party general election fund, 1978–79

Source	Contribution (in £000s)	% of total
TGWU	150	12
GMWU	150	12
AUEW	102	8
NUM	100	8
ASTMS	50	4
NUPE	50	4
Other union donations	496	41
Total union donations	1,098	91

SOURCE: M. Pinto-Duschinsky 'Financing
the British General Election of 1979' in
H. R. Penniman, *Britain at the Polls, 1979*
(Washington 1981).

Other Forms of Expenditure. Although most of union money at an election is channelled through the Labour Party, unions may also incur expenditure in support of the party, but independently of the party machine. In *McCarthy* v. *APEX*[30] the union published a special election issue of its journal. The issue, which was devoted exclusively to election matters, urged members to vote Labour, and contained a list of all Labour candidates who were members of the union, together with a list of all Labour candidates in marginal seats. The Certification Officer held that the issue of the journal was distributed in support of these candidates and that the expense must therefore be met by the political fund, as it was made in furtherance of a rule giving effect to s.3(3)(b). An interesting feature of that decision was the rejection by the Officer of a submission that the words 'any such candidate', in paragraph (b) of s.3(3) are to be read subject to paragraph (a) and thus mean that the former provision only applies where the union is supporting a candidate whose election expenses it is helping to meet. The preferred view was that 'the word "such" relates only to the words "for election to Parliament or to any public office" and was used by the draftsman simply to avoid repetition'. In any event, some of the candidates referred to in the journal were sponsored by the union so that paragraph (b) would have applied even if the submission had been accepted.

Apart from this kind of expenditure incurred by unions individually, the 1979 general election witnessed the formation of an *ad hoc* committee of trade union leaders, the Campaign for Labour Victory, in what was described as being the most intense effort in union history[31] to secure a Labour victory. The Committee cost £50,000 to maintain, a cost which was met mainly by eight unions including TGWU, GMWU, SOGAT, and ASLEF. The money was used to print and distribute pamphlets explaining the policy of the committee and these were sent to leading union officials to help them with their speech-making. The committee also published a broadsheet and considered the idea of newspaper advertisements in marginal seats and even national advertising.[32] The distribution of this literature would no doubt fall within s.3(3)(e) and in some instances, following *McCarthy* v. *APEX*, it might fall within s.3(3)(b) of the 1913 Act. The position relating to advertisements encouraging people to vote Labour is not so clear. If this expenditure is to be covered, then it could only be on the ground that advertising for the Labour Party is an expense incurred indirectly by all Labour candidates, within s.3(3)(a). But although this may achieve a reasonable result, in the sense that the expenditure would need to be financed by the political fund, a problem arises by way of analogy with the Representation of the People Act 1949, s.63 which provides that no expenses may be incurred, with a view to promoting or procuring the election of a candidate at an election, by any person other than the candidate or his election agent. The expenses in question are the holding of public meetings, the issuing of advertisements, circulars or publications, or otherwise presenting to the electors the candidate or his views or disparaging another candidate. This provision was considered by the Central Criminal Court in *R.* v. *Tronoh Mines Ltd*[33] where six days before a general election the defendant company published an advertisement in *The Times* criticising the financial policy of the Labour Party, and encouraging people to vote for a government other than a socialist one. In holding that the expenditure did not breach s.63 of the 1949 Act, McNair J. said: 'the section is not intended to prohibit expenditure incurred on advertisements designed to support, or having the effect of supporting, the interest of a particular party generally in all constituencies, at any rate at the time of a general election, and not supporting a particular candidate in a particular constituency'.[34]

So national party advertising will constitute expenses incurred by a candidate for the purposes of the 1913 Act, but not for the purposes of the 1949 Act. Yet although it may appear otherwise, this is not necessarily an unreasonable position. The decision in *Tronoh Mines* seems consistent with Parliament's intention in introducing s.63 and its predecessor, s.34 of the Representation of the People Act 1918. The latter measure was enacted following a Speaker's Conference which recommended legislation to deal with the 'mischievous practice' whereby at an election outside bodies would swoop down on a constituency and incur expenditure on behalf of one of the candidates.[35] This expenditure would not form part of the candidate's legally permitted election expenses under the Corrupt and Illegal Practices Act 1883, and in many cases would not even be approved by him. It is clear from the nature of the problem, from the recommendations of the Conference and from the subsequent parliamentary debates that the legislation was intended to deal with pressure group expenditure at constituency level, with little if any thought being given to expenditure in support of a party nationally. The absence of any such intention is further supported by the context in which what is now s.63 appears in the statute. As McNair J. pointed out in *Tronoh Mines*, it forms part of a group of sections (ss.60 to 78) which deal with an election for a particular constituency and not a 'panoply of elections commonly known as a general election'.[36] In the absence of any clear indication to the contrary, it would thus be unreasonable to construe s.63 as applying to general elections, an argument which is reinforced by the fact that s.63 imposes a criminal penalty for breach and so should be narrowly construed to protect the individual. Different considerations apply to the 1913 Act, a major purpose of which was to enable trade union members to contract out of any obligation to support the Labour Party. If necessary, the Act should be construed reasonably and widely in order to accommodate this goal, and not narrowly to frustrate it.

Other Forms of Support. Apart from donations to the Labour Party, and other forms of expenditure incurred in support of the party, there are still other ways by which trade unions may support the party's election campaign. During the 1979 election, trade unions provided the party with office accommodation, and speeches were made by trade union officials to encourage the electorate to vote Labour. The unions also encouraged their full-time officials to take annual leave to campaign on behalf of the Labour Party and shop stewards were asked to promote the Labour cause in the work-place.[37] Much of this activity would clearly not be covered by the 1913 Act for the simple reason that it involved no expenditure of money. The 1913 Act does not regulate the purposes for which union officials may take leave, nor does it require that unions charge reasonable rent for office accommodation, though any overhead expenses such as heating, lighting or the use of secretarial resources would no doubt constitute expenditure for the purposes of the Act.

An interesting point which arises from these activities concerns the position of shop stewards who canvass on behalf of the Labour Party while at work. Sections 23 and 58 of the Employment Protection (Consolidation) Act 1978 provides that every employee has a right not to be dismissed or to have action short of dismissal taken against him for the purpose of preventing or deterring him from taking part in the activities of an independent trade union at an 'appropriate time'. This last phrase is defined as meaning any time outside the employee's working hours, or a time within working hours, which, in accordance with arrangements agreed or consent given by the employer, it is permissible for the employee to take part in these activities. The effect of this definition is that a worker may take part in the activities of his union while he is on his employer's premises but not actively working, as during meal-breaks.[38] So far as working hours are concerned, it seems reasonable to speculate that the courts would require an express consent to engage in this activity, save in exceptional circumstances, and that they would be unwilling to imply such a consent from a general term in a collective agreement by which the employer permits shop stewards to engage in union activity during working hours.[39]

The crucial question, however, so far unanswered, is whether political canvassing by stewards is a trade union activity. The question is made difficult by the fact that there is no definition of this central phrase. But if a trade union has political objects, it can hardly be denied that the promotion of these objects on behalf of the union is a trade union activity. A difficulty arises in the form of a dictum of the EAT in *Lyon* v. *St. James' Press Ltd*[40] where it was said that the 1978 Act might not apply to activity which was 'wholly unreasonable, extraneous or malicious'. Although it may be argued that the stewards are taking part in a trade union activity, it may also be argued that it is unreasonable that they should do so at the workplace. The employer might be concerned about any dissension or unrest which such action might cause, although the employee could equally argue that it is reasonable to use the workplace for this activity because it gives access to members which would not otherwise be available.

3. PARLIAMENTARY REPRESENTATION. There are at least three different ways by which a trade union can secure the representation of its views in Parliament. The first is if the union is affiliated to the Labour Party, it may sponsor official Labour Party candidates. This involves paying up to 80 per cent of the candidate's legally permitted election expenses and the payment of an annual grant towards the upkeep of the candidate's constituency. If elected, the candidate may receive help from the union by way of secretarial assistance and he may, in addition, receive a modest financial payment. Under an agreement reached at the party conference in Hastings in 1933 a number of controls were introduced to regulate union sponsorship of Labour

candidates, in an attempt to 'avoid the fierce competition which had grown up between trade unions . . . for a declining number of safe seats'.[41] The most important of these controls is that the annual maintenance grant payable by the union to the constituency party should not exceed £600 in borough constituencies and £750 in county constituencies.[42]

A second way of securing parliamentary representation is to retain the services of a sitting member of Parliament. This is a technique which is adopted mainly by unions which are not affiliated to the Labour Party and which do not have political funds. In the 1974 Parliament NUBE paid a retainer of £400 per annum to a Conservative member of Parliament, David Maddel, and to a Labour member, John Cartwright. Similarly, NALGO engages what it calls parliamentary consultants, who are members on both sides of the House of Commons, together with one peer in the House of Lords. These consultants give advice on the best way of tackling any parliamentary problem, which very often consists of introducing the union to members on either side of the House of Commons who have a particular interest in a subject with which it is concerned. For these services the consultants receive an honorarium and although the amount is undisclosed, NALGO takes the view that these payments are not in breach of the 1913 Act because they are too small to be bothered about so far as the Act is concerned. NALGO also engages a firm of parliamentary agents who advise it on the likely effect of any proposed legislation and who draft amendments if these are called for.

A third method of securing the representation of a union's views in Parliament is by lobbying members of Parliament. A number of smaller unions continue to resort to this method. These include ACTT which although it has a political fund, nevertheless, relies upon sympathetic rather than sponsored members to represent its interests in the House of Commons. Others, although claiming to be non-political, have developed working relationships with groups of members of Parliament. Thus BALPA maintains a close relationship with the aviation groups of the political parties and presents its views to the members of Parliament concerned on any subject which concerns the Association. Similarly, EIS sustains direct liaison with the secretaries of the Scottish Parliamentary Groups. The main platform for this liaison is formal annual meetings with each of the Scottish Parliamentary Groups in the House of Commons over a two-day period. At these meetings EIS speakers address members of Parliament briefly on a number of topics and this s followed by a wide-ranging question and answer session. Between these formal annual meetings, which provide a platform for the Institute's views on all mattters concerning education and the teaching profession, EIS has informal meetings with individual members or groups of members whenever these are necessary.

It is reasonably clear that much of the expenditure on this activity does not need to be financed by political funds. This seems particularly true of expenditure incurred by unions on the third of the above categories. Although the lobbying of members of Parliament is expensive, with EIS spending £1,004 on this activity in 1978, it does not involve the maintenance of members and so would not be regulated on that ground. Similarly, although it could be argued that the lobby meetings are political meetings and so fall within s.3(3)(c), the latter provision has been narrowly construed and would not apply to non-party political lobbying of this kind. It is equally clear, however, that expenditure on the sponsorship of members of Parliament would be regulated by the 1913 Act. Election expenses would be covered by s.3(3)(a) and expenditure on maintaining the constituency party could no doubt be construed as being in furtherance of the political objects generally. What is not so clear, however, is whether, or to what extent, the payment of a fee to sponsored or retained members of Parliament is covered by s.3(3)(c) as being expenditure which can only come from political funds because it is concerned with their maintenance.

One problem which has arisen in this context relates to the position of union sponsored members who retain their office in the union, while also sitting as members of Parliament. Although many unions now prefer to support the candidature of a professional politician rather than compromise the services of a leading official, it is nevertheless true that many recent Parliaments have included trade union general secretaries. Examples of this are Mr Frank Cousins (TGWU), Mr Douglas Houghton (IRSF) and Sir Tom O'Brien (NATTKE). A question which arises under the political fund rules is whether a union which continues to pay the salary of its General Secretary in such circumstances can do so from the general fund or whether it must use the political fund. In *McCarthy and National Association of Theatrical and Kine Employees*[43] the complainant objected that Sir Tom O'Brien, a member of Parliament as well as General Secretary of the Association, continued to draw his salary from the general fund of the Association. O'Brien replied that his political expenses were met by his parliamentary salary and that he maintained himself out of his salary as General Secretary. Counsel on behalf of McCarthy submitted that this expense should have been met by the political fund and that the words 'maintenance of any person' should not be construed as meaning the maintenance of any person in his capacity as a member of Parliament, and he contended that the fact that a General Secretary subsisted on his salary from his union established that the union was spending money on the maintenance of a member of Parliament. However, the Chief Registrar dismissed the complaint and said:

> I am not satisfied that the Association has expended money on the maintenance of Sir Tom O'Brien, whether in his capacity as a Member of Parliament or as General Secretary. The money which the Association has paid him was salary paid for the purpose of obtaining his services. He has sold his services to the Association which has paid the purchase price. I therefore hold that Sir Tom O'Brien has maintained himself out of his earnings as General Secretary and not out of the funds of the Association and his salary is rightly paid out of the general funds of the Association.

It is thus clear that a union may use its general fund to pay the salary of a General Secretary who combines his office with that of member of Parliament. However, the reasoning employed in *McCarthy* means that a union can use its general fund to pay members in many other different situations. Thus, although the union in *McCarthy* was making a regular payment to O'Brien, this did not amount to maintenance: the union had paid a salary for services, had not expended money on maintenance, and O'Brien maintained himself from his own salary. As we have seen, many unions make modest payment to sponsored and retained members. In some cases this is paid from general funds, because the union in question has no political fund. Yet following *McCarthy* such expenditure is not unlawful, for the members of Parliament concerned are paid a fee in return for services rendered in the Chamber of the House. They will be expected to promote the interests of their union in a variety of ways, whether in debates, by tabling questions, by introducing Bills or by lobbying ministers. In such cases the union is paying a salary for services rendered and is not expending money on maintenance. It is submitted that such a conclusion makes the decision in the *McCarthy* case very difficult to justify. If the distinction between the payment of a salary and expenditure on maintenance is sustained, s.3(3)(c) will become a dead letter for there does not now appear, if indeed there ever was, a union which makes a gratuitous payment to members of Parliament without expecting some return. If only for this reason it would seem that s.3(3)(c) should bear a wider construction. This is not to say that the decision in the *McCarthy* case was wrong for there seems no reason in principle why someone who continues as General Secretary should be paid wholly from the political fund if he is genuinely performing his duties as an officer of the union. But *McCarthy* could have been decided on the narrower and more acceptable ground which was in fact presented to the Chief Registrar that O'Brien was being paid and maintained, not in his capacity of member of Parliament, but as

General Secretary. It is true however that this approach might present a difficulty in the sense that the General Secretary's duties may be reduced to enable him to take time off for his parliamentary duties. It could therefore be argued that in such circumstnces the official was in effect being paid and maintained by the union in both of his capacities, unless his salary was reduced to take account of any falling work-load. But this is a minor problem which could be resolved either by a pro-rata reduction in salary or by a portion of the salary being met by the political fund, where the union has such a fund.

4. POLITICAL MEETINGS AND POLITICAL LITERATURE. Section 3(3)(e) of the 1913 Act applies to the expenditure of money on the holding of political meetings and on the distribution of political literature. In practice, the largest single item of expenditure which falls under this heading is the financing of the Labour Party conference. Otherwise, this paragraph accounts for only a very small proportion of union political spending, a matter which is demonstrated by table 4.

Table 4. Trade union expenditure (£) on political meetings and literature, 1980

Trade Union	Total political expenditure	Labour Party Conference expenses	Other meetings & conferences	Printing, publications & propaganda
FTAT	30,231	976	323	155
GMWU	427,169	14,493	4,351	1,456
NUR	128,405	7,859	944	1,253
USDAW	221,632	8,496	3,954	1,653

SOURCE: The Income and Expenditure Accounts of the respective unions.

But although in practice paragraph (e) accounts for a small proportion of spending, it perhaps gives rise to more difficulty in interpretation than any other provision of the Act. One problem is that the word 'political' as it qualifies meetings and literature is not defined. Consequently, those responsible for adjudication under the scheme have a wide discretion to determine the frontiers of this remarkably vague term. One possible approach to interpretation and perhaps the most obvious would be to have regard to the context of the rest of section 3(3). This would mean that political is qualified by paragraphs (a)–(d) of subsection 3 and so relates to meetings and literature which are in some way connected with these issues. But the difficulty with this is that it would be too narrow and would lead to unreasonable results. For example, it would mean that a trade union could finance its contribution to the holding of a special Labour Party conference from its general funds. Moreover, such an approach would be inconsistent with the parliamentary history of the 1913 Act. During the preparatory stages of the Bill, before it left Cabinet, s.3(3)(e) read as follows: 'on the holding of any political meeting during the continuance of a general election of members to serve in a new Parliament or in any constituency during the continuance of a parliamentary by-election for that constituency, or on the distribution of any political literature or documents during the like period, whether in support of any particular candidate or not'.[44] The paragraph did not deal with other forms of meeting or literature. It must be presumed that the present provision, which is much less qualified, was intended to be wider in effect.

On the other hand, it is important that the definition should be carefully drawn so that it does not apply to an unreasonably wide range of activity. One danger which paragraph (e) always presented relates to trade union involvement in pressure group campaigns and in matters of international controversy. In recent years, trade unions have expressed concern about oppression in Chile, apartheid in South Africa, and racism in the UK. It would bear no relation to the function of the 1913 Act if unions were obliged to meet any expenditure in furtherance of such activity from their political funds, or if a union was obliged to establish such a fund in order to express its concern. However, the decisions of both the Chief Registrar and the Certification Officer have combined to exclude expenditure in furtherance of this activity from the scope of the Act by imposing rather narrow limits on the discretion embraced in the sub-section. In the first of these cases, *Forster and National Amalgamated Union of Shop Assistants, Warehousemen and Clerks*, the Chief Registrar said:

> 'political', as it is used in this section, is not the adjectival form of 'polity', but the adjectival form of 'party politics'. This view . . . receives powerful support from the words in Section 3(1) which contrasts 'the furtherance of the political objects to which this section applies' with 'the furtherance of any other political objects'. This recognises that there are two batches of political objects, one of which has to be paid for out of the political fund, and the other of which may be paid for out of the general fund. The first class, therefore, is a special class and does not embrace everything which can be described in the ordinary way as 'political'.[45]

He continued by qualifying the provision still further by suggesting that like paragraph (b) it deals with the placing of a bundle of party-political hay in front of the electors' nose. In other words, he suggested that the paragraph only applied to election matters of a kind which were not caught by paragraph (b). But this too seems unreasonably narrow. It means that again trade unions could finance the Labour Party conference from their general funds.

However, when this issue was next discussed in any detail, the Chief Registrar's latter qualification was implicitly rejected, though his general approach was followed. In *Coleman* v. *POEU*[46] the Canterbury branch of the union paid from its general fund an affiliation fee of £8 to the Canterbury and District Trades Council Campaign Against the Cuts. During the Campaign, meetings were held and leaflets and a newsletter were distributed, the general theme being an attack on government spending cuts and opposition to any government which fails to provide adequate public services. The Certification Officer dismissed the complaint that the affiliation fee should have been met by the political fund on the ground that the meetings and literature in question were not political. In reaching this conclusion he accepted the Chief Registrar's view that the word 'political' in paragraph (e) meant the adjectival form of party politics but said that the paragraph was 'primarily aimed at expenditure on literature or meetings held by a party which has or seeks to have members in Parliament, or directly and expressly in support of such a party'.[47] This is rather wider than the view of the Chief Registrar for it would clearly cover any party meeting or literature and not only those held at election time. Yet although it stretches the limits of the *Forster* case, the frontiers of the definition may continue to be too narrowly drawn. Still excluded would be activity financed to support a caucus within a party; a candidate for the party leadership election; a party, on the right or left, which does not run parliamentary candidates; and expenditure undertaken to criticise the government to the intended and indirect benefit of the opposition parties. There seems no reason in principle why such activity should be excluded from the Act or why *Coleman* could not be slightly redrawn to apply to expenditure on meetings held and literature distributed by a political party, or in relation to the activities of a political party, or which is undertaken, whether directly or indirectly, but intentionally, in support of such a party.

The Holding of Political Meetings. Having discussed what the crucial adjective 'political' means, we can now consider the activities which it qualifies. The first of these is the expenditure of money on the holding of political meetings. This is an issue which was considered in *Richards* v. *NUM*,[48] and is one which so far has been relatively uncontroversial. In that case it was held that three different types of gathering fell within the Act and the rules made thereunder. These were a mass meeting at Hyde Park, a meeting at Central Hall, Westminster, and meetings with members of Parliament in the Palace of Westminster. Expenditure in furtherance of the *holding* of a meeting would include such items as the hiring of a hall and any payments to stewards. In *Richards* it was also held that this phrase included payments to delegates to attend the meetings, even though it is arguable from the wording of the rules that payments to delegates are not payments on the holding of a meeting. But the Certification Officer was correct to reject this narrow construction because otherwise a union could pay delegates expenses to the Labour Party conference from its general funds. The type of expenditure which was held to be covered was the cost of hiring a special train to send delegates to the meetings, the payment of delegates for loss of wages, and a payment to the National Coal Board to cover contributions to the miners' pension scheme for those attending. The Officer also held that the payment to a colliery band to attend the meeting was incurred in the holding of the meeting and so should be met by the political fund.

But not all the activity of the kind in *Richards'* case would be covered by the political fund rules. The reason why the activity in *Richards* was so covered was because the meetings were political in the sense that they had been organised by the Labour Party as part of a campaign against public spending cuts. Where activity of this kind is undertaken by, say, the TUC or trade unions individually and is not designed to further the interests of a political party, then any expenditure may be financed from general funds. In *McCarroll* v. *NUM, Scottish Area*,[49] the pursuer sought a declarator and interdict to prevent the union from meeting from its general fund the expenditure incurred in a lobby of Parliament. Many union members were taken to London: they interviewed members of Parliament, the leader of the Opposition, and the Minister of Fuel in order to protest about threatened pit closures. In dismissing the action, Lord Kilbrandon said:

> It is plain as can be that although an expedition to London to lobby M.P.s and Ministers can be described in one breath as having a political objective, at the same time it is clearly an industrial objective in the context in which the lobby took place. In one sense any dispute between employer and employee in a nationalised industry takes on the complexion of a political dispute since the employer is in some sense the State, which is a political body. Nevertheless I have no doubt whatever that the mainspring of the lobby was the fear that miners were in danger of losing their employment in consequence of an industrial policy of closing pits, and it is against this policy that the demonstrations were being mounted. This, in my view, is fundamentally an industrial demonstration.

This decision was upheld on appeal to the Inner House of the Court of Session.

The Distribution of Political Literature. This item of political expenditure gives rise to two general problems. The first is to determine what is meant by distribution, and the second is to establish what amounts to political literature for the purposes of the Act and the rules. Distribution has been held to apply not only to distribution of literature to the electors as a whole, but also to distribution to the members of the union only, or to a selected group of union members.[50] This means that special issues of the union journal, or circulars to branches would be covered. However, both the Chief Registrar and the Certification Officer have held that costs incurred in preparing literature do not amount to costs incurred in its distribution, the latter taking the view in *McCarthy* v. *APEX* that 'if the intention had been to include preparation costs it would have been a simple matter to do so in specific terms'.[51] Consequently a union can finance the publication of all forms of party political literature from its general funds, a sum which depending on the circumstances may not be insignificant. It is difficult to believe that this is consistent with the policy of the Act and one cannot but agree with Citrine that to construe this provision as relating solely to the cost of actual circulation is to deprive it of substantial effect.[52] Indeed, on a proper construction of the Act and the rules, this interpretation must surely be wrong. They apply to expenditure in *furtherance* of the distribution of political literature. The word 'furtherance' presumably applies to all the means by which that object is achieved. This would include, for example, grants to the publishers of the literature, the taking of advertising space in literature, and the other costs of production of the literature. It is difficult to argue that such expenditure does not promote or further the distribution of literature.

The most pressing question in determining what constitutes 'political literature' is whether newspapers are covered. The government clearly intended that they would not be, with a Lords' amendment designed to include this item being rejected.[53] However, in the absence of other considerations this was unlikely to be influential and within a few years of the Act appearing on the statute book the following observation was made by Warrington J. in *Bennett* v. *National Amalgamated Union of Operative House and Ship Painters and Decorators*:[54]

> If I had to consider that point I think that I should come to the conclusion that the printing, publishing, and circulating of a newspaper such as the *Daily Citizen*, the paper published by Labour Newspapers Limited, came within the provision of subsect. 3(e) of sect. 3 as 'the distribution of political literature or political documents of any kind', words which are extremely wide, covering, I think, as much the distribution of a newspaper

as any other political literature or any other political document,
and if so, then the application of the funds of the Society would
be prohibited by sect. 3 of the Trade Union Act 1913.

This approach was rejected by the Chief Registrar in the *Forster* case
where one of the complaints was that the TUC to which the complainant's union was affiliated, had spent over £40,000 in connection with
the *Daily Herald*. The Chief Registrar could not see how a publication, which served the purpose of an ordinary newspaper for a certain
portion of the population, could be described as political literature or
a political document. He then proceeded to distinguish the *Bennett*
case, first by asserting that Warrington J.'s observation turned on the
memorandum of association of the proprietors of the *Daily Citizen*,
and secondly by claiming that these remarks were made *obiter* in a case
which was primarily concerned with whether the union had acted
ultra vires in investing in Labour Newspapers Limited.

So there are two views about whether newspapers are a class of
document to which the Act applies. The third and most recent case,
McCarthy v. *APEX*[55] tends to support Warrington J., with the Certification Officer dismissing doubts whether a newspaper or periodical
can be literature and holding that the expressions 'literature' and
'document' between them cover just about every sort of written
material. It is difficult to resist the conclusion that this interpretation
is correct for the Chief Registrar's view presents a number of difficulties. Why should newspapers alone of literature be excluded in this
way? What is a newspaper for this purpose? The *Morning Star*, *Mili-
tant* and *Labour Weekly* serve as newspapers for a certain portion of the
population yet they are clearly identified with the interests of political
parties. Would trade union support of these fall outside s.3(3)? And
how is one to tell whether literature serves the purpose of an ordinary
newspaper? By reference to its readers or its publishers? But although
these difficulties tend to support the Certification Officer in preference
to the Chief Registrar, it does not follow that all financial support of a
newspaper would constitute the expenditure of money on the distribution of political literature. The newspapers in question would have
to satisfy the test of 'political' laid down in *Coleman*. Not all payments
would do so for in the past some have been to newspapers which were
sympathetic to the Labour movement but were not directly in support
of the party. Other donations have been to newspapers run by political
parties which eschew the parliamentary process so that if *Coleman* is
followed literally in subsequent cases, it will be perfectly proper for
this expense to be met from general funds.

The Statutory Proviso. Section 3(3)(c) provides an escape route for
unions who wish to use their general funds for political meetings or
literature. They may do so if the main purpose of holding the meeting

or distributing the literature is the furtherance of statutory objects. Statutory objects are defined by s.1(2) as meaning 'the regulation of the relations between workmen and masters, or between workmen and workmen, or between masters and masters, or the imposing of restrictive conditions on the conduct of any trade or business, and also the provision of benefits to members'. So action which otherwise falls within the term 'political' may fall outside the Act because it was incurred for a statutory purpose. However, because of the limited definition of political, this is unlikely to prove very important in practice. It will be recalled that the paragraph applies only to activity held by a political party or in support of a political party. As was recognised in *Richards,* 'where a union makes payments on the holding of a meeting organised by another person or body it is the purpose of that other person or body in organising the meeting which must be considered in deciding whether the statutory objects exclusion applied, and not the purpose of the union in making the payments. This is perhaps unfortunate from the union's point of view because, although it is not impossible that persons or bodies other than the union should have the statutory objects as the main purpose of their meetings, they are in the nature of things less likely to do so.'[56] But nevertheless there are potentially some circumstances in which the proviso would apply. This might include trade union involvement in a Labour Party meeting called to demand the repeal of the Employment Act 1980 or to consider the unemployment problem. These are items which deal with statutory objects, and not only with the promotion of the Labour Party. To ignore the proviso in such cases would be to deny it any effect, a result which would be extremely difficult to justify, no matter how narrowly the term 'political' is construed.

The other major difficulty to which the proviso has given rise is how to determine the 'main purpose' of the distribution of literature or the holding of a meeting. In *Forster,* the Chief Registrar adopted a highly questionable approach. Although he held that the *Daily Herald* was not a political document, he continued by saying that even if it was, it was not distributed for a political purpose. He reached this conclusion by examining the contents of one copy of the newspaper in which '34½ columns out of fifty [were] quite outside the Act'.[57] This approach seems deficient for two reasons. First, it simply establishes the content of one edition of the newspaper, but not the general purpose of its distribution. Secondly, it seems inadequate to impute purpose from a cursory review of the content of the newspaper. In dealing with this question there are two issues that must be considered. The first is content and the second is the intention of those responsible for distribution. The second issue must surely be the most significant, with the first being relevant only as evidence, but far from conclusive evidence of intention. The inadequacy of the Chief Registrar's approach was implicitly suggested by the Certification Officer in *McCarthy* v. *APEX*[58] where he hinted, without deciding, that a wider approach would be called for, perhaps embracing both of these questions. The *McCarthy* case was important for another reason, namely that it established that it is irrelevant that a union distributes literature in support of the Labour Party because it believes that the election of a Labour government is the best way of promoting statutory objects. In rejecting such an argument for the union the Certification Officer said: 'Although the words "the main purpose . . . of the distribution" imply a test which is primarily subjective, it is . . . straining the rule to suggest that the main purpose was to further the statutory objects where that purpose could only be indirect and the direct and obviously apparent purpose was to bring about the election of a Labour Government'.[59] To have held otherwise would have been to render paragraph (e) a dead letter, for as we will see in chapter 7, the reasons why most unions support the Labour Party is simply because they believe that the party in government can provide the legal and economic framework in which their activities can flourish.

OTHER POLITICAL EXPENDITURE

As the discussion so far suggests, the Trade Union Act 1913 is limited in its application. For although most of the items of political expenditure which unions incur in practice are covered by its terms, these are not exhaustive. Section 3 of the Act clearly contemplates that trade unions may incur expenditure in pursuing a wide range of political activity, it being specifically stated that the controls imposed by that Act are 'without prejudice to the furtherance of any other political objects'. Some trade unions use their general funds to affiliate to organisations such as the Anti-Apartheid Movement, Amnesty International, the Anti-Nazi League, the Chile Solidarity Campaign, the National Abortion Campaign, and the British Soviet Friendship Society. The application of the 1913 Act to payments of this kind was considered in *O'Neil and NATSOPA*[60] where the complainant alleged that two payments from the general fund should have been financed by the political fund. The first of these was a donation of £100 to the Defence and Aid fund, a fund formed and administered by Christian Action with the aim of safeguarding freedom and human dignity in South Africa. The second was a donation of £25 to the Medical Aid Appeal organised by the Printers' Movement for Peace (Vietnam) for the purpose of raising money to provide an ambulance to be used by the National Liberation Front in the war in Vietnam. The complaint was dismissed, the Chief Registrar holding that the payments in question were not made in furtherance of the political objects to which s.3 of the 1913 Act applied.

But although unions are not required to finance this activity from their political funds, several unions in fact do so. NUR has used its political fund to pay the cost of affiliating to the Chile Solidarity Campaign, the Fabian Society, and Liberation. Similarly, USDAW finances expenditure incurred in subscribing to a host of organisations from its political fund. These organisations include the Defence and Aid Fund (South Africa), the European League for Economic Co-operation, the United Nations Association, Amnesty International and the Eastern European Solidarity Campaign. The political fund rules of neither of these unions expressly permit the funds to be used for such purposes and indeed very few other unions extend the purposes for which their political funds may be used beyond those which are expressly required by statute. Yet despite the lack of authority for such expenditure in the political fund rules, the Chief Registrar has held that such payments are lawful. In *Corrigan and USDAW*,[61] the Executive Council of the union made a donation of £1,000 from the political fund to a Hungarian Relief Appeal. Corrigan contended that the object of this payment was humanitarian or charitable, and that it should have been financed by the general fund. But the Chief Registrar rejected the argument that the union was thereby in breach of its political fund rules, and said:

> The rule merely prohibits payments in furtherance of the specified political objects from being made out of any fund of the union except the separate fund. Since clearly the donation to the Hungarian Relief Appeal does not fall within the political objects to which the rule applies it is equally clear that a breach of the rule cannot have been committed. The rule does not contain a provision limiting the objects to which the separate fund shall be applied.[62]

Yet although there was no limitation upon the objects for which the rules could be used, Corrigan's complaint was not without substance. If the rules of the union merely reproduced the provisions of s.3(3), it may be argued that the expenditure was *ultra vires* the political fund rules and a breach of the trust for which the fund was established. A not dissimilar problem arose in 1929 when NUS, then in the vanguard of a short-lived non-political trade union movement, announced that its political fund would be wound up and the money transferred to the general fund. Legal advice was tendered to the Labour Party by Henry Slesser that such a transfer would be unlawful on the ground that the political fund is a trust for the political objects and could not be used for any other unspecified purpose. This conclusion is readily supported by the decision in *Sansom* v. *London and Provincial Union of Licensed Vehicle Workers*[63] where money which was raised to help cabmen on strike by the payment of extra benefit was used to meet the contractual obligations of the union under the rule book. The court held that this application could be restrained and said that it 'was the duty of the union to carry out the trust in which they held the monies'. So notwithstanding the decision in the *Corrigan* complaint, it would appear that the use of the political fund for a purpose not provided in the rules would be unlawful.

The effect of this is that unions could be required to meet these payments from their general funds. And here the union may have to tread a careful path to avoid such payments being restrained at common law as being *ultra vires*. Under the *ultra vires* rule, payments of the kind in question can only be made if the union is acting in accordance with express powers under its rules or if the payment is reasonably incidental to any of the objects in its constitution. Several union rule books expressly provide that the union may make charitable donations, or donations to newspapers, or may further political objects of any kind. But where there are no such express powers, the response of the courts is unpredictable for in the absence of clear and unequivocal language, the judges will be vested with considerable discretion in determining what is reasonably incidental to the constitutional objects of the union. For example, in *Bennett* v. *National Amalgamated Society of Operative House and Ship Painters and Decorators*,[64] Warrington J. held that the power to aid societies whose objects included the promotion of interests of workmen was limited to the provision of aid to societies like the defendant union which were established primarily in the interests of workmen, and not companies like Labour Newspapers Limited which were established for a purely political object. In contrast, in *Kelly* v. *Wyld*[65] Luxmoore J. held that the objects of the Civil Service Clerical Association, which included the protection and promotion of the interests of its members, enabled the Association to make a donation to the National Council of Labour to help relieve distress during the Spanish Civil War. In his judgment, Luxmoore J. said: 'the Association's objects were of a wide and elastic character. The court could not give an exhaustive definition of the interests of the Association. That was a matter for the members themselves. If they decided to adopt a certain course the court could not interfere. Nothing here made the payment of money for a charitable purpose, whether at home or abroad, *ultra vires*.' This decision was followed in *Bolton* v. *Durham Miners' Association*[66] where in an even more generous construction of a union's powers, the Durham Chancery Court upheld a payment by the union of £1,000 to a Finnish Relief Appeal to help victims of the Russo-Finnish War. The Chancellor did so, apparently on the ground that the payment could be justified, following *Kelly* v. *Wyld*, as being in furtherance of the union's rule to provide mutual support and advance the cause of trades unionism generally. But in reaching this conclusion the judge was clearly influenced by the fact that the action by the plaintiffs was one which he considered regrettable and which he alleged had been brought for political reasons and in order to gain revenge for their expulsion from the union.

TRADE UNION POLITICAL ACTION
AND MEMBERS' RIGHTS

In the previous chapter, we considered the type of expenditure which is regulated by the 1913 Act. In this chapter, it is proposed to look at the methods of regulation which were introduced by the 1913 Act. These are three in number. First, expenditure by a trade union on the regulated activity must have been approved as an object of the union by a ballot of the members held for that purpose. The ballot must be conducted in accordance with rules approved by the Certification Officer. Second, the union must then adopt political fund rules to establish a separate fund from which any payments made in the furtherance of the regulated objects must be met. Any member of the union is to be entitled to be exempt from contributing to this fund. Third, the political fund rules must provide that those members who are exempt from the obligation to contribute to the political fund are not to be discriminated against by reason of their exemption, and membership of the union is not to be made conditional on the applicant contributing to the political fund.

THE BALLOT

At first sight the ballot requirements seem both obvious and reasonable: if a trade union wishes to adopt political objects, it is not inappropriate that it should first seek the approval of its members. But on closer examination, it may be questioned why Parliament interfered with union autonomy in this way, particularly at a time when domestic arrangements were thought appropriate to deal with other, equally pressing, matters relating to internal union affairs. Trade union members are not bound by the ballot, even though they voted in it, and can freely claim exemption from the obligation to pay the political levy. Secondly, the provisions are a singularly inappropriate method of ensuring that trade unions engage in politics only with the consent of their members. Not only is a simple majority of a small number of members voting enough to establish the fund, but that initial vote may in practice bind all future generations of members. As we will see, there is no formal requirement to renew political fund ballots periodically. The result is that trade unions may pursue political objects with the support of a minority of their membership, a conclusion which may be presumed from the fact that in at least two unions, SLADE and ASTMS, only 33 per cent of the membership contributes to the political fund.

In practice, the ballot requirements have been a formality for most unions. However, some of the votes have been very close, and some unions have been required to ballot their membership on more than one occasion before obtaining the necessary majority. Several unions it is true, have been frustrated by the ballot requirements. For example, NUHKW has tried on a number of occasions to introduce a political fund, but this has always been resisted by its membership notwithstanding overwhelming support at conference.[1] This is despite much publicity and canvassing of the rank and file by the leadership of the union, which in a ballot held in 1980 included the publication of a glossy newsheet written not only in English but also in Hindi, Gujarati, and Urdu in an obvious endeavour to gain support from people of ethnic minorities who are members of the union. Canvassing of this kind is by no means uncommon with a committed leadership often trying to persuade an apathetic or hostile membership to support the adoption of political fund rules. In some cases the leadership campaign is carried right through to the ballot itself, with individual ballot papers containing a recommendation to support the proposed adoption of political fund rules. Although such behaviour is perhaps improper, it is probably not unlawful.[2]

1. THE BALLOT RULES. If a union determines to hold a ballot on the introduction of political objects, it must adopt rules to regulate the ballot and these rules must be approved by the Certification Officer. The latter is instructed by s.4(1) of the 1913 Act not to approve such rules 'unless he is satisfied that every member has an equal right and, if reasonably possible, a fair opportunity of voting, and that the secrecy of the ballot is properly secured'. In order to facilitate compliance with the statutory provisions, the Certification Officer like the Chief Registrar before him has issued Model Rules.[3] These rules anticipate a system of postal voting, though there is no reason why a union should conduct its ballot by such means if it chose not to. Under the Model Rules both the Chairman of the Executive Committee and the General Secretary of the union are required to ensure that every member is supplied with a ballot paper, a copy of the ballot rules, and an envelope addressed to the general office of the union.[4] In addition, the Executive Committee is under a duty to publish in the first available copy of the union journal the date by which ballot papers should be returned, and the date and time when the votes shall be counted.[5] It is also provided that every member shall be entitled to only one vote.[6]

There have been no reported complaints of any breaches of the ballot rules. However, there are two incidents which demonstrate that the Chief Registrar imposed strict conditions on the holding of ballots. The first concerns eligibility to vote. When in 1938 the Amalgamated Society of Lithographic Printers proposed to ballot its members, a question arose as to whether it was required to send a ballot paper to superannuated members, who were not required to pay dues, and who did not vote on any other issue; whether apprentices were entitled to vote; and whether members residing in Eire were entitled to vote. The Chief Registrar replied in the affirmative to each of these questions, taking the view that the ballot rules require ballot papers to be sent to all members irrespective of their voting rights under other rules and notwithstanding the fact that the Act of 1913 did not then apply in Ireland. The political fund proposal was defeated in the ballot, the General Secretary of the Society being left to lament that it was scandalous that superannuated members and boys of 16 and 17 should have been permitted to vote on a matter of this kind.[7] The second incident which demonstrates the adoption of a rather formal approach by the Chief Registrar occurred in 1949 when the Civil Service Clerical Association ballotted its membership on the adoption of political fund rules. The ballot was declared void by the Chief Registrar because the ballot papers did not each contain a branch stamp, as was required by the rules.[8]

2. THE STATE SUBSIDY AND POLITICAL FUND BALLOTS. In s.1 of the Employment Act 1980, the Thatcher government introduced a scheme whereby public money could be used to finance trade union ballots.[9] The scheme applies to ballots held for a number of purposes, one of which is the amending of the rules of a trade union. Under the scheme, a trade union may apply to the Certification Officer for reimbursement of any printing and stationery expenses, and postal costs where a postal ballot was conducted. Before a payment will be made under the scheme, the Officer must be satisfied that the ballot was secret; that all members had, so far as reasonably practicable, a fair opportunity of voting; and that those engaged in the vote were allowed to do so without interference or constraint. An interesting question which arises under the scheme is whether it extends to ballots to adopt political fund rules. It seems to have been assumed by Lord Wedderburn when the Act was in the House of Lords that such expenditure would be excluded.[10] This is a view which gains some support from the fact that one of the other types of ballot to which the Act applies are those held under the Trade Union (Amalgamations, etc.) Act 1964. It might be implied that the failure to mention the 1913 Act, while the 1964 Act is specifically referred to, implies an intention to exclude these ballots.

Equally, however, trade union amalgamations are not simply an amendment of the rules of a trade union and could not easily have been subsumed under this provision. An amalgamation is something qualitatively different from a rule change and it is not unreasonable that this matter would be specifically referred to if there was an intention to include it. It can be further argued that if there was an intention to exclude the 1913 Act, then this could have been done explicitly. The clear and natural language of the Act would include ballots held under the 1913 Act and it would not be unreasonable that this construction should be applied, particularly since this is one of very few issues on which the State actually compels a union to hold a secret ballot. Moreover, the scheme presumably would apply to any attempt by a union to delete its political fund rules. If so, on what reasonable grounds can it be argued that it does not apply to their adoption? However, such considerations are likely to remain of academic interest in view of the determination of the TUC to boycott the ballot provisions. But it would be an interesting rebound on the Conservative government if the TUC was to qualify its boycott to permit unions to take the money to finance ballots held under the 1913 Act.

3. REVOCATION OF POLITICAL FUND RULES. As we have already noted, trade unions are not required to ballot their members on a regular basis to ensure that there is continuing support for the promotion of political objects. However it would be difficult to justify such a distraction and inconvenience, particularly since members are not in any event required to pay the levy and are not in any personal sense bound by the ballots. Yet this is a feature of the law which has provoked some criticism. For example, a memorandum compiled by a Cabinet Committee in 1925 complained that the ballot taken soon after the enactment of the 1913 Act does not need to be repeated even though the membership of the unions may have changed considerably and grown enormously.[11] But it should be noted that unions are not pledged forever by the political fund vote. The 1913 Act provides by s.3(4) that the political fund rules 'may be rescinded in the same manner' as any other rule of the union. So no ballot is needed to rescind the political fund rules.[12] However, as Harrison has argued, 'although renunciation of political action is simple on paper, in practice once a political fund has been established it rapidly becomes a union tradition with all the advantages that sheer inertia and the argument that "we've always had it" can give'.[13]

Short of revocation of the political fund, there are a number of other ways by which a non-existent or declining party-political commitment may manifest itself. It may be that political funds are not used to affiliate to the Labour Party. Similarly, there is evidence that there have been trade union political funds which were not used for any of the regulated political objects,[14] though as we have seen this is arguably unlawful. Examples of this include the old Association of Scientific Workers which used its political fund to finance expenditure on such matters as circulating memoranda among members of Parliament on questions of direct concern to scientists, and on conferences which had the purpose of preparing the ground for legislation on issues of scientific interest.[15] And there are numerous examples, among both trade unions and employers' associations, of political funds becoming obsolete. Between 1927 and 1946 several trade unions gave up collecting political levies and permitted their funds to run down. It seems however that the problem has become more common with employers' associations which despite being regulated by the 1913 Act do not now display any great enthusiasm for political objects of the type covered by the 1913 Act. There is clearly no obligation on unions or employers' associations to collect money for their political funds. In *Edwards and National Federation of Insurance Workers*,[16] the Chief Registrar rejected a contention to the contrary, holding that the political fund rules simply confer a power on trade unions to impose and collect a political levy, but do not create a duty to do so.

THE POLITICAL FUND

The 1913 Act and the rules made thereunder provide for the establishment of a separate political fund from which all expenses incurred in pursuing the regulated political objects must be met. This means that unions cannot finance political action from any of their other funds. So when in 1948 the Llanelly Bar Mill branch of BISAKTA donated one guinea to a Divisional Labour Party from a general fund used for local matters, such as the purchase of wreaths for deceased members of the branch, the Chief Registrar held the expenditure to be unlawful, following a complaint by an aggrieved member of the branch.[17] But although the Act and the rules require all political spending to be financed by the political fund, they do not specify how money is to be raised for that fund. The largest single source of income of trade union political funds is the contributions which are paid by members who are not exempt. But there are several other ways by which unions may augment their political funds. These include the sale of items such as Labour Party diaries and, in the case of ASTMS, donations from wholly owned companies. And on occasion, unions may introduce a voluntary levy to supplement their political fund income. For example, in 1978 the General Secretary of EETPU asked his members to donate one week's wages to the political fund of the union in order to help the Labour Party's election campaign.[18] It is not known how many members responded to this request. Such levies are perfectly lawful so long as their purpose is clear. What unions cannot do is what ETU did in 1931 when it introduced an education levy and transferred the proceeds to its political fund. The union was instructed by the Chief Registrar to place the money in its general fund.[19]

The only occasion when any other controls have operated to regulate the sources of income of trade union political funds was under the 1927 Act. Section 4(2) provided that no assets of a trade union other than the amount raised by the political levy were to be carried to the political fund. This would seem to have precluded a union from transferring interest from political fund investments to that fund, though in practice it seems that most unions continued to do so. But perhaps more importantly, it would have precluded unions from lending money from general funds for political purposes. The repeal of s.4(2) would appear to render such transfers lawful, and it is perhaps interesting to note that despite his general support for the repeal of s.4 of the 1927 Act, the Chief Registrar supported the retention of this provision because it introduced certainty into an otherwise vague area of law. However, unions do not now appear to transfer money in this way and the only point of contention in current practice arises from the fact that some political funds show a deficit of income over expenditure.[20] These deficits are financed it seems by the use of credit facilities. Any interest which must be repaid with these debts must presumably be met by the political fund for otherwise the general funds will be used indirectly to promote the political objects.

THE RIGHT OF EXEMPTION:
PRACTICE AND PROCEDURES

The right of exemption in the 1913 Act and the political fund rules is a right available only to trade union *members*. In practice, however, notice will often be given by prospective members, normally on the application form. In *Wilson and AEU*,[21] the complainant had signed a form proposing him for membership in which he indicated his unwillingness to pay the political levy. He was admitted to the union but was never again asked to sign an exemption notice, and several years after his admission he was asked to pay arrears of the political levy which had built up since his admission. The Chief Registrar dismissed his claim that he had validly contracted out, saying: 'Under section 5 of the 1913 Act, an exemption notice can be given only by a member of the trade union concerned. It follows that . . . no valid exemption notice was given by the claimant since when he signed the proposition form he was not a member of the union.' Although *ex facie* consistent with the 1913 Act and the rules, this decision has the effect of rendering an exemption notice on an application form a nullity. Few trade union members will be aware that they can be legally required to complete two such exemption notices before their right takes effect. In practice, however, unions almost invariably respect any indication made clear in the application form, though it is true that the decision in *Wilson* would enable a union to be difficult or obstructive if it so chose. For this reason it is perhaps unfortunate that the Chief Registrar adopted such a formal approach to construction in the *Wilson* case.

1. THE PROCEDURE FOR CLAIMING EXEMPTION. The 1913 Act and the rules made thereunder adopt a simple form of procedure for the exemption of individual union members. Thus it is provided that members of a trade union may at any time give notice in the form set out in the Schedule to the Act or in a form to the like effect that they object to contributing to the political fund. The Model Rules provide that the form of exemption notice shall be as follows:[22]

> Name of Organisation
> Political Fund Exemption Notice
> I hereby give notice that I object to contribute to the political fund of the .... and am in consequence exempt, in manner provided by the Trade Union Act 1913, from contributing to that fund.
> Signature
> Name of Branch
> Address
> Date

Members should also be notified by the union that they may claim exemption, and that an exemption form can be obtained by the member cr on his behalf either by application or by post to the Head Office or branch office of the union, or from the office of the Certification Officer.[23] He receives a steady flow of such applications each year; in 1980 there were 84.

So the member need not use forms officially provided by the union. But if he does so, he need not make a personal application. This latter point was considered in *Flexton and AEU*[24] where the rules of the union appeared to depart from the words of s.5 by providing that exemption forms 'shall be delivered either by the Executive Council or by the secretary of any branch to any member on his request, or on request made on his behalf either personally or by post'. Flexton's complaint was that the branch to which he belonged had adopted a practice whereby one member could not request an exemption form on behalf of another. Consequently, when he presented to his branch secretary a list of forty-one names and asked for forty-one exemption notices to be issued to him, he was advised that the individuals concerned should make personal applications. In upholding Flexton's complaint that the branch procedure was unlawful, the Chief Registrar took the view that the union rule required that an exemption notice was to be delivered not only when the request was made by a member himself, but also when the request was made on the member's behalf. 'The word "personally"', he said, 'is used [in the union's rules] in contradistinction to "by post" and indicates that the person acting on behalf of a member may make personal application'. The Chief Registrar continued by saying: 'It is inconsistent with the Act for the union to require a member personally to apply for a form of exemption notice, or, when application is made on a member's behalf by some other person, to require a written authority of the member authorising that person to make the application'. However, although the Registrar held that the practice of the branch was in breach of the rules, no order was made because there was no evidence 'that any particular member has failed to receive an exemption notice for which Mr. Flexton was authorised to apply on his behalf'.

Allegations of obstructive tactics of the type displayed in the *Flexton* case are not new. Claims are frequently made that trade unionists encounter difficulties at times in seeking exemption forms from their union. However, in responding to complaints of this kind, the Donovan Royal Commission said that they were founded upon a misconception, and added: 'No stereotyped form is necessary. The Act of 1913 prescribes a form, but enacts that any other form "to the like effect" will do. Any trade unionist so minded can therefore write out his own, saying that he objects to contributing to the political fund of his trade union and claiming exemption accordingly.'[25] Yet although the Act clearly does provide that union forms are not necessary, this does not appear to be widely understood, and the instant question has caused some controversy. The problem has arisen largely because of the activities of outside influences seeking to encourage trade union members to exercise their right of exemption. The Webbs noted that: 'the railway companies went to the expense of printing and distributing hundreds of thousands of forms by which dissentient members could claim exemption . . .; and in the A.S.R.S. in particular, thousands of such claims were made'.[26] Similar steps have been taken by the Conservative Party and by right-wing business organisations. Much of this activity seems intentionally provocative. For example, in 1978 it was reported that the Conservative Central Office was giving away 10,000 contracting out forms a year to its supporters in the unions.[27] Mrs Margaret Thatcher was also reported to have boasted that: 'Contracting out used to be a trickle, now it is becoming a flood. Central Office used to issue a few contracting out forms a year. In the last week alone they have issued a thousand.'[28]

Some unions, particularly at local level, react to this activity by refusing to accept exemption notices other than those which they themselves publish. The issue was dealt with by the Chief Registrar in the complaint of *Hewett and Johnson and ETU*[29] where the complainants handed their branch secretary forms which had been issued by the Conservative Party. The forms were returned to them by the secretary with an accompanying note which said that the union could not accept forms issued by outside bodies. He also enclosed one of the union's contracting out forms. In upholding the complaint made by Hewett and Johnson, the Chief Registrar said:

> At the hearing of these complaints the union's representative did not seriously dispute that the type of form used by the complainants was 'a form to the like effect' within the meaning of rule 5 of the political fund rules and section 5(1) of the 1913 Act. Nor indeed is there room for any serious doubt on this question. The words 'or in a form to the like effect' must be taken to intend and mean exactly what they say. There might be difficulty in deciding whether a particular form was or was not 'to the like effect', but as a general principle I think that these words would cover any form which gave the same particulars as the prescribed form and which would convey to a reasonable person that the signatory did not wish to contribute to the political fund.

It has since been held that it is sufficient for the purposes of the rule if the member writes out his own form and hands it to the appropriate union official,[30] and it has also been suggested that there may be circumstances where an oral notification would suffice.[31]

2. THE EFFECT OF THE NOTICE OF EXEMPTION. The Model Rules provide by rule 5 that any member may submit an exemption form to his branch secretary, who on receipt of such notice must send the member an acknowledgement. It has been held that the latter duty is not satisfied by sending the member a membership card which records the member's exemption: the rule 'requires a contracting-out member to be given a separate acknowledgement over and above the membership card'.[32] Model Rule 6 then provides that having given notice of exemption:

> a member shall be exempt, so long as his notice is not withdrawn, from contributing to the political fund as from the first day of January next after the notice is given, or, in the case of a notice given within one month after the date on which a new member admitted to the organisation is supplied with a copy of these rules under Rule 12 hereof, as from the date on which the member's notice is given.

So new members can be given exemption immediately if they give notice within one month of receipt of the political fund rules. Other members must wait until the beginning of the next calendar year before their exemption becomes effective. This means that a member, who was unaware of the existence of the political levy, may, on finding out about it, be required to pay a contribution for the best part of a year before he will be treated as exempt. The rules do not permit a member to back-date his exemption,[33] and only one union, NUR, departs from the Model Rules with a provision which implies that the exemption of all members can take effect immediately on receipt of an exemption notice. Thus, the rule simply provides that on giving notice, 'a member shall be exempt . . . from contributing to the political fund of the union'.

3. RELIEVING EXEMPT MEMBERS FROM PAYMENT OF THE POLITICAL LEVY: THE PROBLEM OF THE CHECK-OFF. The 1913 Act provides two different means whereby unions can give effect to the exemption of non-contributors. These are either by a separate levy of contributions to the political fund or by relieving those members who are exempt from the payment of whole or part of a periodical contribution to the union. The latter method is the most usual, and the Model Rules make the following provision for this method of exemption:

7. The executive committee shall give effect to the exemption of members to contribute to the political fund by relieving any members who are exempt from payment of part of any periodical contributions required from the members towards the expenses of the organisation as hereinafter provided and such relief shall be given as far as possible to all members who are exempt on the occasion of the same periodical payment.

For the purpose of enabling each member to know as respects any such periodical contribution what portion, if any, of the sum payable by him is a contribution to the political fund, it is hereby provided that   p. of each (quarterly) (monthly) (weekly) contribution is a contribution to the political fund, and that any member who is exempt as aforesaid shall be relieved from the payment of the said sum of   p. and shall pay the remainder of such contribution only.

A controversial issue in the operation of this rule has been the practice of some unions of levying the total sum of the general and political levies from all members, and to make a rebate of the latter levy to exempt members either in advance or at the end of the contribution period. Although this is by no means a recent development, it having been used as early as the 1920s as a means of dissuading potential exemptors,[34] the practice grew rapidly in the 1970s in response to the growth of the check-off as a means of collecting union dues. The check-off is a system whereby employers agree to deduct union dues from their employees' wages and to transfer the money to the unions of which these employees are members. As the Donovan Royal Commission recognised, this method of collection has obvious advantages for trade unions, providing them with 'a steady and assured income' and eliminating 'the need for personal collection of subscriptions, which is often a time-consuming task, unpopular among the voluntary workers who do it'.[35] However, many employers are only willing to extend check-off facilities where the dues of union members are fixed and regular. As we have seen, most unions operate a system whereby both levies are compounded into a single contribution, with exempt members being relieved from payment of the political component. The problem that arises with this is that the political levy is not a fixed weekly or monthly sum but may be a portion of the first or last contribution in each quarter or in each year. The result is that many employers will not deduct a smaller sum from the wages of exempt members in the weeks or months when the political contribution is due by non-exempt members. So unions have responded by requiring contracted out members to have the political levy deducted from their wages and to be paid a rebate of the excess sum.

This practice has given rise to numerous complaints to the Chief Registrar and to the Certification Officer and it has also provoked some adverse comment:

> Under these [check-off] arrangements the political levy is also deducted, and continues to be deducted, not only without any pretence of an authority, but in the face of a duly signed contracting-out form. The member's only recourse is to go to his union from time to time, and reclaim the money. Apart from the fact that this comes near to fraudulent conversion, it means that a union member has to repeat what may well be to him an act of courage, time and again for ever.[36]

But notwithstanding such criticism, the EAT held in *Reeves* v. *TGWU*[37] that the practice of rebates in arrears was lawful, though in so doing, it reversed an earlier decision of the Chief Registrar[38] and two subsequent decisions of the Certification Officer.[39] The latter had held in *Reeves* that the crucial provision of the Model Rule, which had been adopted by TGWU, was the phrase 'relieved from payment' and concluded that this phrase does not in the ordinary meaning of the English language cover a situation where a member has to pay and then claim or be given a refund. Such a person is not relieved from payment, thought the Certification Officer: he has to make a payment even though the money is given back to him later. The Officer did qualify this, however, by holding that it was perfectly lawful to make the rebates in advance, rather than at the end, of the contribution period, and accepted that a member who receives a refund in advance is never out of pocket and that there is no time when he has paid more to the union than the rules oblige him to pay.[40]

In its decision, the EAT rejected an appeal by Reeves that rebates in advance were unlawful and upheld a cross appeal by the union that rebates in arrears might also be permitted under the rules. The EAT's position was determined by the provision in the rules that 'relief shall be given *as far as possible* to all members who are exempt on the occasion of the same periodical payment'. It was held that this provision:

> means that for each periodical payment to the union, relief must be given as far as possible in respect of the political contribution when the periodical payment is made . . . this rule does not lay down an absolute rule, as was contended for on behalf of Mr. Reeves, that the relief must be given when a periodical payment is made, so that it can only be paid and may only be collected by the union in the net amount.[41]

The EAT consequently held that if it is not possible because of the operation of the check-off, to relieve exempt members when dues are actually paid, there is no breach of the rules if the union adopts a system of rebating the political contribution to exempt members. The EAT added that the rebate should be paid in advance where possible, yet accepted that there would be sufficient compliance with the rule if in circumstances where rebates in advance were not possible, the union paid the rebate in arrears at a time as soon as reasonably possible after the date when collection was made by the employer. But the EAT concluded by making clear that for the purposes of its decision, it was presumed that the rebates would be made automatically without the need for the exempt member to make a claim. If the complainant in a future case was required to claim a rebate, 'that might wholly change the position'.[42]

The flexibility which the decision in the *Reeves* case brings to this question, in permitting rebates to be paid in arrears in some circumstances, will be important to trade unions which collect dues by means of the check-off. Although it is true that there will not normally be any reason why rebates cannot be paid in advance, there are several circumstances in which this could be difficult. As we have seen the political fund rules of most unions provide that a member who gives notice of exemption is entitled to be exempt from payment immediately if notification is given within four weeks of membership. One difficulty which arises here relates to the member who gives notice towards the end of the fourth week of his membership of the union. He may already have given his consent to the check-off which, moreover, may already be operating in his case. Yet he will be entitled to be relieved from the payment of the political levy immediately even though, depending on its administrative practices, the union cannot possibly arrange for a rebate at such short notice. Another problem with rebates in advance relates to notices of exemption given after the four-week period has elapsed. The rules of most unions provide that notices given after the first month of membership become operative from the following January. Yet it may be difficult for a union to arrange for a rebate in time if the exemption notice is not given until the end of December; in some unions the rules provide that a portion of the first contribution of each quarter is a contribution to the political fund.

It could be argued, of course, that these difficulties are not fatal to the effective operation of a system of rebates in advance. Unions could respond to the first problem by postponing the implementation of the check-off in the case of new members for a period of about six weeks from the commencement of employment.[43] In relation to the second problem, unions could change their rules so that the political contribution is deducted from the last rather than the first quarterly contribution.[44] But while the Certification Officer's view could thus have been upheld without any substantial inconvenience to the unions, it is perhaps difficult to justify any requirement that unions should alter their existing arrangements. Thus, even if the exempt member insisted on paying his dues by means of the check-off, and even if he was required to receive a rebate in arrears, it is important to note that the practice of the union in the *Reeves* case, as with other unions, was to place all contributions into the general fund until the end of each quarter when money would then be allocated to the various funds for which it was collected. Thus, the exempt member would never make a contribution to the political fund and would never be in the position of financing his union's political activities; he would get his money back, and would have an effective remedy via the Certification Officer if the union was difficult or dilatory in the matter.

PROTECTION FROM DISCRIMINATION

The need for some measure to protect those who exercised their right to claim exemption was clearly demonstrated by the evidence provided in the aftermath of the *Osborne* judgment. There were instances of trade union members being expelled or otherwise discriminated against for seeking injunctions to restrain the political activities of their unions or for merely refusing to pay the political levy. In responding to this need, the Act provides by s.3(1)(b) that a member who is exempt from the obligation to contribute to the political fund:

shall not be excluded from any benefits of the union, or placed in any respect either directly or indirectly under any disability or at any disadvantage as compared with other members of the union (except in relation to the control or management of the political fund) by reason of his being so exempt, and that contribution to the political fund of the union shall not be made a condition for admission to the union.

However, because this provision was included in the 1913 Act in order to protect those members who are exempt from contributing to the political fund, it follows that the measures extend only to protect against discrimination on the ground of non-contribution to that fund. No provision is made to deal with other manifestations of political discrimination. Thus EETPU continues to prohibit members of the Communist Party from holding any office in the union.[45] TGWU revoked a similar rule and replaced it with a provision which reads: 'Membership of an organisation which in the opinion of the E.C. is contrary, detrimental, inconsistent or injurious to the policy and purpose of the Union will render the member liable to be declared ineligible to hold any office within the Union'. It may also be noted that there are some unions which require by their rules either directly or indirectly that certain officers be individual members of the Labour Party.[46] Moreover, in some unions it is not only eligibility for office which will be affected by the political affinities or activities of the individual. In some cases, membership itself carries with it certain political obligations. GMWU prohibits any member from associating with, or co-operating with, or supporting 'any person or body of persons or any organisations whatsoever which the NEC has declared to be acting prejudicially to the union or its policy, whether industrial or political'.[47]

It was clearly demonstrated by the complaint to the Chief Registrar in *Cleger and Amalgamated Union of Operative Bakers, Confectioners and Allied Workers*[48] that the 1913 Act cannot deal with such discrimination. Cleger complained that his nomination as a delegate to the London Trades' Council had been refused by the Chairman of the London District branch of the union. It would appear that this had been done in order to comply with instructions issued by the TUC which had instigated a purge of trades' councils which were infiltrated by 'disruptive elements'. Cleger's nomination had been refused because of his alleged connection with the Bakers' Rank and File Movement, which was regarded as a disruptive body. In dealing with Cleger's complaint, the Registrar found himself bound to hold that no order could be made under the political fund rules. There was no evidence that his nomination had been refused because he was exempt from paying the political contribution. It was impossible to say, noted the Registrar, that if he had contributed to the fund and had still pursued the course which he pursued, his nomination would not have been refused all the same.

1. DISABILITY OR DISADVANTAGE. Although the existence of the discrimination rule is clearly necessary to make the right of exemption a realistic one, the form of the rule is extremely wide in scope. An exempt member is not to be placed in any respect whether directly or indirectly at any disability or disadvantage compared with other members of the union. 'Disability' has been held to refer to 'such rights as the right of a member to vote or to be elected to office in the union',[49] while the word 'disadvantage' would seem to cover almost any other conceivable form of discrimination. However, in *Johns and NUR*[50] the Chief Registrar dismissed a complaint that Johns, an exempt member, had been discriminated against by a branch rule which declared all such members ineligible to hold branch office. The Chief Registrar took the view that until the branch had in fact refused Mr Johns' nomination to any office, the rule in question could not be construed as placing him at a disability, even though it would be *ultra vires* or inconsistent with the union's political fund rules. The reason why the Chief Registrar adopted this course is not clear, though it may well have been an attempt to control vexatious complaints by refusing to adjudicate on hypothetical questions. But although that is an approach with which many would sympathise, it is no justification for the decision in the case of *Johns*. There is no reason why a complaint should never be made before the rule has crystallised to the detriment of the complainant. If for no other reason, the rule in the *Johns* case placed Johns at a disability because it might dissuade or discourage branch members from nominating him for any office. If that happened, he would never be able to complain because the branch would never be given the opportunity to refuse his nomination!

But although it may be argued that the Chief Registrar in *Johns* showed a rather cavalier disregard for the member's right under the discrimination rule, it is nevertheless the case that such a wide rule calls for delicate construction so that the claims of the individual are not permitted to frustrate unreasonably the legitimate interests of the union. One particular problem is the extent of the attack on indirect discrimination. All forms of such discrimination appear to be unlawful. Yet the modern legislation on sex and race discrimination also aims to regulate indirect discrimination but permit discriminatory practices which can be justified on grounds other than the race or sex of the people to whom they are applied. So in *Singh* v. *Rowntree Mackintosh Ltd*[51] for example, a rule in a confectionery factory forbidding the wearing of beards was held to be lawful as being justifiable on grounds of hygiene, even though the rule effectively excluded Sikhs from such employment. The importation of such a defence into the political fund rules could be justified partly by the fact that those responsible for adjudicating on rules made under the 1913 Act will inevitably be influenced by standards of discrimination operating under the 1975 and 1976 Acts, which are probably much more sophisticated than the standards anticipated by Parliament in 1913. If the interpretation of the political fund rules is to be influenced by these standards, it is not inappropriate that the unions should enjoy the limited defences which the modern statutes provide. A defence of justification could well be a valuable device which in some cases might enable those charged with the adjudication of the rules to weigh the need to protect the individual against the wider interests of the union.

The introduction of a justification defence would not appear to be beyond either the Certification Officer or the EAT, for the adjudication of the scheme at the time of writing has witnessed the introduction of two qualifications of the clear and unequivocal terms of the rule. The first was in *Reeves* v. *TGWU* where the EAT held that the rule applies only to material disadvantages or to disadvantages of substance. Like a justification defence, this exception imports a very flexible standard into the interpretation of the rule and permits some considerable scope for manoeuvre. It remains to be seen how effectively this qualification will be used, though it is perhaps significant that a second complaint in the *Reeves* case, that the union practice was also in breach of the discrimination rule, was rejected on the ground that 'what is said to be a disadvantage, if money is paid in advance, is not really something which the ordinary man would regard as being a material or substantial disadvantage'.[52] The second limitation to emerge in the decided cases is much less certain, probably much less significant, and will generally only apply to restrain frivolous or vexatious claims. In *Richards* v. *NUM*,[53] Richards unsuccessfully claimed that he had been discriminated against as an exempt member because he had not been permitted to inspect the political fund account of the union. As we will see, the Certification Officer held that the rule had not been breached because Richards had not suffered any disability. But he added:

> Even if there was a disability or disadvantage in this case, I take the view that it was technical only and not a disability or disadvantage which amounted to a breach of rule 47(8). The provision in the 1913 Act on which that rule is based was intended to protect exempt members from being victimised on account of their exempt status but not, as I see it, to enable them to require information about an area of union activity from which they have deliberately chosen to exclude themselves.[54]

2. CONTROL OR MANAGEMENT. A third limitation of the discrimination rule is that permitted by the 1913 Act, namely that unions may
discriminate against non-contributors in the control or management
of the political fund. It is important to note, however, that unions are
not obliged to discriminate against exempt members. The statutory
provision is permissive and not mandatory, and several unions choose
to involve their whole membership in political matters. In *Hobbs and
CAWU*[55] the Chief Registrar was faced with a complaint that exempt
members were permitted to vote at the annual conference of the union
on a resolution to nominate Mr Aneurin Bevan as Treasurer of the
Labour Party. Hobbs argued that the matter related to the control or
management of the political fund and that exempt members were thus
prohibited from voting on the question. Unsurprisingly, the Registrar
dismissed the complaint and held that the union rule, which adopted
the statutory discrimination provision, only enabled the union to discriminate in the control or management of the political fund, but did
not require it to do so. The Chief Registrar added that if the union was
to take advantage of its power of exclusion 'it must do so by passing a
rule excluding the non-contributing members from such control and
management'.

If taken literally, this last remark could have important consequences. Not only would contributing members be unable to restrain participation by exempt members, but exempt members could not be
lawfully excluded from any say in the control or management of the
political funds unless there was an express rule by which exclusion
was permitted. Yet it may be thought that the right of exclusion is
implicit in the discrimination rule and that although the words in
parenthesis in the rule (except in relation to the control or management of the political fund) do not require unions to discriminate, they
nevertheless confer discretion to do so for otherwise there would be no
point in repeating them. It may also be argued that if this last remark
in *Hobbs* is to be read literally, it was strictly *obiter*: it is possible to
construe the rule as meaning that there is no duty to discriminate
against exempt members without denying that there is a right to do so
should the union so elect. However, the way in which the decision in
Hobbs is construed may now be of little significance. The Certification
Officer has recently held that exempt members can be excluded from
political fund questions on the alternative ground that they are not
exposed to any disability or disadvantage by reason of such exclusion.
In *Richards* v. *NUM* the Certification Officer rejected a complaint
that Richards had been discriminated against as an exempt member
because he had been denied the opportunity of inspecting his union's
political fund account: '. . . someone who does not contribute to the

political fund and has no say in how it is spent has no interest in the books of that fund; and consequently . . . he suffers no disability or disadvantage by being denied the opportunity to inspect them'.[56]

So there are potentially three ways by which exempt members can be excluded from any participation in the control or management of the political fund. The first is on the ground that they have not suffered any disability or disadvantage. The second depends on the construction of *Hobbs*, but it would not be unreasonable to say that a power of exclusion is implicit in the words in parenthesis in the rule itself. There are a number of unions which at least until the decision in *Richards*, justified their practices on this ground. Thirdly, unions may expressly exclude exempt members by formal rules to this effect. APEX and ASTMS exclude exempt members from voting on matters relating to the fund while unions such as NUR and NGA provide that decisions on matters relating to the fund will be taken only by officers who contribute to it. The decision of the Certification Officer in the unreported case of *Parkin* v. *ASTMS*[57] facilitates the writing of wide exclusion rules in view of the generous contribution of the term 'control or management' which was adopted, with the specific aim of protecting the union from the unreasonable demands of exempt members. One of the questions which arose in that case was whether an exempt member could be lawfully excluded from moving an amendment to or voting on a motion for the annual conference of the union which concerned the re-selection of Labour members of Parliament. In answering this question in the affirmative the Certification Officer rejected the narrow construction argued by the complainant, namely that the phrase was restricted to matters affecting the amount of expenditure from the fund, changes in the persons managing the fund, changes in auditing arrangements for the fund and changes in the investments of the fund. The Officer's view was that where a union spends money from its political fund which could not lawfully be spent from any other fund of the union, matters of policy on which the union has a decision to take only because of that expenditure, for example decisions which solely relate to the internal affairs of a political party, are matters within the expression 'control or management of the political fund'. This reasoning was partly justified on the ground that 'to give exempt members a voice in such matters would have the paradoxical result that the internal decision making of a political party could be indirectly affected by the votes of union members who were indifferent or hostile to it'.

The Limits of the Statutory Exception. Although the Certification Officer has rejected a narrow construction of the term 'control or management', it should be noted that there is a corresponding concern to ensure that this statutory exception to the discrimination rule is not pushed too far. This is evident in the controversy which led to the decision of the High Court in *Birch* v. *NUR*.[58] The rules of the union prohibited exempt members from holding any office which involved control or management of the political fund. This was a departure from the plain language of the statute which simply enables trade unions to discriminate against members in relation to the control or management of the fund. However, the instant rule had been approved by the Registrar who had also suggested in the earlier case of *Vaughan and National Association of Operative Plasterers*[59] that such a rule would be lawful. As a result of this rule, Mr Birch was removed from his post as branch secretary when it was discovered that he did not pay the political contribution. He complained to the Chief Registrar but his complaint was dismissed. The Chief Registrar took the view that Birch had been excluded within the terms of the union rule, and that it was entirely outside the scope of his inquiry to consider whether the rule complied with the provisions of the Act. As far as he was concerned, a rule was enforceable once it had been made and approved.[60]

Mr Birch then sought a declaration that the rule did not comply with the requirements of the Act. However, he was faced with the argument by Sir Walter Monckton on behalf of the union that the Act did not confine the exception to the discrimination rule to functions concerned with control or management of the political fund and that exempt members must suffer disabilities of the kind contained in the instant rule since, 'as a matter of practical administration of the affairs of the branch it is necessary to combine the control and management of the general fund and the political fund in the hands of the same officials of the branch'. This appeal to collective interest was firmly rejected by Danckwerts J., who replied that the argument of the union appeared to be:

> equivalent to the exception swallowing the provisions of para. (b) which were primarily designed to prevent disability from being imposed on the exempted member. In other words, as long as the constitution of the union fails to separate the control and management of the political fund from other functions of the union, there is no limit to the area of the exception and an exempted member might find himself excluded from practically all the activities of his branch. I cannot believe that this is the result of an exception introduced into a provision designed to protect the exempted member. It is entirely reasonable that a non-contributor should be excluded from control or management of the political fund; it is quite another matter that he should be excluded from any office in his union or branch.[61]

Danckwerts J. concluded, therefore, that the rule was inconsistent with the terms of the Act and a declaration to that effect was granted.

Such a conclusion appears unexceptional for it is difficult to see how the rules could seriously bear any other construction. The words of the rule are clear and unequivocal: exempt members may be discriminated against only in relation to the control or management of the political fund. Yet the practice of NUR in this case discriminated against exempt members, not only in relation to the control and management of the political fund, but in relation to much else besides. If, however, the decision would create problems for the administration of union affairs, a departure from the plain meaning of the rules might not have been unreasonable. But despite Sir Walter Monckton's argument to the contrary, it is difficult to see what problems this decision would present for the union. Few if any other unions were known to have adopted this practice and if NUR wished to take advantage of its right to exclude exempt members from participating in political fund matters, it could easily have done so by ensuring that only contributing members participated. This can apply equally to exempt members who are officers as to those who are not. In fact the union did revise its rules after the *Birch* case by withdrawing political fund matters from the branches and transferring them to its District Councils. Under the rules of the union 'Each District Council shall set up a Political Fund which shall be governed and controlled by delegates from branches who are contributors to their respective branch Political Funds'.[62] Yet it seems that branches have not lost complete control over political fund questions for they are still allocated money for political purposes. However, the rules of the union no longer require branch chairmen to contribute to that fund and provide that various matters relating to its management can only be decided by the branch members who in fact do contribute.[63]

3. THE OPERATION OF THE DISCRIMINATION RULE.

Contributions. As we saw in chapter 3, the Asquith government's intention in 1912–13 to create a right to contract out of paying the political levy raised the implacable hostility of Labour members of Parliament. One objection to the government's proposal was that trade unionists would thus be able to take the benefits of political action without contributing to its cost.[64] After the enactment of the 1913 Act several unions sought to deal with this problem by levying the same weekly contribution from both exempt and non-exempt members. Non-exempt members would then have a portion of their dues transferred to the political fund so that in effect exempt members were paying a higher general contribution than non-exempt members. Although this practice was not uncommon, it was clearly unlawful, and the Chief Registrar held accordingly in *Griffiths and GMWU*.[65]

Yet notwithstanding this decision, the practice continued to operate, and in the 1930s the Chief Registrar was required to remind several unions that it was unlawful because it effectively required exempt members to pay more than other members for general purposes. However, the practice no longer appears to exist, though it is clear that the free rider continues to concern trade union officials who in some unions request exempt members to pay a sum equivalent to the political levy into the union's benevolent fund. Although exempt members are not under a legal obligation to make such payments, those in at least two unions, NUR and TSSA, generally do so.

The Method of Payment of Contributions. A second question of discrimination under the 1913 Act concerns the way in which unions require exempt members to pay their dues. The problem here relates again to the growth of the check-off. As we have seen the Certification Officer held unlawful a system whereby exempt members paid both the general levy and the political levy and received a rebate of the latter. He did so not only because this practice was in breach of the rules made pursuant to s.6, but also because it was in breach of the discrimination rule. The Officer adopted this position on the ground that the exempt member was required to make a temporary additional payment to the funds of the union. However, the Officer did hold that this practice would not be unlawful if the rebate was paid in advance rather than in arrears of the contribution period. In reaching this conclusion he rejected the argument that the exempt member was placed at a disadvantage because the administration of the scheme might go wrong and that he might not in fact be relieved from payment owing to a breakdown in the system.[66]

As we have seen, the EAT reversed the Certification Officer's decision on the question of rebates in arrears. Apart from the reasons discussed earlier in this chapter, the EAT did so on the further ground that the practice did not involve any material or substantial disadvantage. However the EAT did indicate that a different conclusion would be reached where the rebate was not paid automatically or where there was an inordinate delay in making the rebate. So there may well be cases where the operation of the check-off could still indirectly lead to a breach of the political fund rules. And apart from the practice of rebates, this could also arise in circumstances where rather than deal with rebates, the union refuses check-off facilities to exempt members and requires them to pay their dues manually. The Certification Officer has held that a requirement to pay dues by cheque in such circumstances would be unlawful because it gives rise to a degree of inconvenience not suffered by non-exempt members in the sense that the exempt member must keep a check of payments due and a record of payments made.[67] It may be questioned, however, whether this last decision is open to challenge in view of the subsequent decisions of the EAT that only material disadvantages are appropriate for the purposes of the discrimination rule.

The Question of Fair Representation. A third problem to which the discrimination rule gives rise relates to the question of fair representation in collective bargaining. In other words, to what extent can a union discriminate against non-contributors in the bargaining process or in the protection of job security? This is the unlikely problem with which the Chief Registrar was faced in the complaint of *Bond and Parker and TGWU*[68] where the complainants alleged that they had been dismissed following representations which had been made to their employer by the local union branch to the effect that the other members of the union could no longer work with them because they were in arrears with their political fund contributions. The Chief Registrar dismissed the case on two grounds. In the first place, he could not see how it could be said that the union's action was taken because the complainants were non-contributors to the political fund and therefore that they had been placed under any disability or at any disadvantage compared with other members of the union because they had not contracted in. In other words, he held that the discrimination rule applies only to those members who are exempt from the obligation to contribute to the political fund, and this must be construed as referring to those who have given notice of exemption in accordance with the terms of the Act. In this case, the complainants had undertaken to pay the levy.

The second ground for the Chief Registrar's decision was that the discrimination provision relates only to cases 'where a member has been deprived of his rights or put under some disability or at some disadvantage within the union itself, as compared with other members'. This view, he thought, was supported by the fact that the application of the Act could not extend to cases where no effective order could be made. This was not a case in which he could make an order. 'Obviously', he said, he 'could not order the company to take [the men] back into its employment'. Yet it may be noted that one purpose of the discrimination rule was to ensure that trade union members did not lose their jobs because of expulsion where the right of exemption had been exercised. It is difficult to believe that Parliament would have endorsed a situation in which a member could lose his job not because exemption had resulted in loss of union membership, but because exemption had directly resulted in union pressure for his dismissal. Moreover, it seems to be reasonably clear that the provisions of the statute do not permit such a contingency. An exempt member is not to be placed 'in any respect' at 'any disadvantage' as 'compared with other members of the union'. It would seem that union pressure for an exempt member's dismissal from employment comes squarely within this formula.

However, even if this breach had been established, it is clear that there would have been a difficulty in providing a remedy for the complainants in this case. Although the jurisdiction of the Registrar is wide, 'he may make such order for remedying the breach as he thinks just under the circumstances', his jurisdiction stems from the provisions of union rule books. This would not give him any authority to make an order which directly involved a third party employer. In any case, his ability to order a reinstatement of the employees would necessarily be qualified by the fact that at that time, the common law was unable to countenance any such notion.[69] However, there is no reason why he could not have either ordered the union to stop acting in breach of the rules or made a recommendation that it seek the reinstatement of the complainants or seek to find them suitable alternative employment.

Participation in Union Affairs. Perhaps one of the most obvious forms of potential discrimination relates to the exclusion of non-contributors from participation in union affairs. In the *Parkin* case[70] one of the complaints was that the complainant had been denied the opportunity to vote on a motion calling for the abolition of the House of Lords. The Certification Officer rightly concluded that this action was unlawful, taking the view that a motion does not relate to the control or management of the political fund simply because it may be a matter of political controversy. However, he adopted a rather wide construction of the term, 'control or management', holding that it did not apply only to financial matters but might include issues relating to the internal affairs of the Labour Party. As a result of the construction of the discrimination rule in the *Parkin* case, it is clearly open to unions to exclude exempt members from voting on a motion to increase the political levy; on questions as to how the political fund should be spent; on who should be the delegates to the Labour Party conference; and on questions to be discussed at the conference. But as we have seen the unions are not obliged to exclude such members, unless there is a duty in their rules to do so. Consequently, several unions allow a wide franchise, which includes exempt members, to vote on political fund matters. A good example of this was during the Healey-Benn battle in 1981 for the Labour Party deputy leadership contest. Some of those unions which balloted their members allowed contracted-out members to vote in what many observers believe was a device to increase the support in the union concerned for Healey, the more 'moderate' of the candidates. A number of Labour Party members rightly objected to this outside involvement in the affairs of their party. But as the decision in the *Hobbs* case shows, it seems that there was little that the law could do for them. In any event, it should be pointed out that simply allowing contributing members to vote would not necessarily stop outside involvement, for it is not only Labour supporters or Labour Party members who pay the political levy. The point was made on several occasions during the campaign that members of the Communist Party and other left-wing groups would almost certainly have been involved in the election.

Union Office. It is clear that the denial of union office would be a disability within terms of the 1913 Act and the rules made thereunder. However, in those unions which are affiliated to the Labour Party, it may be appropriate that some officials should attend the Labour Party conference. This is particularly true of national leaders who will be closely involved in the formulation and administration of union policy and who might normally be expected to be sympathetic with the broad aims of the union and the methods it pursues. It is not surprising then that some unions make attendance at the Labour Party conference a condition of holding some senior offices. But the difficulty with such requirements is that since 1962 the constitution of the party has provided that delegates to party conferences must be individual members of the party.[71] Under the rules of the Labour Party 'A person who does not contribute to the political fund of his or her Trade Union may not be an Individual Member of [the] Party'.[72] So, following the test of indirect discrimination which has been adopted by both the Sex Discrimination Act 1975 and the Race Relations Act 1976, the rules in question indirectly discriminate against non-contributors. They impose a condition for office which is such that the number of non-contributors who can comply is considerably smaller than the number of contributors who can comply. It might be argued, of course, that the trade union member was discriminated against, not because of his exemption, but because of his non-membership of the Labour Party. However this would be like requiring all employees to be members of an all male club and then claiming that the 1975 Act has not been breached because women are not discriminated against on account of their sex, but on account of their non-membership of the club. In both cases eligibility for the job or office is based upon a condition with which the protected group is unable to comply.

The issue of indirect discrimination in the operation of the political fund rules was raised in *Vaughan and National Association of Operative Plasterers*[73] where in exercising its discretion to reject unsuitable candidates, the NEC of the Association rejected the nomination of the complainant for the post of Assistant General Secretary on the ground that he did not contribute to the political fund and so would be unable to perform all the duties of office. Under the rules of the Association, the Assistant General Secretary could be required to act as General

Secretary and one of the duties of the latter was to attend the Labour Party conference, though this was not formally required under the rules of the union. Under the rules of the Labour Party at that time, it was not required that trade union delegates to the party conference be party members, but it was required that they paid the political levy of their union. Yet although it would appear that Vaughan had been indirectly discriminated against because of his exemption, his complaint was rejected by the Chief Registrar. The latter seemed to sustain the view that Vaughan was discriminated against not because of his exemption but because of his potential inability to perform the duties of office. In sustaining this distinction the Chief Registrar further held that it had been drawn by the NEC as reasonable men and with good faith, and was neither arbitrary nor capricious.

So *Vaughan* would appear to establish that trade unions can require the General Secretary to attend the Labour Party conference, even though this means that this officer must pay the political levy of the union. On a strict construction of the political fund rules, the decision in *Vaughan* is extremely difficult to justify. The facts presented a clear and obvious case of indirect discrimination: Vaughan could not perform the duties of office because he was an exempt member. In exercising its discretion under the rules, a body such as the NEC of a union is required not only to act reasonably and in good faith, but to take account of lawful and not unlawful considerations. In the *Vaughan* case, the Committee acted unlawfully because it imposed a condition of eligibility with which exempt members could not comply. The decision was all the more remarkable first for the fact that it was only exceptionally that the Assistant General Secretary could be required to stand in for the General Secretary, and secondly because even if he did stand in, the union was not required by its rules to send the General Secretary to the Labour Party conference. However, the broad proposition for which *Vaughan* is authority, that trade union officials can be required to be contributors to the political fund because of the conditions of office, is not unreasonable in some cases. As we have seen, it would be unrealistic, particularly in the case of major unions, that these unions fail to require senior officials to attend the Labour Party conference. However, this could be done by a more acceptable device than that used in *Vaughan*, and by means which do not quite so openly neglect the protection from discrimination which is guaranteed by the political fund rules. The necessary result could be achieved by the use of the justification defence, that it is necessary for leading officials of the union to assist in forming Labour Party policy and to be in attendance at conference. However, justification is a flexible concept, and what might be justified in one union, might not be in another. The onus would be on the union to establish its case.

POLITICAL FUND COMPLAINTS AND
THE ADJUDICATION OF DISPUTES

In the previous two chapters in this section we have examined the
substance of the 1913 Act. It is the purpose of this chapter to examine
procedural aspects of the jurisdiction. Any member of a union who is
aggrieved by a breach of his union's political fund rules may complain
to the Certification Officer who, 'after giving the complainant and any
representative of the union an opportunity of being heard, may, if he
considers that such a breach has been committed, make such order for
remedying the breach as he considers just under the circumstances'.[1]
This function was originally performed by the Chief Registrar of
Friendly Societies but was transferred under the terms of the Industrial Relations Act 1971 to the Chief Registrar of Trade Unions and
Employers' Associations.[2] On the repeal of the Industrial Relations
Act in 1974, the Chief Registrar of Friendly Societies resumed his
duties for a brief spell until 1976 when jurisdiction was transferred to
the Certification Officer, a post which had been created by the Employment Protection Act 1975.[3]

THE ORIGINS AND AIMS OF THE JURISDICTION

In chapter three we saw that, as originally drafted, the 1913 Act
contained provisions to protect the individual trade unionist who
objected to paying the political levy of his union. Thus, unions were
required to establish a separate fund; to allow for the exemption of
objectors; and to ensure that exempt members were not exposed to
any discrimination or disability. However, the Bill neglected to make
any provision for the enforcement of these rights. It was only because
of Conservative pressure and Labour fear that somehow the courts
might become involved in adjudication under the 1913 Act that the
government was induced to accept a procedure whereby complaints
could be made to the Chief Registrar.[4] Labour members of Parliament
saw several potential advantages in this procedure.

In the first place, the Chief Registrar was not expected to expose the
unions to much expense: it was anticipated that he would operate a
'very simple and inexpensive tribunal' in which costly legal representation would not be necessary. Legal costs would be minimised still
further by the fact that there would be no appeal from a decision of the

Chief Registrar. A second advantage of the Registrar over the courts was his expertise in trade union affairs and his sensitivity to the problems which arose in the field. Since 1871, he had been responsible for the registration of trade unions and the supervising of their accounts. The creation of this jurisdiction was consequently commended by the Attorney-General in the following terms:

> At the same time it is quite right that there should be some tribunal with the simplest possible procedure to provide a remedy without any difficulty of any sort or kind, and where there is no expense and no appeal. The matter goes before a man who is used to dealing with trade unions, who lives in the atmosphere of trade unions, and knows fully all the points which sometimes may look a little small in Courts of Justice, but which are real points to trade unionists. The Registrar of Trade Unions is a man who can understand those points and deal with them. For that reason I think my hon. Friend is perfectly wise and right in the interest of trade unions in his proposal.

A third advantage of the Chief Registrar over the courts was that he could be more flexible in his approach to dispute settlement. During the Second Reading in the House of Lords, the Earl of Selbourne questioned whether the Registrar should be given a judicial or quasi-judicial status since he would now be performing a judicial function. The Lord Chancellor replied to this by saying:

> The Registrar of Friendly Societies will have a great deal of work to do, much of it of an administrative character, and to make him a Judge would probably be to spoil him as an administrator. It is essential that he should be an administrator, and I think that what reconciled Labour members to this clause was that the Registrar would be largely an administrator and that no hard and fast rules of law were likely to be applied in this case.[5]

THE CHIEF REGISTRAR
OF FRIENDLY SOCIETIES AND HIS SUCCESSORS

In view of the wide powers granted to the Chief Registrar by the 1913 Act, concern was expressed in the House of Lords, both in the Second Reading and in Committee, about his status. The Chief Registrar was a civil servant who held office during the pleasure of the Treasury.[6] This prompted some criticism on the ground that he thereby held tenure under the discretion of a government department and could be exposed to political pressure by ministers, to whom he owed obedience. The Marquess of Salisbury moved an amendment to the effect that the Chief Registrar could be dismissed only for incapacity or misbehaviour, a step which would 'not only give security to him, but [would] also exalt his office and give people confidence in his decisions'.[7]

The government was not prepared to accept this amendment. The Lord Chancellor argued first that the matter raised questions of constitutional principle: he knew of no case where a civil servant had been given the authority of a judge. He added that the amendment, if carried, would introduce difficulties into the administration of the civil service: 'either all the important people would ask for this new tenure, or they would say "None of us ought to have it"'. Secondly, the Lord Chancellor assured the House that civil servants in fact had a firm security of tenure and that he had not heard of civil servants being dismissed except for incapacity or misbehaviour. The amendment was withdrawn, but not before Lord Balfour said:

> This may not be a proper occasion for making a protest, but I believe there is a very strongly growing feeling that this practice of putting Civil Servants and those who are more or less under the power of the Executive Government into these *quasi*-judicial positions has gone about as far as is judicious.

Until 1981 the Chief Registrar was normally required to be a barrister of at least twelve years' standing.[8] In recent years the position has been filled by men who have pursued a legal career in the civil service.[9] The incumbent in 1981, Mr Keith Brading, was appointed in 1972 and had responsibility for trade union political funds for a brief period between 1974 and 1976. Brading was born in 1917, educated at Portsmouth Grammar School and was called to the Bar in 1950. He appears to have spent his time since then first in the Solicitor's Office at the Inland Revenue and then as Assistant Registrar of Friendly Societies. Brading's immediate predecessor was Mr Samuel Musson, who held the position between 1963 and 1972. Musson was born in 1908, educated at Shrewsbury School and Trinity Hall, Cambridge, and was called to the Bar in 1930. He practised as a barrister for sixteen years and later became Principal Assistant Solicitor in the Ministry of Health.

Responsibility for the administration of the 1913 Act passed to the Certification Officer on February 1976.[10] His other functions include the listing of trade unions; the granting of certificates of independence to trade unions; and the handling of complaints of irregularities about trade union amalgamations.[11] He is not subject to direction of any kind from Ministers of the Crown.[12] Indeed, the government was anxious that the Certification Officer should be: 'someone who commands . . . widespread respect and standing and who has not been involved with matters of controversy concerning unions or employers' associations, but someone who is of considerable standing, independence and impartiality'.[13] The first Certification Officer was Mr John L. Edwards, who retired in 1980 to be succeeded by Mr Alan Burridge, formerly an Assistant Secretary in the Industrial Relations

Division at the Department of Employment. Mr Edwards was born in 1915 and educated at Marlborough and Corpus Christi, Oxford. He is not a lawyer and has spent most of his working life as a civil servant in government departments closely involved in industrial relations. He was Principal Private Secretary to the Minister of Labour in 1956; Secretary to the National Economic Development Council from 1968 to 1971; and Under Secretary in the Department of Employment from 1971 to 1975.

AGGRIEVED MEMBERS

Under the 1913 Act only a member who alleges that he is aggrieved by a breach of a political fund rule may complain to the Certification Officer. This means that the Officer can hear only complaints from a member who was himself adversely affected by the action complained of. So it is not possible, for example, for a contributing member to bring a complaint that exempt members were unlawfully treated in terms of the discrimination rule by not being permitted to vote on a matter which did not relate to the control and management of the political fund.[14] The complainant himself must have been wronged; there is no vicarious right of complaint; nor will a mere allegation of irregularity suffice. There is no scope whatsoever for permitting a right of complaint to all members. Apart from anything else, if this was the intention of Parliament it seems unlikely that it would have referred to 'a member who alleges that *he is aggrieved*' when defining who could bring a complaint (emphasis added).

THE APPROACH TO DISPUTE SETTLEMENT

Concern has been expressed in recent years about the limits of the traditional legal approach to adjudication in the field of industrial relations. In 1968, the Donovan Royal Commission recommended the creation of new labour tribunals to hear disputes between employers and employees. The Commission anticipated that:

In all proceedings between employers and employees it should be a primary duty of the tribunal to bring about an amicable settlement, and the procedure should be designed so as to make this as easy as possible. Each hearing should be preceded by a 'round table' meeting in private between the parties and the tribunal, or one or two of its members, in order to settle the case. If this fails, further attempts at a settlement should be made in the course of the further proceedings. Experience abroad has shown that labour tribunals can settle a very large proportion of all cases before them. There is no reason to believe that a similar result would not follow here.[15]

It is well known that the industrial tribunals, the bodies that inherited

the role prescribed by Donovan, have failed to fulfil this expectation.
A rigid distinction is maintained between pre-hearing conciliation and
adjudication, with different actors in the different processes, and with
little conciliation apparently taking place in the adjudication process.[16]

In contrast to the rather traditional approach adopted by industrial
tribunals, a bold experiment has been undertaken by the voluntary
TUC Independent Review Committee which was set up in 1976
under the chairmanship of Lord Wedderburn to consider complaints
from workers who have been excluded or expelled from a trade union
in a situation where a closed shop exists.[17] The IRC has eschewed
traditional adjudicatory methods and attaches great importance to
conciliation in its work. Not only is an attempt made to conciliate in
complaints before they come to a full hearing, but the Committee may
engage in a process called post-hearing conciliation. In its report for
1978, the Committee explained:

> Subsequent to the hearing . . . the Committee has found it useful
> to ask both or all the parties if they will agree to discussions
> between the Committee and each party separately . . . The Com-
> mittee tries, in most cases in which it engages in post-hearing
> conciliation, to ensure that the complainant does not remain
> unemployed if he is at the time of the hearing and to ascertain
> whether the union or unions involved are willing to assist in any
> way to this end, and if so, on what terms. The Committee be-
> lieves that this approach is often more valuable than merely stat-
> ing an 'award' or 'decision' and leaving the parties to go away and
> solve their difficulties unaided by the goodwill which frequently
> emerges at the hearing.[18]

Unlike the Independent Review Committee, the Certification Officer,
like the Chief Registrar before him, adopts a formal legal approach to
dispute settlement. Disputes are settled by means of adjudication,
and conciliation is not even attempted at the pre-hearing stage. In
evidence to the Donovan Commission, the Chief Registrar said:

> I would follow the normal arbitration procedure very much as in
> the courts, although not being bound strictly to the rules of
> evidence; I have statutory obligations as an arbitrator.[19]

and then explained:

> The Chief Registrar has to be a barrister of standing unless al-
> ready an assistant registrar. I have been at the Bar for ten years,
> and I hold my hearings in exactly the same way as for example I
> held sittings as a Deputy Recorder.[20]

But although it would be unrealistic to expect a statutory office
holder like the Chief Registrar or the Certification Officer to display
the same informality in settling disputes as a voluntary body like the
Independent Review Committee, it might nevertheless be argued that

there is no reason in principle why the Chief Registrar in particular could not have adopted a rather more flexible approach to dispute settlement. In the first place there was no appeal from the Registrar and there was only limited scope for review of his decisions, particularly before the development of a recognisable system of administrative law in the country. Secondly, the Chief Registrar had a wide discretion regarding remedies: he could make 'such order . . . as he [thought] just under the circumstances'.[21] Yet it can be said of only one occasion that he took full advantage of this provision. This was in *Newman and BISAKTA*[22] where the complaint was upheld but no order was made, the Chief Registrar explaining that:

> The complainant brought this case before me in order to establish a principle and that purpose seems to me to have been sufficiently achieved by my findings. Bearing further in mind that the sum wrongly paid was a small one . . . I feel in the circumstances justified in making no order.

But even though a more flexible approach to dispute settlement had been adopted, it is quite possible that many attempts at conciliation would have floundered. It seems that many complainants are fighting to assert a political principle,[23] often with third party support, and have little need to compromise, particularly since, unlike complainants to the Independent Review Committee, their future employment will not normally be in issue. Yet it cannot be assumed that all attempts at conciliation would fail. Some indication of what might be achieved is provided by *Gasson and NACODS*[24] where the parties reached agreement at the end of the hearing, without the need for a formal order by the Registrar. However, it is perhaps too late in the day to begin experimenting with new procedures. If anything, the right of appeal, which was introduced into this jurisdiction in 1971, may tend to reinforce rather than discourage the use of traditional techniques for the settlement of disputes.

PROCEDURAL INFORMALITY

The Certification Officer has no power to initiate an investigation into the practice concerning a union's political fund. He can only take action when a formal complaint is lodged by an aggrieved trade union member. It appears to have been intended in 1913 that the Chief Registrar would only take action after the complainant had first exhausted all internal union dispute settlement machinery.[25] In practice, however, neither the Chief Registrar nor the Certification Officer have imposed this requirement. The Certification Officer will hear complaints even though the member has failed to take steps within the union to resolve his problem.

A complaint is made by writing to the office of the Certification

Officer in Page Street, London. Details of the right to complain and of the address of the Officer are to be found in the political fund rules of the relevant trade unions. It has been recently pointed out, however, that many trade unions have been slow in changing their rules and that several unions still refer to the right to complain the Chief Registrar.[26] But although this may be inaccurate and untidy, it gives rise to no serious problem. Any correspondence on this matter to the office of the Chief Registrar is automatically passed on to the Certification Officer.

Table 5. Political fund complaints

Year	Total no. of complaints	Total no. of formal hearings
1969	20	2
1970	5	2
1971	0	0
1972	6	1[27]
1973	4	0
1974	n/a	n/a
1975	2	1
1976	3	0
1977	18	0
1978	12	0
1979	105	4
1980	20	1

SOURCE: Annual Reports of the Chief Registrar of Friendly Societies; the Chief Registrar of Trade Unions and Employers' Associations; and the Certification Officer.

The number of complaints varies from year to year, but in practice there has been only a handful of complaints each year. In the first ten years, there were only 68 complaints in all, 26 of which were outside the Registrar's jurisdiction.[28] More recent figures are shown in table 5. The sharp increase in the number of complaints in 1979 which is shown in the table can be explained partly on the ground that 76 of the 105 complaints in that year came from members of the same union in the same workplace.[29]

When a complaint of some substance is made by an individual to the Certification Officer, the latter writes to the union concerned explaining the nature of the member's complaint. In many cases, especially with the most common form of complaint which alleges a failure at local level in the union's procedures for contracting out, the union proposes a course of action satisfactory to the complainant who then withdraws his complaint.[30] Almost all cases are settled in this way and so it is only rarely that a formal hearing is necessary. Thus, although table 5 shows that there were 158 complaints to the Certification Officer between 1976 and 1980, it is salutary to note that he held only five formal hearings in that period. As we have seen, he does not take any further steps at the preliminary stage and in particular does not actively seek to conciliate in complaints.

Where complaints cannot be dealt with in this way, a formal hearing may still be unnecessary to dispose of the matter. In one reported case the Chief Registrar did not call the union because the complaint was clearly of no substance.[31] In another case, at the request of the parties, the Chief Registrar dealt with the complaint without an oral hearing but simply on the basis of correspondence.[32] The formal hearings which have been held by the Certification Officer have all taken place at his headquarters in London. In contrast to this, the Chief Registrar adopted a rather more flexible approach to his choice of venue, indicating at an early stage that there might be cases where a hearing in London would not be satisfactory owing to the expense and that in such cases he would hear the complaints locally.[33] In recent years complaints have been heard as far afield as Durham and Canterbury. Hearings conducted by the Certification Officer are not conducted in private.

In complaints where a hearing is held, the matter proceeds on traditional accusatorial lines, with both parties presenting their case, examining witnesses, and cross-examining the witnesses of the other party.[34] However, within the confines of such a formal structure, the Certification Officer, like the Chief Registrar before him,[35] endeavours to maintain a very informal procedure, and compared with, say, industrial tribunals, this is probably achieved reasonably well.[36] As a measure of the procedural informality before the Certification Officer, it may be noted that there is no formal originating application; there is no time limit for the lodging of complaints; and witnesses cannot be compelled to attend, nor can the Officer order the discovery of documents. It is also the case that witnesses do not give evidence under oath and that written statements will be accepted without the need for affidavits. Moreover, the Officer adopts a relaxed approach to the admissibility of evidence and has said that in order to facilitate informality and representation in person, complainants will be allowed to produce evidence of a kind which would not normally be admissible in a court of law.[37] Finally, it is worth noting that although the two parties to the complaint and the Certification Officer (together with his legal adviser) all sit at different tables, unlike industrial tribunals no one sits on a raised platform.

REPRESENTATION

When this jurisdiction was created, it was intended that the procedure should be simple so that neither party would need representation. This was done primarily with the unions in mind in an attempt to save them from the harassment of expensive litigation by members who might be promoted by unscrupulous employers.[38] But the intention that parties should not be represented has clearly not been fulfilled. It is difficult to determine the extent to which legal representation has taken place, with many of the reports of the early hearings being laconic in the extreme. However, in the first two reported complaints, the unions were represented by counsel.[39] And recent evidence suggests that legal representation of unions is now the norm. Between 1974 and 1981, there were eight recorded hearings. In six of these the unions were legally represented, three times by counsel and on three other occasions by a solicitor. On the two occasions where the unions were not legally represented, they were represented by the General Secretary in one case and by the Assistant General Secretary in the other.

Representation of complainants, on the other hand, has not been so prevalent, a consequence, perhaps, of the fact that legal aid is not available in proceedings before the Certification Officer. In the seven formal hearings which have been heard all but one of the complainants represented themselves. Indeed, there is evidence of only three other cases in which complainants have ever been represented. In two of these cases counsel have appeared for complainants and in the other, the complainant was represented by a university lecturer in labour law. However, it is clear that some complainants have been helped by outside organisations, though it is uncertain to what extent and in what form such assistance takes place. Thus, two of the recent complainants have been assisted by *Aims*, the Free Enterprise body,[40] and it is clear that Conservative Central Office keeps an eye on these proceedings. Nevertheless, it would appear that the informality of this tribunal is not now necessary so much to protect the union as it is to provide a cheap and straightforward method for union members to process their disputes.

DECISION-MAKING

Apart from providing a cheap and informal forum for the adjudication of complaints, a further rationale for the creation of this jurisdiction was the expertise of the Registrar and his awareness of trade union interests. The decision to give the Registrar jurisdiction over political fund disputes was clearly motivated by the need to find an alternative to the ordinary courts to settle disputes, a need which was largely based on the distrust of the courts which was present in the labour movement at that time.[41]

The relative success of the jurisdiction in this respect has already been traced.[42] For present purposes, it is sufficient to note that the unions have generally not found their activities obstructed by any unreasonable or unusual interpretation of the political fund rules. There is clear evidence of flexibility in decision-making and the Chief Registrar not only tended to respect union autonomy in cases where the political fund rules were equivocal, but he was also prepared to deviate from the clear terms of the rules on several occasions. On one occasion, such a step was justified by express reference to the collective goals of the union.[43] In fact, the only hint of legalism in the approach to dispute settlement or in the handling of issues which arose in disputes came during the tenure of S. D. Musson as Chief Registrar. In one case he proceeded on the basis that he had to examine a complaint 'as a lawyer and as a matter of principle',[44] while in a later case he introduced the legal doctrine of estoppel to prevent a union from claiming arrears of political fund contributions from a member who alleged that he was exempt from paying the political levy.[45] Although the latter decision was unexceptional and involved no great point of principle, the disposal of issues on such a formal basis as this was nevertheless unusual.

It would not be unreasonable for the Certification Officer to adopt a rather less flexible approach to the construction of the rules than the Chief Registrar because unlike the latter, who for a long time was effectively the final arbiter in these disputes, there is an appeal from the Certification Officer first to the EAT and then to the Court of Appeal and ultimately to the House of Lords. However, although decisions are now accompanied with more careful reasoning, such caution cannot yet be unequivocally identified in the seven decisions of the Certification Officer to date. Two of the complaints which were upheld concerned matters which clearly breached the principles of the 1913 Act: one was whether a union could use its general fund to finance the Labour Party headquarters and the other was whether a union could use its general fund to distribute election material.[46] In both cases it is difficult to see how the policy of the Act or the rules gave much scope for manoeuvre. Two of the other complaints were covered by a precedent that had been set by the Chief Registrar (S. D. Musson), and which by practice had subsequently been followed by his office.[47] However, in cases where the Certification Officer's room for manoeuvre was not so restricted, he has construed equivocal rules to the advantage of the respondent,[48] and he has shown a willingness to depart from the plain meaning of the rules in appropriate circumstances.[49]

THE POWERS OF THE
CHIEF REGISTRAR AND THE CERTIFICATION OFFICER

If the Certification Officer finds that a breach of a union's political fund rules has been committed, he is empowered to make such order to remedy the breach as he thinks just in the circumstances. Any such order may be recorded in the county court and may be enforced as if it had been an order of that court.[50] This latter provision was included in the Act to ensure that 'the order shall not be mere wastepaper, which it would be if the Registrar had no means of enforcing his decision'.[51] The powers of the Officer are limited in so far as he has no jurisdiction over third party employers. He cannot for example, order an employer to re-engage a dismissed employee.[52] It should also be noted that it was not intended that the wide powers of the Registrar would include the power to award damages.[53] No such award has yet been made.

To date, there have been thirty-three complaints to the Chief Registrar and the Certification Officer which have been reported in one form or another.[54] Fourteen of these complaints were upheld at least in part; one was conciliated during the hearing; and the remaining eighteen were dismissed. Of the fourteen complaints which were upheld, the Chief Registrar and the Certification Officer have made orders on nine occasions.[55] Unions have been ordered to transfer money from the general to the political fund;[56] to stop discriminating against an exempt member;[57] to return money wrongly obtained from an exempt member;[58] and to regard a complainant as an exempt member from some named date prior to the hearing.[59] In one case where no order was made, this was because the union had already taken remedial action[60] while in another, the Certification Officer took no action because the breach complained of took place some time in the past and could not now be remedied.[61] We have already seen that in yet another complaint no order was made because the Registrar thought that the decision on the substantive point was sufficient to dispose of the matter.[62]

One difficulty concerning the powers in this jurisdiction is whether the Certification Officer may award costs. Although the 1913 Act and the rules made thereunder do not expressly deal with this question, the Act does enable the Officer to make such order to remedy any breach as he thinks just under the circumstances. At least one Chief Registrar seemed to take the view that his orders could consequently make provision for costs. Thus in the complaint of *Gasson and NACODS*,[63] the union reimbursed the complainant for lost wages and travelling expenses. The Chief Registrar, S. D. Musson, said that this is a step which he would have ordered anyway had the union not taken the initiative. In contrast, the Certification Officer now takes the view that there is no scope to grant costs,[64] though it was clearly anticipated by the Attorney-General in 1913 that there would be power to award reasonable expenses.[65] With the growing practice of hearing complaints in London, it is essential that the Certification Officer should adopt a flexible approach to this question, such a flexible approach being clearly permissible under the Act.

THE ROLE OF THE COURTS

Parliament intended that the courts should be excluded from disputes in this area and, in order to ensure this, the 1913 Act included a remarkably wide ouster clause. By s.3(2) it was provided that a decision of the Chief Registrar 'shall be binding and conclusive on all parties without appeal and shall not be removable into any court of law or restrainable by injunction'. It seems, at least in the early stages of this jurisdiction, that the courts would have been willing to respect the intention of Parliament. In the *Forster* case,[66] Eve J. said:

> In considering these matters one must not omit to notice what was the effect of that procedure on the plaintiff's part. Had the complaint resulted in the making of an order for remedying the breach, the union would have had no alternative but to give effect to that order. It is clear that there could have been no appeal, and that by no procedure in this Court could the union have evaded the statutory duty imposed upon it of obeying the order.[67]

It is important to note, however, that the wide ouster clause in the 1913 Act would not have been enough to exclude the courts completely. The courts could clearly have intervened in cases where there was excess of jurisdiction,[68] and judicial review to correct errors of law within jurisdiction would obviously have been available after the Tribunals and Inquiries Act 1958 enacted that exclusion clauses in legislation passed before 1 August 1958 would not be effective to prevent review by *certiorari* or *mandamus*.[69] However, these points are of academic interest only because a right of appeal now exists in the jurisdiction. Provision for appeal was first made in the Industrial Relations Act 1971 which permitted an appeal from the Chief Registrar of Trade Unions to the National Industrial Relations Court against any order made by the Registrar or against any refusal of the Registrar to make an order.[70] The right of appeal was re-enacted in the Employment Protection Act 1975 which provides for an appeal on a point of law from the Certification Officer to the EAT.[71] A further appeal lies to the Court of Appeal or the Court of Session.[72]

Apart from this appellate function of the superior courts, it is possible that the ordinary courts may also have an original jurisdiction in political fund cases. An interesting question is whether a complainant could elect to bring proceedings in the courts rather than before the Chief Registrar or now the Certification Officer. Proceedings in the ordinary courts would be obviously advantageous to a complainant who wished to raise additional matters which were beyond the jurisdiction of the Certification Officer. A recent example of this is the complaint in *Reeves* v. *TGWU* where the complainant alleged that a union practice contravened not only the political fund rules, but also the terms of the Truck Act 1831, ss.2 and 3.[73]

The right of a complainant to elect to bring proceedings in the courts was a question which was left open by Eve J. in the *Forster* case. However, the principle in *Barraclough* v. *Brown*[74] suggests that the member has in fact no right of election: 'it is a general rule that where Parliament has created new rights and duties and by the same enactment has appointed a specific tribunal or other body for their enforcement, recourse must be had to that body alone'.[75] It was certainly intended by the government in 1913 that the Chief Registrar would have exclusive jurisdiction. At the Report stage of the Bill, the Attorney-General said: 'The remedy will be given in the Statute in that Section [section 3], and if that is the case there is no doubt that the remedy which is given exhausts the remedies for any breach under that Section'.[76] Following this assurance, Labour members seemed to feel that there was no need to pursue a suggested amendment to the effect that '. . . the method of redress set forth [in section 3] shall be the only method of redress open to an aggrieved member'.[77]

If, as seems likely, the Certification Officer has an exclusive jurisdiction, the courts may nevertheless be called upon to deal with political fund matters. In the first place, as in *Birch* v. *NUR*[78] it is still open to a trade unionist to seek a declaration that the political fund rules of his union do not comply with the terms of the 1913 Act. Secondly, the Certification Officer has only a limited jurisdiction over political fund rules. Thus, he can hear only complaints alleging a breach of a rule which was made in pursuance of the 1913 Act. Should a union expand its political fund rules to include matters not required by the 1913 Act, the only remedy for a breach would lie in the ordinary courts.[79] Similarly, the Certification Officer has no jurisdiction to determine the manner in which the political fund is spent.[80] All he can do is to ensure that where a union has political fund rules, the union does not use its general fund to finance the political objects. So a member who wishes to challenge the payment from the political fund of legal expenses to a union-sponsored parliamentary candidate must bring his action in the High Court.[81] So too must the member who claims that his branch may use union funds to support the Conservative Party, even though the union nationally is affiliated to the Labour Party.[82]

Conclusion

This jurisdiction was established for the benefit of the unions at a time when it was feared that they might be exposed to harassing litigation. The Chief Registrar was seen to have three advantages over the ordinary courts: flexibility; cheapness and informality; and expertise in trade union affairs. It may be, however, that under the weight of various pressures and developments, the Certification Officer will come to exercise a jurisdiction far different from that originally envisaged in 1913. The first of the perceived advantages of this jurisdiction was never fully realised if it was intended that the Registrar should be flexible in his approach to dispute settlement: he adopted a traditional adjudicatory approach and his proceedings followed an accusatorial model. But despite this, both the Chief Registrar and the Certification Officer have managed to conduct fairly informal proceedings. However, informality has largely outlived its purpose so far as the unions are concerned, with more recourse now being made to legal representation. The informal procedure now seems to serve the needs of complainants rather than respondents, though it is undermined to a large extent by the fact that hearings are now generally held in London and by the fact that costs are not being awarded. The third perceived advantage of this jurisdiction has to a large extent been met. The Chief Registrar and the Certification Officer have brought a flexibility to the construction of the rules and have shown an understanding of trade union interests in their reasoning. However, this too may gradually change with the Certification Officer being forced to adopt more formal reasoning in his decisions in view of the supervision over his work by the EAT and the higher courts. It is one of the inexplicable facts of life of the post-Franks era that an appeal will lie from a specialist jurisdiction to a body with little or no expertise in the subject-matter of the dispute.[83] It is also the more remarkable when the degree of expertise often exists in inverse proportion to the position of the appeal body in the hierarchy of courts.

PART THREE

THE 1913 ACT IN PERSPECTIVE

THE FUNCTION OF
POLITICAL ACTION AND
THE EFFECT OF LEGAL CONTROL

In its report, the majority of the Houghton Committee on Financial Aid to Political Parties said 'Effective political parties are the crux of democratic government. Without them democracy withers and decays.'[1] In the modern British Constitution political parties play a crucial role, and the operation of the present political system depends upon at least two strong political parties in competition with each other. At a general election, the electorate will vote for candidates adopted by political parties, and these candidates will generally present the views of the party which they represent. The parties embrace different ideologies, articulate different policies and they vie with each other for the support of the electorate. The party which gains more seats than any other will generally form the government of the nation for a period of up to five years. During that time, the party in office may claim to translate into positive law the policies which it presented to the electorate. In view of the role of party government in British politics, it would be impossible to overstate the importance of trade union finance of the Labour Party.

In 1979 the income of the Labour Party's head office general fund was £2,151,238 of which £1,842,383 was paid by trade unions in affiliation fees.[2] The unions finance the party in a host of other ways. As we have seen, they have accepted responsibility for providing the party with its new premises. Moreover, delegates are charged a fee to attend the annual conference of the party; grants are made to constituency parties of sponsored members of Parliament; and union branches affiliate to constituency parties. In an election year the unions will heavily finance the party's general election fund. In 1974, a year of two general elections, £914,998 was donated to the fund and it seems that most of this was donated by the unions.[3] Unions sponsoring candidates would incur the additional expense of financing their election campaigns. Under the rules of the Labour Party, first formulated at the party conference at Hastings in 1933, trade unions may pay up to 80 per cent of the expenses of parliamentary candidates and may make a grant towards the upkeep of the candidate's constituency of £600 in a borough constituency and £750 in a county constituency. A union may also make a contribution of 70 per cent of the salary of a full-time agent if such an officer is employed in the constituency in question. It should be noted however that affiliation fees normally contribute by far the largest single item of political expenditure, a point which is illustrated in table 6. It may also be noted that political spending generally accounts for a very small proportion of a union's total budget, usually in the range of about 1–3 per cent. Some idea of the money available to unions for political purposes and the number of trade unionists who contribute to this action may be gauged from table 7.

Table 6. Trade union affiliation fees to Labour Party

Trade union	Total political fund expenditure, 1980	Total paid in national affiliation fees
APEX	57,305	40,082
FBU	8,458	5,955
FTAT	30,231	26,305
GMWU	427,169	208,000
NUPE	531,216	220,000
NUR	128,405	57,600
NUS	10,862	8,000
TGWU	616,338	400,000
USDAW	221,632	139,662

SOURCE: The Income and Expenditure Accounts of the respective trade unions.

THE FUNCTION OF TRADE UNION POLITICAL ACTION

In chapter one it was argued that trade union political action was undertaken largely to protect the liberties of unions and their members, and as a means of promoting industrial interests. The same theme was identified by Perlman, an American commentator on the British trade union movement. In his *Theory of the Labor Movement*, he wrote: 'the heart of British unionism is still in those jealously revered organisations that stand guard over the collective economic opportunity of each group – the jobs and the working conditions that go with jobs'.[4] It was the commitment to this basic purpose that led unions to show 'periods of enthusiam for politics'.[5] In a similar vein, Flanders has observed that unions prefer to rely upon industrial rather than political methods to achieve their aims.[6] Political methods exist as a second string to the union bow and are resorted to in order to support and supplement their industrial methods. Although unions must be involved in politics 'in order to establish and maintain the legal and economic conditions in which they can flourish',[7] the extent to which unions could adopt political action is limited by the need not to threaten their industrial unity. Thus 'when political divisions within a trade union become too acute and occupy too much attention, the result is paralysis and possibly disruption'.[8] It is for this reason, he argues, that union intervention in party politics is 'largely confined to questions in which they have a direct interest as trade unions'.

But although trade unions have needs which can be dealt with in the political arena, it may be argued that they no longer depend on the Labour Party for the satisfaction of these needs. Since the formation of the party the style of government has changed remarkably in this country with much more open consultation with interest groups before any legislation is enacted. Indeed one political scientist has seriously claimed that organised groups now have a right to take part in making policy related to their sector of activity.[9] So far as the unions are concerned, a number of factors encouraged this process. Although several government ministers in the early years of this century involved the unions in questions of policy-making,[10] this was not widely extended until the demands of the First World War compelled the political leaders to recognise that the full participation of organised labour was an indispensable condition of maximum public support for the war-time policies. For their part in backing the war effort, the unions had demanded and secured: 'the right to be represented on the many Committees established to administer the distribution of national relief funds, the Munitions and Pensions Acts, rationing and food control. At a higher level the Parliamentary Committee had been in constant consultation with members of the Cabinet and heads of Government departments on all manner of subjects'.[11] The value of the war-time consultation was widely acclaimed. In its report in 1918 the Haldane Committee on the Machinery of Government recommended that in order to secure and retain public and parliamentary confidence, it was imperative that departments should avail themselves of the advice and assistance of advisory bodies which could represent the knowledge and experience of all sections of the community.[12]

But notwithstanding these recommendations, much of the machinery of consultation was dismantled and union participation in government was not again commonplace until the advent of the Second World War when the nation faced such problems as manpower shortages, production delays and wage inflation. Citrine, then General Secretary of the TUC, recalls that it was taken for granted that in practically everything which at any point involved the workers, the advice of the TUC had to be sought.[13] In underlining this develop-

Table 7. Political funds of trade unions, 1979

Unions each with a political fund of £10,000 or more	Total membership	Number of members contributing to political fund	% of total membership contributing to political fund	Political fund			
				Income £000s	Expenditure £000s	Fund at beginning of the year £000s	Fund at end of the year £000s
TGWU	2,086,281	2,024,749	97	620	812	1,032	840
NUM	372,122	244,304	66	465	395	750	820
Durham area	42,218	16,759	40	34	30	223	227
AUEW							
Construction	36,073	26,320	73	12	8	16	20
Engineering	1,217,760	1,010,335	83	491	488	360	363
Foundry	55,720	41,677	75	21	29	22	14
TASS	200,054	98,750	49	98	85	110	123
GMWU	967,153	897,396	93	627	522	396	501
NUPE	691,770	678,197	98	657	719	301	239
NUR	170,294	163,875	96	179	205	230	204
USDAW	470,017	436,445	93	211	284	207	134
ASB	129,712	78,859	61	70	48	108	130
APEX	150,611	117,458	73	96	114	135	117
NUSMW	73,482	56,765	77	31	71	100	60
POEU	125,723	89,567	71	82	95	66	53
SOGAT	205,784	50,700	25	30	58	78	50
NUDBTW	56,843	56,660	100	20	28	22	

FTAT	85,036	51,872	61	16	12	25	29
EETPU	443,621	380,770	86	121	150	53	24
ASLEF	27,478	26,001	95	25	34	31	22
ISTC	110,276	95,617	87	45	64	38	19
NGA	111,541	50,949	46	12	18	21	15
NATTKE	64,744	58,034	90	25	34	23	14
NUFLAT	18,000	12,500	69	3	1	12	14
NACODS	19,146	18,648	97	18	16	11	13
COHSE	212,930	195,151	92	91	83	4	12
FBU	41,533	26,100	63	13	13	11	11
NUTGW	117,362	106,083	90	52	26	−15	11
NUIW*	2,985	221	7	n.d.	n.d.	11	11
TWU	19,685	10,116	51	6	8	12	10
Total, above 32	8,713,191	7,353,482	84	4,310	4,575	4,475	4,210
39 other unions	1,229,773	746,814	61	358	467	138	29
Total, all 71	9,942,964	8,100,296	81	4,668	5,042	4,613	4,239
72 unions, 1978	9,887,597	8,082,361	82	4,045	3,417	3,902	4,530

SOURCE: Annual Report of the Certification Officer 1980.

* Liverpool Victoria Section only

ment, one historian has revealed that as a result of the active involvement of the unions in the war-time administration, 'the annual reports of the TUC General Council began to read like the records of some special government department responsible for coordinating policy in the social and industrial spheres'.[14] But unlike the experience of World War One, the norms established during the Second World War long outlived the hostilities, and the position now is that trade unions, like other pressure groups, are represented at many different levels in the decision-making process, and are consulted on a wide range of issues. The TUC is represented on a host of advisory committees and there are regular contacts between TUC representatives on the one hand and departmental officials, government ministers, including the Prime Minister, on the other. In its evidence to the Donovan Commission, the TUC claimed:

> Whilst there can be no obligation on the Government to consult the TUC or individual unions on questions which closely affect the interest of their members, over the last fifty years there has grown up a pattern of consultation the scope of which is very wide ranging. All Governments recognise that it is not possible to run a country purely through a Parliament. It might be said that Governments treat the TUC as a sort of industrial Parliament; in the first place to obtain the benefit of the views and experience of the trade union Movement in framing legislation or developing policies in general, and second, to secure the approval or endorsement of the TUC for the broad terms of legislation which will have a day by day influence on the work of trade unions.[15]

Because of the access to government which the TUC now has, and the influence which it wields, several large white-collar unions, including NALGO and NUT, chose to affiliate in the 1960s, despite their reservations about identifying with large groups of manual workers and despite their fear that their political neutrality might be compromised.[16] Attempts to set up a rival body for white-collar workers failed, lacking the authority and power of the TUC which speaks on behalf of some 12 million workers. The reasoning of EIS was symptomatic of the attitude of a considerable number of white-collar unions in the 1960s:

> In recent years, the Institute has become increasingly involved in matters concerning salaries and conditions of service. Our affiliation to the TUC and STUC was motivated by the need to influence trade union policy on educational and professional matters and to gain access to the Ministers of the Crown at the highest possible level and I think we can claim that we have so far benefited in these ways from affiliation.

But it should be noted that contact with ministers and officials is not the sole preserve of the TUC. It is reported that if Arthur Deakin, one time General Secretary of TGWU, 'wanted to speak to the Minister of Labour he simply telephoned or called in at his room in St. James' Square'.[17] Access may also be available to much smaller unions. In 1977 the General Secretary of National Union of Wallcovering, Decorative and Allied Trades, a union with less than 4,000 members, said:

> One thing that the recession has brought home to me is that a Union's traditional role, that of bargaining with the member's employer on matters affecting his or her terms and conditions of employment, has changed. During the past year I have regularly met with Government officials. Our efforts to establish a joint committee of Department of Industry representatives, Employers and Trade Unionists, under the auspices of the National Economic Development Council, to consider the plight of the British Wallcoverings Industry, has been one of the main reasons for this development.[18]

Yet although consultation is valuable and should not be underestimated, it is nevertheless of limited potential. It oils the machinery of government on matters of routine administration but does not always guarantee that the trade union view will prevail on major matters of policy. There are many occasions when consultation is an empty procedure, particularly when conducted by an administration which is more responsive to the needs of other groups, and particularly during periods, which appear to occur all too frequently, when the trade union question is one of acute political controversy. Yet if consultation is limited, it may still be argued that it is too simplistic to see the links with the Labour Party as merely a means of pursuing the interests of trade unions and their members. The unions which are affiliated to the party are inevitably involved in the formulation of policies which at best can be described as peripheral to their industrial interests. It may be further argued that affiliation represents the support of a political ideology. By clause 4 of its constitution, the Labour Party is committed to socialism and again it may be argued that this is only remotely related to the daily business of trade unions. Certainly, when compared with a union such as BIFU, the Labour Party link seems to assume an added dimension. The objects of BIFU include:

> To watch over all legislative measures which may affect, or tend to affect, the interests of its members; to use its influence with Members of Parliament; to attempt to secure the promotion, rejection or amendment of legislation affecting Banks and Financial Institutions and their employees, as circumstances may require, *but the Union shall not belong to or subscribe to any political party*.[19]

The union adopted this latter measure in pursuit of an ideology of 'pure and simple trade unionism' divorced from any direct link with a political party.

But because one union can operate politically without any formal identity with a political party is not to deny that the close links of others exist to a large extent for reasons of self-protection. The form of political action is essentially a question of judgment and there is good reason to believe that affiliation to the Labour Party is a more effective tactic than the neutrality of bodies such as BIFU. For simply in negative terms, a Labour government is an insurance policy which guarantees freedom from legal restriction, whether from the courts or from Parliament.[20] Equally, a Labour government is more likely than any other to create a social and economic climate in which the activities of trade unions can flourish. Union growth, freedom from unemployment, and effective collective bargaining are now more likely to be consequences of a Labour government than a Conservative one. And while these are important features of the link with Labour, the alliance provides the unions with rather more. Thus, ASTMS has claimed that 'Labour party policy on the whole . . [reflects] the views of the trade union movement';[21] POEU reported that it affiliated to the party in 1964 so that it would have 'a significant voice in the determination of policy within the Party';[22] and GMWU has claimed that the party is the natural political vehicle for the aspirations of trade unionists.[23] The advantages of affiliation have not been lost on NALGO, which at the time of writing is holding a ballot for the adoption of political fund rules, with a view to eventual affiliation to the Labour Party. One of the arguments in favour of affiliation was expressed as follows:

> The main argument for affiliation to the Labour Party is similar to that advanced for joining the T.U.C., . . . that N.A.L.G.O. should ensure that it is involved, and its influence felt, where crucial decisions affecting the membership are made. Although the T.U.C. is not financially linked to the Labour Party, connections historically between the two have been close and the process of policy formulation overlaps to some extent. It is maintained that when a Labour Government is in office its links with the trade union movement ensure that policies and legislation favourable to the interests of union members are pursued and that there is ready access for union leaders at very senior levels in Whitehall. It is argued that N.A.L.G.O. should take full advantage of this situation by joining other unions in the Labour Party. When the Labour Party is in opposition policy making on a wide range of issues of importance to N.A.L.G.O. continues and the outcome of this process is likely to affect the programme of the next Labour Government. Thus, for example, there is every

possibility that work done by the Labour Party on regional policy and local government structure will eventually be translated into practice. In these circumstances it can be maintained that N.A.L.G.O. has a responsibility to its members to ensure that their interests are represented.[24]

So not only does the Labour Party provide an economic and legal climate conducive to the interests of the unions, it also provides them with a platform for the formulation of the policies of one of the major parties of the state, which indeed at one time was thought by many to be the natural party of government. The trade unions are thus in a profoundly powerful and influential position to mould policies which will best suit the needs of their members. And in this respect it is important to note that the Labour Party's constitutional changes of 1980 have considerably increased the power of the unions within the party. Whereas before, the party leader was elected by the PLP, he is now elected by an electoral college of which the unions have 40 per cent of the votes. This compares with 30 per cent held by the PLP and constituency parties respectively. Secondly, unions hold by far the largest number of votes at party conference, with 6½ million votes in 1980 compared with the 689,000 in the hands of constituency parties. Under the constitution of the party, Conference is to decide what specific proposals of legislative, financial or administrative reform are to be included in the party programme. Thirdly, the unions are guaranteed by the Standing Orders of the party at least 12 of the 29 seats on the National Executive Committee and may nominate candidates for five of the other places which are reserved for women. The NEC is an important body, for not only does it keep the machine in operation, but it is also partly responsible for drafting the party's election manifesto.

Finally, it should be noted that the unions are influential within the PLP. Although it is sometimes argued that 'the sponsoring of candidates for Parliament is of secondary and quite limited importance', sponsorship shows no sign of declining.[25] At the general election in 1979, the unions sponsored 165 candidates, of whom 133 were elected. This compares with 127 elected at the second general election in 1974 which was a figure which had been surpassed on only one previous occasion. Details of the 1979 sponsorship are shown in table 8.

A number of factors help to explain the continuing commitment of the unions to the sponsorship of members of Parliament. It is sometimes suggested that the activity is undertaken for reasons of prestige or status;[26] or in order to ensure that there is some genuine working class representation in the PLP,[27] though many unions are now turning to professional politicians to represent them, rather than to their own members. But to deny that sponsorship performs any practical

Table 8. Trade-union-sponsored candidates
at the 1979 general election

Trade union	No.	Elected
NUAAW	1	1
NUB	1	1
ASB	2	2
UCATT	4	2
EEPTU	4	4
AUEW	18	16
AUEW (Construction)	1	1
AUEW (TASS)	5	4
NUFLAT	1	0
FTAT	1	1
GMWU	14	14
NGA	1	0
COHSE	6	3
ISTC	2	2
ASLEF	1	0
NUM	18	16
POEU	4	3
UPW	2	2
APEX	6	5
NUPE	8	7
NUR	13	12
ASTMS	12	8
NUSMW	1	0
NUS	1	1
USDAW	6	5
TGWU	29	20
TSSA	3	3
	165	133

SOURCE: Labour Party Report 1979.

function would be misleading. In evidence submitted to the Houghton
Committee on Financial Aid to Political Parties, ASTMS claimed:

> The practice of sponsoring parliamentary candidates is an impor-
> tant one for the trade unions. The unions sponsor candidates in
> order to see that their interests are represented in Parliament.
> Sponsored MPs keep a watch on legislation that might affect

their union, they can send delegations to Ministers, ask questions in the House, and even sponsor legislation of their own.[28]
Similar sentiments have been expressed in recent years by such unions as TGWU, COHSE and NUR, and trade unions which neglect the parliamentary dimension may find their positions considerably weakened particularly when Labour is in Opposition. Equally important, sponsorship plays a potentially crucial role in the special context of Labour Party politics. As we have seen, the party leader is now elected by an electoral college in which the PLP has 30 per cent of the votes. Sponsorship gives the unions some influence over the way in which at least some members of Parliament exercise their vote and may be important where a union sponsored member is a candidate. More importantly perhaps, the presence of a large group of sponsored members provides a potential veto in the event of a Labour government proposing any steps which are thought to weaken the position of the unions. This was admirably demonstrated when in 1969 the Wilson government ignored union advice and proposed to legislate along the lines outlined in the White Paper, In Place of Strife.[29] These proposals were only abandoned when it was made clear that many union sponsored members of Parliament were unlikely to support the government on the issue.[30]

THE EFFECT OF LEGAL REGULATION

So political action is central to the work of the trade unions. In this light it becomes imperative to establish to what extent, if at all, the 1913 Act undermines the power of the unions freely to develop their political arm. It is not unreasonable to presume that the Act must have operated as some form of constraint. Trade unions may only finance political activity from a separate political fund. Consequently, political expenditure will be conditioned to a large extent by the income of the fund. It is perfectly conceivable then that political funds will not be large enough to bear the level of political expenditure in which unions might wish to engage, or to meet any unusual or unforeseen expense such as requests from the Labour Party to help with the financing of a general election campaign, or the costs incurred in the building of the party's new premises.

Yet several authors take the view that the Trade Union Act 1913 has been advantageous to the development of the political activities of trade unions. The historian A. J. P. Taylor argued, wrongly on this point, that the Liberal government had intended by the 1913 Act to impede union political activity. He claims, however, that it has had just the opposite effect, concluding:

> Instead it proved an advantage. The political fund could not be used for anything else. In the old days a union felt generous when

it subscribed £100 to the Labour party. Now it thought nothing
of handing over £5,000, if the money were lying in the political
fund . . . Thus the act of 1913, designed to cripple the Labour
party, accidentally gave it a watertight guarantee of a regular and
fairly substantial income.[31]

But this appears to be mere speculation, and the author provides no
evidence to support his view. However, in a similar vein, Richter has
argued that in relation to the extended political commitment of the
AEU in the post-war years:

The growth of the political fund may itself have been an independent influence in the E.C.'s decision to enlarge the group (of
sponsored MPs). 'Parkinson's law' states that expenditures rise
to meet income. Here, as in other unions, growing amounts of
unexpended funds helped to create a demand for political expression.[32]

Richter also concludes that the growth in the number of candidates
sponsored by TGWU in the 1960s was determined largely by the
amount of money available in the political fund of the union.[33]

But inevitably perhaps, not all the evidence is consistent with the
view that unions do not operate under restraint because of the existence of the 1913 Act. Harrison noted that in the 1950s several political
funds ran into difficulties and that, for example, the Typographical
Association could spare nothing for the general election campaign of
1955.[34] Similarly, Rush has argued that whereas the large unions can
comfortably afford to sponsor several parliamentary candidates, 'their
smaller rivals must consider whether their political funds can adequately support even a single candidature'.[35] He concluded:

Thus it is that some small unions, like the Tobacco Workers'
Union or the National Union of Furniture Trade Operatives,
supported only one candidate each between 1950 and 1966; or
others, such as the United Patternmakers Association or the
National Union of Tailors and Garment Workers, were each
represented by a single M.P. during part of this period. Con-
versely, finance accounts to a considerable extent for the ability
of the N.U.M. to support nearly 200, the T.G.W.U. over a
hundred, and the A.E.U. over eighty candidatures between 1950
and 1966.[36]

Some idea of the costs involved in an election may be obtained from
the permitted expenditure of candidates under the Representation of
the People Act 1978. The maximum expenditure of candidates at a
parliamentary election in a borough constituency is £1,750 together
with an additional 1½p for every entry in the register of electors to be
used at the election.[37] In a constituency with 70,000 electors the maximum expenditure of each candidate would be £2,800 and, as we have

seen, the Hastings Agreement permits trade unions to pay up to 80 per cent of the candidate's maximum expenses, which in this example would be £2,240. This would clearly be beyond the means of many, but not all, small unions, though it does not necessarily follow that these unions would be willing to use their general funds for this purpose if they were free to do so.

Finally, in his study of ASSET, Richter drew attention to the fact that:

> Unlike our manual model, the A.E.U., where an accumulation of enormous political funds was in itself a factor in its spurious political behaviour, A.S.S.E.T. reached out for greater funds than the levy provided for its genuine pressure activity. First, the political fund was enlarged by calling in branch shares of that fund. Second, general funds were allocated to, and some outside funds were secured for, legislative phases of the political programme. There was also very close co-ordination of the electoral and legislative phases – as one generally finds to be the case in any effective pressure group.[38]

Insofar as he is saying that the 1913 Act presented a problem for ASSET's political activities, this may embrace a mild exaggeration. Richter alleges that 'the pressure phase' of the union's work which was financed by general funds included the cost of monthly luncheon meetings with members of Parliament in a House of Commons dining-room. The union justified this expenditure on the ground that it was not merely political, but also part of its organisational and educational programme. Yet, as we noted in chapter four, such expenditure is not *prima facie* improper. Depending upon the purpose of these meetings, it may be argued that they are in furtherance of statutory objects and so may be met by the general funds. However, the author's general point may be thought to be substantiated by his allegation that: 'The branches formally had access to one-third of the levy. For the 1964 campaign, however, they were informed that because of urgent need in some important constituency elections, each branch share would be 'impounded' and put into the central fund, unless objection should be voiced within seven days of receipt of the letter. It appears that none objected.'[39]

In order to assess some of the points made in the above works, a postal survey of 65 trade unions was conducted by the author in 1977–8. Of these 65 unions, 41 had political funds. The unions in the sample included all those affiliated to the TUC and the STUC with a membership of over 25,000. The remaining unions all had a membership of less than this and were included with a view to establishing whether there were any special problems encountered by small unions. The unions in this latter category were selected on a random basis, but included several which were concentrated on a particular locality, in a particular industry, and on a particular group of workers within an industry. Briefly, the respondents were asked to comment on a number of points, including the following:

i) whether the Trade Union Act 1913 constrained, inhibited, or prevented the union in question from spending as much money on political action as it might otherwise wish to do; and

ii) whether if the legal constraints were lifted, the union in question was likely to increase its political spending in any way.

Details of the response to the survey and the identity of the respondents are to be found in tables 9 and 10.

Table 9. Trade union response to survey

	Unions with political fund	Unions with no political fund	Total
Number that responded	31	20	51
Number that failed to respond	10	4	14
Total	41	24	65

Table 10. Trade union respondents

	Unions with political fund	Unions with no political fund	Total
General Secretary	17	10	27
Assistant General Secretary	1	3	4
Political Organiser	1	–	1
Legal Officer	–	1	1
Research Officers	10	3	13
Other	2	3	5

One union found it difficult to answer the hypothetical questions in the survey, and another said that it had never considered the issues. Rather curiously, it was intimated on behalf of a print union that the Act did present difficulties but that if it did not exist, the union was unlikely to increase the level of its political expenditure. A union representing workers in the ceramic trades said that it would not ask for a repeal of the 1913 Act, but no reason was given. Otherwise, the respondents fell into five main categories. The first, a very small group, were those which thought that the 1913 Act was in some way an advantage to the development of their political activities. The General Secretary of a union representing transport workers said that the Act was a benefit, 'inasmuch as the funds designated for political use can be used as such without question'. Similarly the General Secretary of a union in the entertainment field said that the union's political fund income exceeded its requirements. Consequently, the union was beginning to use the fund for purposes other than to promote its own political interests. In particular, it was being used partly as a service which would be available to those members who had stood for Parliament to help with their election expenses. He said that the union had recently helped a Liberal candidate, and would be prepared to help other non-Labour Party candidates.

The second most common response was that the Act did not impede the political activities of the union concerned. The General Secretary of a large industrial union said that nothing would be gained by that union if the legal restraints were lifted. Similarly, the General Secretary of a building trades' union said that 'the 1913 Act has little significance and effect on the union's political activity and to no great extent inhibits the union in this area'. And it was said on behalf of a large white-collar union that:

> At the present time we consider that [the union's] representation in Parliament is quite satisfactory through our six sponsored Members of Parliament and another two dozen who are individual members of the union. We find this appropriate to our purposes and do not feel that we are operating under any undue restriction in this respect . . . we are experiencing no difficulty through its [the 1913 Act] continued operation.

In a similar vein, the General Secretary of a large general workers union said that the political expenditure of the union was not limited by the 1913 Act but by the size of the fund. It seems that the political fund was large enough to satisfy the needs of the union, because it was said that no significant additional areas of expenditure were feasible. Moreover although it was said on behalf of another white-collar union that 'The 1913 Act clearly does place a limitation on the Parliamentary activity of trade unions', it was also said that the union 'has a Parliamentary Panel of five . . . For a union with 170,000 members this is probably about par for the course'. It may also be noted that a number of other unions expressed the view that they were experiencing no difficulty through the operation of the Act. These unions included those representing boilermakers, bakers, sheet metal workers and communication workers.

A third group of respondents were those which intimated agreement with the present legal framework. The General Secretary of a print union said: 'I do not believe that our particular union's activity would change very much if the Trade Union Act of 1913 was repealed. By and large, I think our members accept that the present separation and distinction for the Political Fund, and for obviously separate political activity, is about right.' A tentative response to this effect was made on behalf of a union in the broadcasting field: 'The issue . . . is not one which I recall active discussion at any level within the union. In the absence of any discussion, the assumption must be that our union accepts the present position'; and by a health service union: 'I think it would be fair to say that in general we support the division of general and political funds'.

A fourth group of respondents implied agreement with the present legal framework, by pointing to informal pressures which would compel them to operate such a scheme, even in the absence of a legal obligation to do so. The General Secretary of another union in the entertainment field said: 'Since we, like many other unions, operate on a close balance of income and expenditure my guess is that we should not significantly increase our political expenditure if we were free to do so'. Similarly several unions which do not operate a political fund at present indicated that the removal of the present legal rules would not induce them to give money to political parties or to sponsor, as opposed to retain, members of Parliament. It was said on behalf of a banking union that if there was any movement to provide funds for a political party, this would be strongly resisted by the members of the union. Other unions which pointed to a similar restraint were those representing school teachers, civil servants, and journalists. Moreover, it may be noted that it was said on behalf of a civil service union that: 'It is clear that there is also a strong feeling, shared by other unions in the Civil Service, that where the employer is the government, constructive negotiations will be hampered if the Union is seen to be at any time politically affiliated to, and owing allegiance to, a party that forms the opposition'.

Most of the respondent unions fell within one of these four categories. There was, however, a fifth and final group of unions which either confessed to some difficulty in raising money for purely political purposes or claimed that they might be more generous in their political spending if the legal restraints were lifted. A print union complained: 'We must be represented in the highest councils in the land if we truly want to fully represent our members. Because of the state of the [political] Fund we have not been able to play our full part.' Similarly, unions representing both tailors and patternmakers reported difficulties in building up their political funds which had been in deficit for a number of years. Perhaps less seriously, it was said on behalf of a union representing iron and steel workers: 'Like other unions we might well increase our political spending if legal restrictions were removed. We are at present inhibited by the limits on the use of our general fund . . . We cannot use this for directly political purposes, though we would like to give more to the Labour Party in order to put it on a sound financial footing at last. We have investigated ways and possibilities of using the general fund.' A union representing post office employees thought that the removal of the 1913 Act would induce them to be 'a little less cautious in their support to the Labour Party in terms of grants etc.' And a textile union indicated that: 'There is no doubt that the 1913 Act does, to some degree, restrict Trade Union spending on political activities although this is most notable when there are election campaigns and demands in quick succession as in 1974'.

The fifth category of respondents was a small one of six unions, only three of which had difficulty in building up funds, and none of which were crippled by the difficulty. There is no reason to believe that the 1913 Act was a major cause of the problems of the unions concerned or that these unions would be able to find any additional money for political purposes if the Act did not exist. One of the unions concerned had a very small political levy, of only 39p per annum, at a time when affiliation fees to the Labour Party were 24p per member. The problems of this union could have been considerably alleviated by a modest increase in its levy. Similarly, one of the other unions, it seems, always had a very temperamental membership so far as politics are concerned. Following the Labour government's White Paper, In Place of Strife, hundreds of its members contracted out and by the early 1970s the union could afford to support only one parliamentary candidate. And even at the height of the unpopular Heath government, the Finance Office of the union continued to be 'bombarded with contracting-out forms'. It was also reported at the union's Biennial Conference in 1974:

> Because of the parlous state of our Political Fund we have not been able to give financial support to [our sponsored M.P.'s] constituency, and we have reduced our affiliation fees by half to the Labour Party and have also reduced our representation at the Annual Conferences considerably in order to conserve the fund. We hope, therefore, that our Political Fund will soon be improved sufficiently to enable us to pay our way and to prepare for the additional financial burden we shall be faced with in the event of an early General Election.

THE FINANCES OF THE LABOUR PARTY

Since the survey was conducted, fresh evidence has come to light concerning the financing of the Labour Party. The finances of the party have never been healthy, particularly when compared with its main rival. Internal party inquiries have repeatedly drawn attention to financial crises and in 1975 the Houghton Committee on Financial Aid to Political Parties estimated that the total income of the Labour Party was less than half that of the Conservatives. But the problem was never quite so acutely demonstrated as by the report of the Commission of Enquiry of 1980 which pointed out:

2.2. It is clear that the party has effectively no reserves, a thoroughly inadequate income and is moving into serious deficit and debt. This problem has been veiled by a traditional method of account presentation. We are dissatisfied with both policy formation and management in respect of the party's finances. It has been difficult for anyone to take, or be empowered to take, responsibility for this problem. The party now has to urgently re-structure all its finances, and to make the gravity of the present financial situation fully understood by the party at large and take the necessary steps to remedy the situation.

2.3. After detailed examination it was apparent that the party's financial difficulties have existed for over a decade and have been exacerbated by persistently high rates of inflation. For the majority of the past ten years, the party has been running at a deficit on its general operations and has had to draw heavily on its reserves. It now has little in the way of realisable assets and the party's expenditure in 1979 grossly exceeded its income.

Yet in 1976, Rose argued that 'Labour finance reflects a particular state of mind more than a lack of cash in the bank'.[40] To justify this assertion, he pointed to the fact that although the general fund of the Labour Party tends to show a nominal deficit each year, this had to be seen in the context of large amounts of money hoarded in the coffers of the Labour movement generally. One example of such hoarding to which he referred was the money held by trade unions in their political fund accounts, which in 1979 stood at a total of £4,239,000.[41] However, this represents the accumulation of funds over many years and even if all this money was transferred to the party, it would simply resolve the problem in the short-term. Labour's cash flow problems would still have to be faced when these funds dried up.

One suggestion to help deal with these problems is that the 1913 Act should be repealed. This has been made on a number of occasions, and most recently by COHSE which in its evidence to the Labour Party Commission of Enquiry said that it believed: 'affiliated unions should not be so restricted as they are at present by the 1913 Act. Either the restrictions should be removed, so as to allow some limited use of General Fund monies for political expenditure, *or* legislation should be introduced to control the political expenditure of companies.'[42] This suggestion was not considered by the Enquiry, but if it was pursued and implemented it would have the advantage of enabling trade unions to respond to their political needs much more freely and without an eye to the constraints of legislation. Yet although superficially attractive as a means of relieving the distress of the Labour Party, such a proposal, if implemented, could have serious political consequences, for although COHSE is not alone in believing that ideally the Act should be repealed, senior Labour politicians were opposed to such a move because of the real danger that opening up the issue might encourage a Conservative administration to introduce even more restrictive measures. In these circumstances, it was thought better 'to let things be'. Some commentators would argue that in any event the proposal to repeal the 1913 Act raises serious questions of principle.[43] Thus, it might be contended that the contracting out provisions of the 1913 Act are necessary to protect the union member who has joined the union, not through choice, but because of the existence of a closed shop. If such a member leaves the union because he dislikes the policy and spending activities of the union, he would do so at the risk of losing his job.

The closed shop was defined by McCarthy in his seminal work as being 'a situation in which employees come to realise that a particular job is only to be obtained and retained if they become and remain members of one of a specified number of trade unions'.[44] The function of the closed shop, despite the unwillingness on the part of some employees to be union members, relates mainly to the need to protect union security. The closed shop may be essential in order to establish an effective and stable bargaining unit or to maximise the strength of the workers involved. Additionally, the closed shop is justified on equitable principles as being a means of distributing the costs of collective bargaining and other union activity. It might be argued that the reasons which require that individual liberty be compromised for the closed shop apply also to union political activities. As a method of union security the closed shop does not stand isolated. It has already been argued that union political activity is undertaken with the main purpose of promoting and protecting basic trade union interests. Sometimes this will be to secure an environment in which stable collective bargaining can be effective and at other times it will be to secure measures to supplement the defects of collective bargaining as a means of regulating working conditions. At any rate it is clear that like the closed shop, political activity makes a major contribution to union security. The closed shop may provide the means for effective bargaining, but the political activities play an important part in supplementing and underpinning the bargaining process. It may be argued then that there is neither logic nor reason in facilitating the growth of the closed shop as a method of union security if to do so is to justify the operation of contradictory pressures.

Yet to insist on compulsory membership is one thing, but to then require that the individual contributes, however indirectly and for whatever purpose, to the Labour Party is something quite different. Nevertheless it is true that membership will be offered on the same terms as it is offered to everyone else. This means in effect that the member will have the same right as other union members to use the democratic machinery of the union to campaign against and to challenge the policy of the hierarchy. However, if a worker has joined a trade union against his will, he should not be obliged to participate in its internal affairs in order to protect his conscience. In any event, his access to the democratic procedures of the union is likely to be ineffective in practice. Trade union members are notoriously apathetic and are unlikely to respond to his efforts. So too, it would be crude and authoritarian to suggest that as a member of a democratic institution the individual must accept and respect the will of the majority and the needs of the institution. A democracy does not seek blindly to enforce majority rule. It also strives to secure the recognition of basic and fundamental interests and to resolve and recognise the interests of the majority within this framework. Yet despite these considerations the weight of the closed shop argument is limited. The argument is inapplicable where the compulsory union membership does not exist, and will be less forceful in view of the wide conscience clause introduced by the Employment Act 1980 which provides by s.7 that the dismissal of an employee will be unfair if the employee 'genuinely objects on grounds of conscience or other deeply-held personal conviction' to being a member of a trade union. And it is not immaterial to note that the other conscientious scruples of the trade unionist are not protected if he finds himself in a minority. It has never yet been adequately explained why this issue demands special treatment, particularly in a society which fails to protect the political conscience of company shareholders, company employees, or consumers who in one way or another indirectly support the Conservative Party.

A more convincing argument against lifting the legal constraints is that such a step is unlikely to make much difference to the level of trade union political spending. The survey referred to above certainly indicates this and it is reasonable to speculate that those unions which might be tempted to use general funds for political purposes would be prevented from doing so by informal pressures operating within the union. Thus, in several unions, many members contract out. In AUEW (Engineering Section), APEX and POEU it is about one-quarter of the total membership; in UCATT and FBU it is about a third; and in AUEW (TASS) it is about a half. If these unions were to use general funds for political purposes there is a great danger of unrest, dissension or resignation among the members, which might detract from the efficiency of the unions concerned. Equally, there is a danger that the use of general funds would rebound on the unions. In some unions including ASTMS, NGA and SLADE the majority of members claim exemption. The removal of the present legal rules would not be an advantage to these unions if it meant that the majority would assert itself and prevent the minority from engaging in any political action. These problems suggest that many unions would be compelled to retain the existing practice by voluntary means for to do otherwise would be to risk potentially very damaging consequences. And in this context it is appropriate to note that Conservative Party influence within the trade union movement seems to be operating with some effect. The party has been active in encouraging members to become involved in the affairs of their union; it is known that a very large number of trade unionists vote Conservative; and a body called Conservative Trade Unionists is strong enough to maintain a full-time administration and to hold annual conferences which in the past have been attended by as many as 600 delegates.[45] In any event, trade unions now have substantial reserves in their political funds, with the total reserves of 71 unions in 1979 being over £4 million. Yet few unions seem anxious to make donations to the Labour Party between general elections, despite its financial plight. There is no reason to believe that most would be any more generous if they were free to use general funds which will in any event be stretched to their limits by the obligations imposed on trade unions by the Thatcher government.

So lifting the legal controls is unlikely to be a money-spinner. It could create a great deal of harm for the unions if any changes were attempted, and it is unlikely to make any practical difference to the financial problems facing the Labour Party. This is not to say that the unions do not have a role to play in helping the Labour Party with its financial difficulties. A number of large unions are not affiliated to the party: these include the civil service unions, NALGO and NUT. All depend on expansive government policies and it would not be inappropriate to encourage affiliation from these bodies. In fact, one of the great failures of the Labour Party has been its inability to exploit changing social and economic trends by selling itself to the growing number of white-collar trade unionists. It is also the case that the unions affiliated to the party get their politics on the cheap. The affiliation fee per trade union member was only 28p in 1978, and it has since risen to 45p per annum. Correspondingly, the political levy of many unions is extraordinarily small. In 1979 the average levy was only 52p per annum, that is 1p per week and there were numerous examples of annual levies being much less than this, with several unions fixed at about 20p and one as low as 8p. The 1980 Commission of Enquiry could reasonably claim that a radical increase in union subscriptions should be implemented in order to deal with the short-term financial crisis facing the party.[46] As one commentator has written:

> The fundamental cause of Labour's financial problems has been the failure to increase union levies in line with inflation. The Donovan Commission found that in 1938 adult male manual workers were earning on average £3 9s a week and their average union contribution was £1 16s 7d a year, which amount to 1.02 per cent of their earnings. By 1966 that figure was down to 0.39 per cent, and by 1977 to 0.32 per cent. It will be a delicate task to hoist union contributions and political levies back to their original level.[47]

In the long term, however, it seems unlikely that the unions will provide sufficient funds to finance a modern political party in a commercial and sophisticated mass democracy. This is a view that several trade union leaders now share and seems to be accepted by the party. David Basnett, General Secretary of GMWU is reported to have claimed that union political funds are reaching the limits of what they can do for the party.[48] Similarly NUR has denied that the solution to the party's crises can be found in 'major new subventions from the trade union movement, particularly at a time of mounting industrial confrontation'.[49] These sentiments seem to be supported by the difficulties which the party has had in obtaining the agreement of the unions to raise affiliation fees. At the 1980 annual conference of the party, the Treasurer suggested that if the party was to operate effectively it would need £1 per annum from each affiliated trade unionist. Yet it has been unable to endorse the recommendation of the Commission of Enquiry that affiliation fees be raised to 50p. Some trade union leaders could not adjust their rules, nor go back to their members, nor succeed in convincing their people to raise the political levy to enable them to affiliate on the basis of 50p per member. Others were prepared to accept the proposal though it would mean reducing the level of their affiliation. The affiliation fee has thus been set at 45p, though there is no guarantee that all unions will be able to raise enough money to bear this cost.

The apparent inability of the unions to provide the level of financing which the party seems to need is not necessarily undesirable. The trade unions provide a remarkably high proportion of the party's Head Office income. For example, while it is now about 90 per cent, in the early 1940s it was rather less, hovering for much of the time round 70 per cent and indeed in 1945 was only 60 per cent.[50] While it is easy to understand that the change in the law in 1946 would induce complacency, the present position is not without its dangers. The Labour

Party is a national party representing a national interest and not a sectional interest when in government. And it owes loyalty as much to the people who vote for it as to those who pay for it. This is not to say that the unions always call the tune. The unions will not always agree on questions of policy, and even where they do, considerable autonomy has been permitted to party leaders in the past, even on occasions where they have followed courses which were contrary to the perceived interests of the unions. Yet there must remain some unease about the freedom of the party in government, for as Minkin has written in his monumental work: 'by the very nature of the Party as an instrument through which trade unionism had sought to secure the freedom to carry out its industrial activities, some policies were simply not open to the Party's leaders'.[51] More seriously perhaps is the fact that union threats to withhold cash are being made with some frequency and it has been suggested that this is not done even more often because 'Labour's awareness of its financial vulnerability if union aid were withdrawn may be sharp enough not to need any public underlining'.[52] A threat to withdraw funds was made in 1969 if the government pursued its industrial relations reforms; in 1971 financial support by UPW was conditional on the party's commitment to repeal the Industrial Relations Act;[53] and in 1980 AUEW, NUR and EETPU threatened to withhold financial support unless the party abandoned its 'silly policies'. Unease about the role and influence of money in Labour politics is certainly not helped by the fact that a number of unions over-affiliate to the party in what seems to be a deliberate attempt to buy more votes at conference. It has even been known for unions to affiliate more people than they actually had in membership.

Major additional sources of income on a scale large enough to support the party thus look neither imminent nor necessarily desirable. The party is clearly in a position where it will need to find money from other sources. Although it is rather stretching the frontiers of the present work, two additional sources seem appropriate. First, the party itself could take steps to reduce its dependence on institutional support. Many fund raising activities can now be successfully undertaken, including the creaming of profits from clubs and national lotteries. Additionally serious steps must surely be taken to increase the number of individual members of the party which at about 250,000 is thought to be the lowest individual membership of any social democratic party in Western Europe. It is difficult to believe that a sophisticated and persistent membership drive could not induce many more Labour voters to join the party. And it is perhaps an issue for the consideration of a future Labour government as to whether party membership dues should attract income tax relief. This would be to the advantage of all the parties and would enable subscriptions to be pitched at a rather higher level than at present. Secondly, in the long term it may well be that the health of the Labour Party can only be properly secured by the introduction of some form of financial aid for political parties from the State. Various forms of State Aid are already available to the parties. These include State responsibility for the registration of voters; free postal services for parliamentary candidates; free broadcasting time; and since 1975 a modest payment has been made to help opposition parties in carrying out their parliamentary work.[54] In 1980 the Labour Party received £290,000 from this last source.

But the financial problems facing the Labour Party suggest that it will need further support from the State if it is to fulfil its potentially valuable role, and do so with greater freedom from institutional financiers. The Labour Party is in fact committed to legislation of a kind which will introduce financial aid for political parties. The Commission of Enquiry argued: 'the introduction of state aid is now essential for the continued functioning of our political parties and therefore for the health of our democratic system. Lack of finance by the party has meant that the party has been unable to employ sufficient agents and its organisation has not had the resources to operate as effectively as it would like. The Commission therefore believes that there must be a commitment to introduce state aid for political parties as a piece of priority legislation.'[55] This was endorsed by the party conference in 1980, though reservations were expressed that such a scheme would weaken the links between the party and the unions and encourage the development of a centre party. However, these reservations were overruled by a substantial majority and the recommendation to adopt a modified version of the Houghton Committee's proposals was accepted. The majority of the Committee had recommended that an annual grant should be paid to political parties from Exchequer funds on the basis of 5p for each vote cast in favour of the party at the preceding general election. On this basis the Committee calculated that during the life of the 1974 Parliament, the Labour Party would have received an annual grant of £573,407.[56] This compares with the head office income of the Labour Party of £1,070,630 in 1974 and an expenditure in that year of £1,147,101. It may be noted, however, that it was not the intention of the majority of the Houghton Committee that political parties should be freed from their dependence upon institutional support. Indeed, the majority said that they had 'deliberately limited the amount of aid which parties would receive to ensure that no party would be able to rest on its oars'.[57] But although State Aid in this form would not remove the dependence and accountability of the Labour Party on and to the unions completely,[58] it might at least give the party greater scope for manoeuvre. Guarantees of the kind embraced in the Houghton plan, with necessary modifications for inflation, would not only help to insulate the party from the threat to withhold funds, but might also help create a climate in which the party was no longer seen or thought to be too responsive to the demands of its paymasters. This would be even more so if the provision of State Aid was coupled with a limit on the amounts which companies and unions, whether individually or collectively, could donate to political parties. Any reform which reduced dependence on institutional sources would be a step forward, for in a healthy democracy money must have no place at the policy making table. As far as is humanly possible public affairs must be conducted free from the suspicion that those in office are influenced by financial considerations. It makes no difference that such people are not in fact so motivated. They must be seen to be above such pressure or temptation.

THE COMPANY AND THE CONSERVATIVE PARTY

Although the case for lifting the legal constraints is thus not compelling, it is as well to remember that trade unions alone of interest groups operate under restraint as to the amount of money which they may devote to political purposes. In particular, limited liability companies, the donations of which swell Conservative Party coffers, are not required to meet any such expenditure from a separate political fund. Despite the great concern for trade union political spending, British policy-makers, rather hypocritically, have failed to turn similar attention to company donations. In fact the only serious ripple caused by such donations occurred in 1906, when the London and North Western Railway Company paid £100 to the London Municipal Society which had promoted candidates at local authority elections. Some members of Parliament reacted angrily when in the following year the railway company sought parliamentary approval for a private Bill.[59] It was argued that Parliament should not oblige, otherwise:

> great companies might, whether secretly or openly, provide funds for Party organisations: there was no limit to it . . . money which was lavished on politics with the sole aim of gaining more money, was a dangerous element in politics. This country had not yet suffered from the employment of corporate funds in politics. In America, railway and other corporations operated in the political market just as they did in the commercial markets. They subscribed largely to Party funds, they paid candidates, they bought votes, they got obedient assemblies to pass laws . . . Let the House not be so foolish in their pride at their present political purity as to suppose that these were not dangers in the future for themselves unless they took precautions against them.[60]

It was also claimed that 'For a public company to be allowed to apply the funds of its shareholders for the benefit of any political Party was to lower the purity of public life.'[61] The matter was only resolved when Lloyd George, then President of the Board of Trade, promised to introduce a Bill prohibiting statutory corporations from making donations of this kind. The promise was apparently unfulfilled.

Yet however much it lowers the purity of public life, companies make substantial donations to the Conservative Party, the total of which, together with donations from wealthy individuals, is generally higher than that which the Labour Party receives centrally from the unions. It was estimated by the Hansard Society in 1981 that about 55–60 per cent of Conservative central income came from company donations, and that in 1979–80, an election year, this had been about 80 per cent.[62] Company donations constitute a much smaller proportion of constituency income, with estimates ranging from 5 to 23 per cent and it has been further estimated that company donations amount to about 30 per cent of the total annual income of the Conservative Party. In its study on the financing of political parties, the Hansard Society notes that there seems to be no particular pattern of industrial donations in terms of size of firm or sector of industry. Fear of nationalisation is thought to be one of the motives which can impel firms to give money, but it is not the only factor involved. Some firms are consistently large donors, while the donations of others vary, and it is interesting to note that in the early years of the Thatcher government many companies withheld funds because of their opposition to government policies. Many large firms, such as ICI do not as a matter of principle make political donations, while foreign-owned multinationals are cautious about making such payments.

Company donations are monitored annually by the Labour Research Department and in the year ending August 1980, it was estimated that over £2.75 million was given by 470 companies, with over 70 per cent of this money going direct to Conservative Party funds. The survey covered only about 1,000 companies and was far from exhaustive. It did not take account of donations made by private companies or individuals and was hampered by the belief that not all companies disclose their political donations, despite the legal obligation to do so. Details of where the company money goes is shown in table 11. It will be seen that although most goes direct to the Conservative Party, a significant amount is directed through Conservative Party front organisations and free enterprise groups. Table 12 gives an indication of the size of the subventions which are made by individual organisations. The figures in table 12 reflect the total payments made to the party, British United Industrialists, and regional Industrialist Councils.

Table 11. Total donations to the Conservative Party and
other political organisations 1979–80

Organisation	No. of companies making donations	Amount £
Conservative Party	370	1,936,660
British United Industries	46	444,254
Industrialist Councils	59	185,330
Economic League	84	117,386
Aims	35	36,494
Centre for Policy Studies	21	26,500
Others	36	16,189
	470	2,762,813

SOURCE: Labour Party Research Department
Information Paper 1980.

Table 12. Individual company political donations 1979–80

1.	Allied Breweries	£62,000
2.	Taylor Woodrow	£61,692
3.	Consolidated Gold	£53,000
4.	Rank Organisation	£50,000
5.	GEC	£50,000
6.	Plessey	£47,000
7.	Sedgwick Forbes Bland and Payne	£41,000
8.	Trafalgar House	£40,000
9.	British and Commonwealth Shipping	£39,071
10.	C. T. Bowring	£36,280

SOURCE: Labour Party Research Department
Information Paper 1980

It is now generally accepted that there are few barriers in company
law to the making of political donations.[63] Although there is no decision expressly approving such payments, the prevailing view is that
they are lawful provided they can be shown to be for the good of the
company. Charitable donations have crossed this hurdle and it is
arguable that payments to the Conservative Party are of even more
direct benefit to commercial companies. The only constraint under
which companies operate was imposed by the Companies Act 1967
which by s.19 requires disclosure by the directors in their annual
report of political donations in excess of £200. For the purposes of the

Act, a company is regarded as having made a political donation if, directly or indirectly, it gives money to a political party or to a person who to its knowledge is carrying on activities which can reasonably be regarded as likely to affect public support for a political party. Such disclosure hardly seems unreasonable, for as was pointed out during the Second Reading of the 1967 Act: 'if the directors want to play at politics with the company's money, they ought in all fairness and honesty tell the shareholders what they are doing'.[64] The same spokesman rightly continued by saying that secret contributions to political parties should have no place in a modern parliamentary and political system. Yet the provision was bitterly opposed by some Conservative backbenchers and some peers. It was claimed that the measure was a mean, spiteful gesture, designed to frighten firms from giving money to political organisations of their choice;[65] that it would lead to discrimination in the giving out of contracts; and that disclosure would lead to politically inspired strikes.[66]

It is crucial to note that there are otherwise no controls on company political spending. So the company shareholder, unlike the trade union member, has no right of exemption if company funds are used for a political purpose of which he disapproves. And, some might argue, there is no reason in principle why he should enjoy the same protection, for he is always free to sell his shares and move to some other investment. This is not a choice which is open to the trade unionist, for whatever the law may say about the closed shop, there will inevitably be cases where an employee is compelled to remain a member of a trade union in order to retain employment. But although superficially attractive, such reasoning is plainly unconvincing. It is based upon the assumption that there will always be someone ready to buy the shares at the price paid by the investor. In many cases that will probably not be difficult, but conceivably it need not always be so. But even if such an option is available: 'this could require a shareholder who wishes to avoid making a political contribution being forced to make a decision which, on commercial grounds, he may believe to be mistaken. Nor is such a choice available to a member of a pension fund which decides to purchase shares in a company making political donations.'[67]

If a trade unionist is to be excused from choosing between his political conscience and his job, there seems no reason in principle why the company shareholder should be denied similar protection. It is not surprising then, in view of the lack of consistency on these issues, that some attempt has been made to bring companies into line with trade unions. A Companies (Regulation of Political Funds) Bill was sponsored by a group of Labour backbenchers in 1978,[68] and attempts were made to deal with this issue as the Companies Act 1980 was completing its parliamentary journey. The 1978 Bill provided that companies would not be permitted to engage in political expenditure unless this had first been approved in a ballot of the shareholders. The company would then be required to establish a separate political fund which would be financed only by dividends otherwise payable to shareholders of the company. The fund would be financed only by those shareholders who voted for the resolution to adopt a political fund or who had not given notice of objection to contributing to the fund. The political objects to which the Bill applied were identical to those in s.3(3) of the 1913 Act with the following additional provision: 'the expenditure of money, directly or indirectly, on payments of any kind to any political party or other organisation one of whose aims is the support of candidates for election to Parliament or to any other public office'.

If successful this Bill would have introduced some measure of consistency and fairness to the present position. But it is doubtful if it would have gone far enough. The equation so far has neglected the position of the company employee, not in his capacity as trade unionist but as employee of the company. In these enlightened post-Bullock[69] days it is now generally accepted that the company is a structure in which the position of the employee demands consideration. As the Bullock Report acknowledged: 'The coming of age of democracy in our society is a process that inevitably affects the whole of people's lives; it cannot be excluded from the work place'.[70] A need to consider the position of the company employee is reinforced by s.46 of the Companies Act 1980 which provides that in the exercise of their duties, directors of a company must have regard to the interests of the employees of the company, as well as the interests of the members. Surely, it is wrong if the protection of political liberty is an issue of policy in this country, as the 1913 Act suggests it is, that not only are shareholders compelled to support the Conservative Party, but that company employees are required to stand back and watch as the profits which they helped to create go to finance a political party to which they may be bitterly opposed. Consistency and fairness demand that both groups be protected. Yet if some attempt is to be made to protect the employee, it is difficult to see how this can be done by a system of contracting out by shareholders as was anticipated by the 1978 Bill. Such a system would also be defective in the sense that it would not properly give effect to the aggrieved members of institutional investors. In such cases it would be the institution which would exercise its right of exemption, not the individual member of the institution.

These complex problems do not arise of course in the case of the trade union. Here the issue is a simple one between the trade union and its members. The member can contract out by a straightforward procedure and there are not other interest groups whose political freedoms are infringed. In such circumstances contracting out is an adequate vehicle for the protection of political liberty. But in the case of the company such a vehicle simply cannot cope with the manifold interests and pressures. In fairness not only to shareholders, but also to employees and the members of institutional investors, the only proper device in the company context is a political fund to which interested parties may contract in. The shareholder can then contribute from his dividend; the employee from his wages; and the institution by some method which suits the needs of its different interests. In view of the lack of protection for those interests, the 1913 Act appears as something of an anomaly. That is a consideration which must inform ideas as to the way in which that Act should be modified or reformed. But before examining such matters, we should first consider the practice in other jurisdictions to see by what other means trade union political expenditure is regulated.

COMPARATIVE APPROACHES
AND SOLUTIONS

It is a common feature of most western democracies that trade unions provide financial support to socialist or social democratic parties. In some cases, as in Britain, the unions are affiliated to the parties concerned and are thus in a formal sense institutional members of them. This is true of the New Zealand Labour Party, the Australian Labor Party and the Canadian New Democratic Party. In New Zealand and Australia, the unions collectively provide most of the funds of the respective parties, by means of regular affiliation fees and occasional donations for elections and other purposes.[1] In Canada, affiliated unions have been a major source of NDP funds and before the foundation of the party in 1961, they made donations to its predecessor, the Co-operative Commonwealth Federation.[2] In other countries unions are not formally affiliated to a political party but may support a party electorally by providing it with financial and other support. This is true of several European countries and also of the United States where Democratic Party candidates receive donations from unions and where union locals are used as an organisational base for campaigning during elections.[3] Although the unions are an important source of Democratic Party funds, their contributions are not nearly as proportionally high as in Britain or Australia. Nevertheless, unions alone donated no less than $8 million to congressional candidates in 1976.[4]

It is the purpose of this chapter to consider how the rights of dissenters are safeguarded in a number of jurisdictions, these being New Zealand, the United States, Canada and Australia. But before turning to this issue, it may be noted that in two of these jurisdictions, the United States and Canada, controls have been introduced to regulate the scale of union support for parties and candidates.[5] This has been done as part of an extensive overhaul of election law in the 1970s which in both countries was inspired by the escalating costs of elections, a growing concern at the scale of corporate, trade union and other 'fat cat' involvement in the political process, and fears of electoral corruption which proved well-founded after Watergate. In both countries steps have been taken to promote greater accountability of those involved in the political process; encourage more widespread individual involvement; and reduce and control the dependence of parties and candidates on institutional finance. Thus, candidates and parties are required to disclose their income and expenditure; tax relief has been introduced for individual donations to political parties; public subsidies have been made available to parties and candidates; and limits have been imposed on the amounts which individuals, corporations and trade or labour unions may donate to parties and candidates. In Ontario contributions by any person, corporation or trade union to a political party must not exceed $2,000 in any one year. A further $500 may be donated to constituency associations, subject to a maximum donation of $2,000 in total to constituency associations. During a campaign period a further $500 may be donated to candidates, subject once again to an aggregate maximum of $2,000 spent on such candidates.[6] Similar provisions operate in Alberta and New Brunswick, though the amounts which may be donated are set rather higher.[7] In the United States, federal election law now provides that union organised political funds may not donate more than $5,000 to any candidate for federal office, though there are no limits on the number of candidates who may be supported in this way.[8] An attempt to further prohibit expenditure in excess of $1,000 per annum in support of a candidate (as opposed to a donation to him) was declared unconstitutional in *Buckley* v. *Valeo*[9] as violating the First Amendment which guarantees free speech, the Supreme Court taking the view that 'the independent advocacy restricted by the provision does not presently appear to pose dangers of real or apparent corruption comparable to those identified with large campaign contributions'.[10]

LEGISLATION IN NEW ZEALAND

Legislation dealing with trade union political spending was introduced by New Zealand's first Labour government in 1936 for two principal reasons. First, the Osborne judgment had been followed and applied by New Zealand courts and although it had not operated to strike down union political action,[11] there was sufficient doubt about the power of unions to engage in such activity to warrant legislation to clarify the position.[12] Secondly, 1936 saw the introduction of compulsory unionism in New Zealand, with the Industrial Conciliation and Arbitration Act of that year providing that it was unlawful for employers to employ non-unionists. In the light of this enactment it was felt that there was a corresponding need to introduce some measure of individual protection in the matter of trade union political levies. So in response to these needs the Political Disabilities Removal Act 1936 provided that the funds of a society could be applied in furtherance of political objects.[13] However, so far as minority rights were concerned, the Act made only limited provision, simply enacting that the promotion of political objects required the approval of a majority of the members of the society voting in a ballot held for that purpose.[14] Unlike Britain, the ballot was conducted in accordance with the rules of the society and not in accordance with statutory requirements under the supervision of an independent official such as the Chief Registrar of Friendly Societies. And perhaps more significantly, the 1936 Act departed from the British model by failing to make provision for individual members to claim exemption from the obligation to contribute to political action. The Prime Minister defended this position in the following terms:

> in the matter of funds contributed to a society it is not always easy to separate one man's contribution of 1s.9d. from the thousands of pounds contributed by other members. Such a distinction is not always practicable. While I desire to treat the conscientious objector with justice, I would not like to say that people would be immune from the operation of the law because of conscientious objections they have raised . . . exemptions have not always been met. They are not easily applied.[15]

So the only device aimed at the protection of the individual was the ballot. But even this proved unduly onerous, for unlike in Britain where political objects could be adopted following the approval of a majority of those voting in the ballot, the 1936 provision required a majority of the members of the union to approve the adoption of political objects. Consequently the Act was amended in 1948 to bring it into line with British law in this respect.[16] But two years later the National Government restored the 1936 position[17] and the law remained in that form until the enactment of the consolidating and amending Political Disabilities Removal Act 1960, which, as amended in 1973, now regulates this question. The Act introduced two major changes to the law. First, it restored the 1948 amendment, which has survived ever since,[18] subject only to the new requirement imposed by the Industrial Relations Act 1973 that any ballot on the adoption of a political levy must be secret and must be either a postal ballot or otherwise approved by the Registrar of Industrial Unions.[19] The second change introduced in 1960 was a right of exemption from the obligation to pay a political levy. By s.3, the Act provides:

> Where any levy to be applied in the furtherance of political objects becomes lawfully payable by any member of [a trade union], he may, within fourteen days after the date on which he receives written notice that the levy is payable, give notice in writing to the Secretary of the [union] that he objects to payment of the levy.

On giving notice, the member is immediately exempt from payment of the levy. The Act further introduces a prohibition against discrimination of exempt members which is similar, though not identical, to the British law.

So the development of New Zealand legislation has been significantly different from the development of British law. There has been a considerable delay in the enactment of comparable safeguards for the individual and the political debate has concentrated on the form of the ballot for the adoption of political objects rather than on the most effective method for protecting the conscience of the individual once political objects have been approved. Equally interesting is the fact that the conscience provisions which have been introduced are potentially very narrow in scope. As Mathieson has observed, the funds of a trade union which may be used for political purposes are not defined in the Act.[20] A union may thus use its general funds in the furtherance of political objects, as well as raise a special fund, by imposing a special levy for that purpose. It is only in relation to the latter that the individual has a right of exemption. Unlike in Britain, New Zealand trade unions are not required to finance their political action from a separate political fund. And even where the right of exemption does apply, the safeguards in New Zealand are significantly different from those in British law. It is true that in New Zealand, exemption may take effect immediately on submission of a notice of exemption;[21] that there is no prescribed manner by which notice of exemption should be given; and that the non-discrimination provision is not qualified to permit unions to exclude non-contributors from any control or management over the way in which the political levies are spent.[22] But otherwise, New Zealand law provides rather less formal protection. The non-discrimination provision applies only to members and not to applicants for admission. Similarly, there is no duty to inform members that they have a right not to contribute, and as Mathieson has pointed out 'It may be that some union members are unaware of their rights'.[23] And even if he is aware of his rights, the member must claim exemption in respect of each levy: he is not exempt from paying until he gives notice to the contrary.

Apart from the provision which it makes for individual protection, New Zealand law is interesting in two other respects. Surprisingly, the 1960 Act does not define the crucial phrase 'political objects' which determines the scope of the Act and is central to its operation. However, Mathieson has suggested that the New Zealand Act would apply to much the same expenditure as the British; for example, payments to political parties, electioneering expenses, and the expenses incurred in distributing political literature.[24] But although there may be similarities in practice between New Zealand and British law, the New Zealand measure has the advantage that it does not require regular revision to keep pace with changing political conditions.

An obvious disadvantage, however, is the power it gives to the courts in cases of uncertainty to determine what is and what is not 'political'. This is not a power which trade unionists in Britain could confidently leave to the courts; there is always a danger that the judges would adopt an unreasonably wide definition of the term 'political' and so require an inordinate level of expenditure to be financed by political funds. New Zealand law also differs from the British with regard to enforcement. The action is one for breach of the statute, and not for the breach of rules made in pursuance of the statute. If a union or its officials commit a breach of the statute, the union is treated as having committed a breach of an award made under the Industrial Relations Act 1973. The matter is enforced not by the individual complainant but by an Inspector of Awards appointed under the 1973 Act and otherwise responsible for ensuring the awards made by the Industrial Commission under the Act are complied with.[25] So there is no direct access to the courts by a worker who claims that the terms of the 1960 Act have been breached.

PROTECTION OF INDIVIDUALS IN THE UNITED STATES

Since the late nineteenth century, concern has been expressed in the United States about the involvement of big business in the democratic process.[26] It has been written that at the turn of the present century 'Politics was largely a Punch and Judy show, but though the puppets and even the voices changed, the hands that held the strings were the same. Business ran politics, and politics was a branch of business'.[27] In an attempt to control the influence of corporations over elections Congress enacted in 1907 that it was unlawful for any national bank or corporation to make a money contribution in connection with any election to any public office. The reason why this and the amending Federal Corrupt Practices Act of 1925 did not apply to unions was quite simply that at the time the unions were 'a faction too small to pull the strings'[28] and were in any event imbued with the philosophy of voluntarism which eschewed any active involvement in the political process. The need for similar controls were not perceived until 1936 when 'organised labor dramatically leaped into the political arena'[29] by investing some three-quarters of a million dollars in Franklin Roosevelt's first re-election campaign. The Mine-Workers alone donated or lent $469,000 which was five times greater than the total amount the AFL had raised for political purposes in the preceding thirty years. In the light of this development and reports that organised labour was hoarding vast sums of money for political purposes, it is not surprising that American opinion should be informed by the belief that just as the corporations had made huge contributions to influence governmental action, the powerful unions were now embarked upon a similar course, with corresponding untoward consequences for the democratic process.

The first measure to control such political spending was enacted during the Second World War. The War Labor Disputes Act of 1943, passed by Congress to protect defence production against work stoppages, was used as a device to prohibit labour organisations from making any 'contribution in connection with any election at which Presidential and Vice Presidential electors or a Senator or Representative . . . are to be voted for, or for any candidate, political committee, or other person to accept or receive any contribution prohibited by this section'.[30] Despite this provision, the unions collectively spent substantial sums of money in the 1944 national elections. The main vehicle for such spending was the Political Action Committee of the CIO which had been established in 1943 to co-ordinate union political expenditures.[31] The Committee was financed by union donations and subsequently by contributions freely given by individual CIO members; by 1944 it had accumulated some $650,000, most of which was spent in the elections of that year. This the Committee could do by skilfully exploiting the loopholes in the 1943 Act: 'it . . . made direct contributions only to candidates and political committees involved in state and local elections and federal primaries, to which the Act did not apply, and . . . limited its participation in federal elections to political "expenditures", as distinguished from "contributions" to candidates or committees.'[32] However, these loopholes were closed by Congress when in re-enacting similar provisions at the end of the war in the Taft-Hartley Act of 1947, it provided that it was unlawful for

> any labor organization to make a contribution or expenditure in connection with any election at which Presidential and Vice Presidential electors or a Senator or Representative in, or a Delegate or Resident Commissioner to Congress are to be voted for, or in connection with any primary election or political convention or caucus held to select candidates for any of the foregoing offices, or for any candidate, political committee, or other person to accept or receive any contribution prohibited by this section.[33]

For this purpose a labour organisation was defined as 'any organisation of any kind . . . in which employees participate and which exist[s] for the purpose, in whole or in part, of dealing with employers concerning grievances, labor disputes, wages, rates of pay, hours of employment or conditions of work'.[34] Violation of this provision was punishable by a fine in the case of the union and a fine or imprisonment in the case of union officials.

Despite its wide terms, this provision did not exclude unions from all political involvement. It applied only to federal elections and did not prevent union participation in state elections. Nor did it affect the use of union money to sponsor or campaign against legislation. Moreover, it did not effectively prohibit all union involvement in federal elections, and it is clear that it was not intended to. The Congressional Records show that Senator Taft, who was partly responsible for piloting the Act, only anticipated that unions would be prevented from using general funds for political purposes. Thus he said that 'If the labor people should desire to set up a political organisation and obtain direct contributions for it, there would be nothing unlawful in that.'[35] He subsequently made a similar claim when he said that 'unions can ... organise something like the Political Action Committee, a political organisation, and receive direct contributions, just so long as members of the union know what they are contributing to, and the dues which they pay into the union treasury are not used for such purpose'.[36] This intention is clearly reflected in the definition of a labor organisation in s.304 and has been respected by the Supreme Court in each of the three cases on this provision which have been before it. In the first, *United States* v. *CIO*[37] the Court recognised that in enacting this measure:

It was felt that the influence which labor unions exercised over elections through monetary expenditures should be minimized, and that it was unfair to individual union members to permit the union leadership to make contributions from general union funds to a political party which the individual member might oppose.[38]

In *United States* v. *UAW*,[39] the second case, the Court referred the matter back to the lower court with an instruction for dismissal of the indictment if the expenditure in question in that case had been met by funds obtained on a voluntary basis. And in the third case, *Pipefitters Local Union No. 562* v. *United States*,[40] the Court accepted, after reviewing the legislative history, that the Senate debate 'compellingly demonstrates that voluntarily financed union political funds were not believed to be prohibited by the broad wording of s.304'.[41]

It is thus on the basis of these interpretations that unions could engage in federal elections through the medium of bodies such as the Committee on Political Education. This body was set up in 1955 following the merger of the AFL and the CIO, and has inherited the work originally done by the CIO's Political Action Committee and the AFL's Labor's League for Political Education. The main function of COPE is to support and endorse candidates for federal elections who are recommended by the AFL-CIO and to this end it reports facts about issues and candidates; publishes voting records of elected officials; carries out drives to help people register and vote; and makes payments to further the interest of the candidates concerned.[42] Yet while COPE is the main agent for union expenditure in federal elec-

tions, s.304 (subsequently codified in 1948 as 18 USC, s.610) has not
prevented individual unions from directly incurring expenditures
during election campaigns.[43] The Supreme Court accepted that notwithstanding the wide terms of s.304, there was still some scope for
direct union involvement. In the *CIO* case, the President of the
Congress, Mr Phillip Murray, deliberately sought to precipitate a
conflict on s.304, taking the view that the provision was unconstitutional. Consequently, he authorised the publication and distribution
of a copy of *CIO News*, carrying on its front page a statement by him
urging all members of the CIO to vote for a named candidate for
Congress. Both the CIO and Murray were indicted for violating s.304
but the indictment was dismissed on the ground that the activity
complained of did not fall within s.304, the Court holding that the
section did not apply to the distribution of a trade journal which
expressed political views in the normal course of publication. Consequently the Court was not called upon to consider whether or not
the section was unconstitutional, though it did say:

> If [s.304] were construed to prohibit the publication, by corpor-
> ations and unions in the regular course of conducting their affairs,
> of periodicals advising their members, stockholders or customers
> of danger or advantage to their interests from the adoption of
> measures or the election to office of men, espousing such
> measures, the gravest doubt would arise in our minds as to its
> constitutionality.[44]

The scope of the *CIO* decision was called into question some eight
years later when the Supreme Court was required to consider whether
UAW had violated what was by then s.610 by using general funds to
sponsor commercial television broadcasts designed to influence the
electorate at the 1954 elections. The lower courts refused to convict,
following *CIO* and an earlier District Court decision where on similar
facts to the *UAW* case, it was held that s.610 had no application.
However, the Supreme Court reversed, the majority holding, after a
review of Congressional history, that the provision was understood
by Congress to prohibit the expenditure of union money to pay for
commercial broadcasts. In reaching this conclusion, *CIO* was distinguished on the ground that:

> unlike the union sponsored political broadcast alleged in this
> case, the communication for which the defendants were indicted
> in *CIO* was neither directed nor delivered at the public at large.
> The organisation merely distributed its house organ to its own
> people. The evil at which Congress has struck . . . is the use of
> corporation or union funds to influence the public at large to vote
> for a particular candidate or a particular party.[45]

The case was thus remanded to the District Court for further proceedings, with the majority refusing to adjudicate on whether or not s.610 violated the union's constitutional rights. In so remanding, Justice Frankfurter, though holding that *CIO* had no application, nevertheless pointed the way to the lower court side-stepping the section when he posited a number of well-known questions, any one of which if answered in the affirmative would have provided a necessary defence:

> was the broadcast paid for out of the general dues of the union membership or may the funds be fairly said to have been obtained on a voluntary basis? Did the broadcast reach the public at large or only those affiliated with appellee? Did it constitute active electioneering or simply state the record of particular candidates on economic issues? Did the union sponsor the broadcast with the intent to affect the results of the election?[46]

On reconsideration by the lower court, it seems that the judge concentrated on the first of these questions in his address to the jury:

> in deciding whether or not the funds used may be fairly said to have been obtained on a voluntary basis, you have a right to take into consideration the fact that these men, in 1954, were delegates to a convention . . . They represented others. The whole membership couldn't go to the convention . . . And at the convention in 1953 [sic] these delegates, acting for the UAW membership, voted as they had on previous conventions, authority for their governing board to use part of the dues for this educational program that the governing board had used and was preparing to use in the future.[47]

The union was acquitted, though it must be said that the directions to the jury were tantamount to rendering the controls imposed by s.610 almost wholly ineffective.

The government was thus having a distinct lack of success in its use of s.610. Not a single successful prosecution had been brought at any level, with the courts showing remarkable agility in their effort to avoid convicting. This led one commentator to remark that 'By the mid-1950s unions had reason to believe that virtually any political activity, short of direct campaign contributions, would be interpreted as lawful by the federal courts.'[48] Following the lead of the Supreme Court, one lower court had held that unions could lawfully take advertisements in national newspapers[49] while another held that a union could pay its employees for time spent on political activity.[50] The dissenting individual might thus justly feel that his interests were not being properly protected in the administration of a provision which was in any event rather limited in scope, particularly when compared with rights available in British law. However, from the date of the decision in *UAW*, the position of the dissenting individual has been improved. First by the emergence of a private right of action fashioned by the courts which, in the absence of any federal legislation, have groped around successfully for a number of convenient causes of action. And secondly, by improving the protection offered by the federal election laws. In each of these developments the influence of the British Act of 1913 is apparent, though perhaps more so in the first where the Act was referred to by the Supreme Court as an appropriate method for the handling of this question.

1. THE EMERGENCE OF A PRIVATE REMEDY. The starting point of any discussion in this area of American law is the landmark decision of the Supreme Court in *International Association of Machinists* v. *Street*[51] where a number of employees were required under the terms of the Railway Labor Act of 1951, Section 2, Eleventh, to either join the union or pay an agency fee to the union in recognition of the fact that they benefited from the union's collective bargaining efforts. The employees refused to do either, objecting to the use of union levies for political purposes. Their claim was sustained, although some five years earlier in *Railway Employés Department* v. *Hanson*[52] the Supreme Court had upheld the constitutionality of section 2, Eleventh. In the *Street* case, however, the majority were not prepared to hold that a union could therefore compel employees to support political action. In delivering judgment for 4 of the majority (the Court divided 5:4), Justice Brennan traced the history of the relevant provisions of the Railway Labor Act and concluded that compulsory unionism had been introduced to force employees to share in the costs of negotiating and administering collective agreements, and the costs of the adjustment and settlement of disputes. He continued by saying that the use of dues or agency fees to support candidates for public office or advance political programs did not help defray such costs and was consequently a use which fell outside the reasons accepted by Congress for permitting the union shop in the railways. In delivering the other majority opinion, Justice Douglas proceeded on slightly different grounds:

> Once an association with others is compelled by the facts of life, special safeguards are necessary lest the spirit of the First, Fourth and Fifth Amendments be lost and we all succumb to regimentation. . . . If an association is compelled, the individual should not be forced to surrender any matters of conscience, belief, or expression. He should be allowed to enter the group with his own flag flying, whether it be religious, political, or philosophical; nothing that the group does should deprive him of the privilege of preserving and expressing his agreement, disagreement, or dissent, whether it coincides with the view of the group, or conflicts with it in minor or major ways; and he should not be

required to finance the promotion of causes with which he dis-
agrees.[53]

Having thus upheld the principle of the complaint, the task of the
Court was to find a remedy. In dealing with this issue, the majority
rejected the argument that an injunction should be issued to restrain
enforcement of the union-shop agreement in the case of the employees
in question: 'Restraining the collection of all funds from the appellees
sweeps too broadly, since their objection is only to the uses to which
some of their money is put'.[54] Rather, the Court decided to send the
case back to the court below for consideration of a proper remedy
which would protect both the interests of the union and its dissenting
members to 'the maximum extent possible without undue impinge-
ment of one on the other'. The Court gave guidance as to what would
be permissible in this respect. It said first that the safeguards should
only be available to those who applied: dissent was not to be presumed. Secondly, it suggested:

> One remedy would be an injunction against expenditure for poli-
> tical causes opposed by each complaining employee of a sum,
> from those moneys to be spent by the union for political pur-
> poses, which is so much of the moneys exacted from him as is the
> proportion of the union's total expenditures made for such politi-
> cal activities to the union's total budget. The union should not be
> in a position to make up such sum from money paid by a non-
> dissenter, for this would shift a disproportionate share of the
> costs of collective bargaining to the dissenter and have the same
> effect of applying his money to support such political activities. A
> second remedy would be restitution to each individual employee
> of that portion of his money which the union expended, despite
> his notification, for the political causes to which he had advised
> the union he was opposed.[55]

The amount of money which the employee would be entitled to recover in this way would be the same proportion that the expenditures
for political purposes which he had advised the union he disapproved
bore to the total union budget.[56]

The decision in *Street* and the approach as to remedies was endorsed
by the Supreme Court in 1963 in *Brotherhood of Railway and Steamship Clerks* v. *Allen*,[57] another case decided under the Railway Labor
Act. The case is important for the further advice which the Court gave
as to remedies. A form of practical decree to give effect to *Street* was
suggested, and on the question of calculating the proportion of political spending to other spending, it was held that since the unions
possess the facts and records from which the proportion of political to
total union expenditure can reasonably be calculated, basic considerations of fairness compel that they, and not the individual employees,

bear the burden of proving such proportion. Equally important is the plea to the unions in *Allen* to keep these disputes out of the courts. The Court recognised that practical difficulties may attend a decree reducing an employee's obligation under the union-shop agreement by a fixed proportion, since the proportion of the union budget devoted to political activity may not be constant. Such difficulties with judicial relief, thought the Court:

> should . . . encourage petitioner unions to consider the adoption by their membership of some voluntary plan by which dissenters would be afforded an internal union remedy. If a union agreed upon a formula for ascertaining the proportion of political expenditures in its budget, and made available a simple procedure for allowing dissenters to be excused from having to pay this proportion of moneys due from them under the union-shop agreement, prolonged and expensive litigation might well be averted. The instant action, for example, has been before the courts for 10 years and has not yet run its course. It is a lesson of our national history of industrial relations that resort to litigation to settle the rights of labor organizations and employees very often proves unsatisfactory.[58]

In delivering the opinion of the Court, Justice Brennan referred to the British Act of 1913 as a precedent for such a plan, suggesting that it might be possible for American unions to adopt something similar without legislation. He continued by saying, however, that he did not mean to suggest:

> that the Act provides a perfect model for a plan that would conform with the discussion in this opinion and in Street, nor that all aspects of the English Act are essential, for example the actual segregation of political funds, nor that the particular boundary drawn by the Act between political expenditures and those germane to collective bargaining is necessarily sound.[59]

So the Supreme Court had made an important move in safeguarding individual interest in the matter of political expenditure. However, the decision in *Street* was potentially of very limited application in view of the fact that four of the majority of five decided on the sole ground that the use of dues or agency fees of dissenting employees in furtherance of political action was not authorised by the Railway Labor Act's union shop provisions. This would be of little value to union members or agency fee payers in industries where that Act did not apply. However, two further grounds of action have been accepted by the American courts. Justice Douglas in *Street* cast the seeds of one such action when he suggested that the use of union levies for political purposes over the objection of individuals would violate the spirit of the First, Fourth and Fifth Amendments. In *Abood* v. *Detroit Board of*

Education,[60] the Supreme Court went further and held that such a practice constituted a violation of the First Amendment, 'at the heart [of which] is the notion that an individual should be free to believe as he will, and that in a free society one's beliefs should be shaped by his mind and his conscience rather than coerced by the State'.[61] In that case, school teachers in Michigan refused to pay agency fees under an agency-shop agreement, partly because they objected to the use of union money to support political action to which they were opposed. In delivering the opinion of the Court, Justice Stewart said:

> We do not hold that a union cannot constitutionally spend funds for the expression of political views, on behalf of political candidates, or toward the advancement of other ideological causes not germane to its duties as collective-bargaining representative. Rather, the Constitution requires only that such expenditures be financed from charges, dues, or assessments paid by employees who do not object to advancing those ideas and who are not coerced into doing so against their will by the threat of loss of governmental employment.[62]

As to how to give effect to the objection of dissenters, the Court followed the approach which had been adopted under the Railway Labor Act cases as a means of 'preventing compulsory subsidization of ideological activity by employees who object thereto without restricting the Union's ability to require every employee to contribute to the cost of collective bargaining activities'.[63]

The decision in *Abood* related to a complaint by local government employees and if read literally the passage from Justice Stewart quoted above would appear to limit its application to such workers. This would not be surprising in view of the special position of public sector employees in American labour law. Nevertheless, there seems no obvious reason why the constitutional argument should be so limited and why it would not apply, for example, to union members operating in the sphere of the National Labor Relations Act. However, lower courts in the United States have been prepared to recognise a right of action available under that Act and it may well be unnecessary to extend *Abood* into this field. In *Seay* v. *McDonnell Douglas Corporation*[64] a District court held that employees who objected to agency fees being used to finance political action could claim injunctive relief and restitution, as in *Street*, on two grounds. First, *Street* was imported by the court to support the view that the agency fee collective bargain incorporated an implied term limiting the use of agency fees to defray collective bargaining costs. Secondly, the action was sustained on the ground that the use of complainants' money over their protest for unauthorised purposes was potentially a breach of the union's duty of fair representation. The duty of fair representation is a device of North American jurisprudence, with its origins in the famous decision of the Supreme Court in *Steele* v. *Louisville & NRR*,[65] and requires the union to represent the bargaining unit, including non-members, in such a manner as to prevent arbitrary discrimination against an individual or a class of people. *Seay* is important not only because the duty of fair representation provided the basis of a remedy, but also because in doing so, the Court extended the duty in a relatively novel fashion. Hitherto the cases concerned with the duty had almost always arisen out of the collective bargaining process, and very rarely from a complaint about the use of union funds. An equally important feature of *Seay* is the fact that for the first time a court gave any serious attention to the type of activity which would be regulated by its decision. Although the Supreme Court had been prepared to create causes of action to safeguard the interests of the individual, it had been remarkably reluctant to state what it was protecting the individual from. A reasonable position seems to have been suggested by *Seay* when the Court said:

> Dissenting employees in an agency fee situation should not be required to support financially union expenditures as follows:
> One, for payments to or on behalf of any candidate for public office in connection with his campaign for election to such public office, or
> Two, for payments to or on behalf of any political party or organization, or
> Three, for the holding of any meeting or the printing or distribution of any literature or documents in support of any such candidate or political party or organization.

So since 1961 the American courts have developed several devices to control union political spending. A number of unions have responded to these developments by adopting voluntary plans to safeguard individuals, as recommended by the Supreme Court in *Allen*. It is not altogether clear how many unions have followed this course, and it may be that only a handful have done so. These include the American Federation of State, County and Municipal Employees, the International Association of Machinists, the United Auto Workers, and the Brotherhood of Railway, Airline and Steamship Clerks.[66] These rebate plans are all very similar: they apply to members and non-members; they require annual notice by the objecting employee by registered or certified mail; they rebate the proportion of dues spent on undefined 'political' activities; and senior union officials are normally responsible for determining how much is to be rebated to dissenters each year. The right of appeal on the size of the rebate is normally limited to bodies within the union, and as Nelson has pointed out, the appeal arrangements raise some important questions of principle.[67] The procedure in most cases gives rise to the suspicion that it is designed to minimise the refund. Thus, as we have seen, the initial determination is normally made by the union leadership, who as a body will have little incentive to reduce the amount of funds the union has to spend. An appeal then normally lies to the international executive board or to a body appointed by the executive board. They too will have an interest in not reducing the funds available to the union. But perhaps of greater concern is the fact that in two unions, the Railway Clerks and the Machinists, the final appeal is made to a body which is itself appointed by the international executive board. It seems that only the Auto Workers make provision for independent review of the amount of the rebate, with aggrieved members having an ultimate right of appeal to the union's Public Review Board.[68] This is a body of seven persons independent of the union which was set up in 1957 to act as the final appeal body to deal with complaints arising under the union's constitution and its Ethical Practices Code. There is always the possibility of course that the operation of the plans could breach the duty of fair representation. However, both the Auto Workers' and the Machinists' have been accepted by the courts as reasonable attempts to comply with the *Allen* judgment.[69] An action on the operation of these provisions is thus likely to occur only where they are operated in a manner which is arbitrary, discriminatory or in bad faith. It has been held that such plans do not violate the duty merely because they make the union the sole judge of what is or is not a proscribed political activity.[70]

THE REFORM OF FEDERAL ELECTION LAW. The second development which has helped the dissenting member is the reform of s.610 which took place in 1971. Although the principles of the 1947 Act have survived, s.205 of the Federal Election Campaign Act of that year (now 2 USC, c.14, s.441b) tightened up the individual safeguards and spelt them out in more detail. This development was precipitated by the decision of a Circuit court in the *Pipefitters'* case, and was inspired as much by the need to protect union freedom in the political arena, as it was by the need to protect individual liberty. In the *Pipefitters'* case the union maintained a political fund between 1949 and 1962 to which all members were required to contribute. In 1963, fearing legal action, the union altered the fund and set it up on a voluntary basis, though no changes were made in the collection of contributions, which continued to be by union agents at the workplace. However, the evidence showed that the political contributions were strictly segregated from union dues and that donation to the fund was not a condition of membership. Contributors were required to sign authorisation cards and no pressure was exerted, or reprisals exacted, in order to secure contributions. Nevertheless the local branch and three of its officers were found guilty of violating s.610 on the ground that the political fund was not a separate segregated fund of the kind which Senator Taft had in mind, but was in fact a subterfuge through which *the union* made political contributions of union money and that the donors to the fund made contributions in the belief that their jobs depended on it, albeit that this belief was mistaken. The union was fined, as were each of the individuals, who were also imprisoned for a year.

The Supreme Court reversed on the ground that the jury had been misdirected and in so doing said:

> We hold that such a fund must be separate from the sponsoring union only in the sense that there must be a strict segregation of its monies from union dues and assessments. We hold, too, that, although solicitation by union officials is permissible, such solicitation must be conducted under circumstances plainly indicating that donations are for a political purpose and that those solicited may decline to contribute without loss of job, union membership, or any other reprisal within the union's institutional power. ... Nowhere, however, has Congress required that the political organisation be formally or functionally independent of union control or that union officials be barred from soliciting contributions or even precluded from determining how the monies raised will be spent.[71]

However, the decision of the Court is now of little practical value in view of the fact that it was clearly influenced by s.205 of the 1971 Act (now s.441b) which had been passed by Congress during argument before the Supreme Court. The Court held that s.205 generally amplified what was in any event intended by s.610 and construed the latter accordingly. The amended provisions apply to contributions or expenditure in connection with the same elections to which the 1947 Act applied. So the scope of the regulated activity remains the same. But the term 'contribution or expenditure' was widened to cover 'any direct or indirect payment, distribution, loan, advance, deposit, or gift of money, or any services or anything of value'.[72] This means for example that the use of union employees or other facilities are now caught by these restraints. However, the provision is expressly qualified in the sense that it does not apply to communications by a labour organisation to members and their families.[73] So the decision in *CIO* now has statutory force.

The most important feature of s.441b is the express provision that it makes for the 'establishment, administration, and solicitation of contributions to a separate segregated fund to be utilised for political purposes'. The administration of the fund may be financed from union general funds. However, the funds are to be voluntary and members are now specifically protected from improper pressures. Thus s.441b (3) provides:

It shall be unlawful:

A) for such a fund to make a contribution or expenditure by utilizing money or anything of value secured by physical force, job discrimination, or financial reprisals, or the threat of force, job discrimination or financial reprisal; or by dues, fees, or other moneys required as a condition of membership in a labor organization or as a condition of employment, or by moneys obtained in any commercial transaction;

B) for any person soliciting an employee for a contribution to such a fund to fail to inform such employee of the political purposes of such a fund at the time of such solicitation; and

C) for any person soliciting an employee for a contribution to such a fund to fail to inform such employee, at the time of such solicitation, of his right to refuse to so contribute without any reprisal.

In addition to the fact that this measure makes provision for a criminal sanction, it contrasts with British law in a number of respects. First, it does not apply to discrimination within the union; so *ex facie* non-contributors could be denied access to office and any other benefit or facility which union membership provides. Secondly and perhaps more importantly, the section seems to anticipate what would be recognised in Britain as a form of contracting in. The member is not presumed willing to donate to the fund: the union must solicit his contributions. However, it does not appear that the member has to be solicited for every contribution. It seems sufficient that he signs an authorisation card of the kind in *Pipefitters*, in which the members consented to making 'regular contributions' to the local political fund.

One important consequence of this latter difference with the British Act was highlighted in *Federal Election Commission* v. *National Education Association*,[74] a case which raised problems not unlike those in *Reeves* v. *TGWU*.[75] The FEC, which is charged with the duty of enforcing 2 USC, c.14, raised the instant action against the NEA, claiming that the Association had violated the Act by adopting an illegal method for the collection of political levies. The NEA had formed a Political Action Committee in 1972 and levied $1.00 per annum to finance the fund from willing members. But because most members paid their dues by pay-roll deduction, the political contribution was deducted from salaries along with membership dues and teachers who did not wish to pay the contribution had to make a written claim for a rebate of their dollar. The Circuit court agreed that the NEA were acting illegally on the ground that the method of collection adopted 'required the dissenter to act to prevent a contribution rather than requiring his affirmative assent to make one'. The court continued by pointing out that its decision did not preclude the defendants from using the payroll deduction for funding its PAC – it simply required that union members be asked beforehand if they wanted a contribution to be deducted with their dues. To the argument that such an approach was impracticable because school districts would only deduct a uniform amount from employees' salaries, the court replied:

> The burden on defendants caused by those that require uniformity should not be shifted onto union members who choose to contribute. Instead, the union should solicit contributions in those districts by cash or check while making unequal deductions a priority item for collective bargaining if it is so important to the success of its fund raising.[76]

ABSTENTION IN CANADA AND AUSTRALIA

Unlike their counterparts in the United States, Canadian unions can devote funds to political purposes without the need to protect the conscience of the individual. The development of the law in this area however has been much more straightforward than in the United States, with there being an almost unbroken pedigree of legal abstention and with no apparent difficulty arising in the courts by aggrieved trade unionists seeking to take advantage of more general labour law remedies. One of few exceptions to this pattern of abstention was to be found in the now repealed s.9(6) of the Labour Relations Act 1960 of British Columbia which, it appears, was enacted with the deliberate intention of limiting the funds available to the infant New Democratic Party. The main concern of the unions was with para. (c) of s.9(6) which provided that a union could not contribute to a political party from any membership subscriptions which were either deducted from an employee's wages or paid as a condition of membership of the union. Para. (d) provided that an employer would be under no obligation to deduct dues by means of the check-off, a facility the union could otherwise insist upon, unless the union sent a written undertaking to the employer that it was complying and would continue to comply with para. (c). If notwithstanding this undertaking, the union failed to comply with s.9(6)(c), the money deducted from employees' wages was to be treated as the property of the employees concerned and recoverable by them.

This provision clearly had an important effect on the powers of unions in British Columbia particularly in view of the fact that 99.8 per cent of the total revenue of the unions was received as payments from members which were made as a condition of membership. In

Oil, Chemical and Atomic Workers' International Union v. *Imperial Oil Ltd*[77] an attempt was made to have the provision declared unconstitutional on the ground that a provincial Parliament had no power under the British North America Act 1867, s.92 to legislate in a manner which would interfere with the growth and development of political parties in Canada, or with the status of trade unionists by curtailing their freedom to participate collectively through their unions in political affairs. Under the 1867 Act provinces have the power to legislate on matters relating to property and civil rights, and in *Toronto Electric Commissioners* v. *Snider*[78] it was established that labour relations fell within this category. In the present case the Supreme Court divided 4:3 in rejecting the challenge, the majority holding that s.9(6) was 'in pith and substance, legislation in respect of civil rights in the Province'.[79] In leading the majority, Martland J. said:

> The *Labour Relations Act* has materially affected the civil rights of individual employees by conferring upon certified trade unions the power to bind them by agreement and the power to make agreements which will compel membership in a union. Such legislation falls within the powers of the Legislature of the Province of British Columbia to enact, as being labour legislation, and, therefore, relating to property and civil rights in the Province. The legislation which is under attack in the present proceedings, in my opinion, does nothing more than to provide that the fee paid as a condition of membership in such an entity by each individual employee cannot be expended for a political object which may not command his support. That individual has been brought into association with the trade union by statutory requirement. The same Legislature which requires this can protect his civil rights by providing that he cannot be compelled to assist in the financial promotion of political causes with which he disagrees.[80]

The minority took the view that s.9(6)(c) had nothing to do with civil rights but concerned constitutional and political rights and had no relationship whatever to collective bargaining conditions of employment or contracts of employment.[81]

Section 9(6) was repealed in 1973 with the result that there is now no legal protection of dissenters' rights in Canadian law. The lack of protection of individual conscience in a jurisdiction where the unions do actively finance a political party, and where union shops are sanctioned by law, has not gone without criticism. In 1968 the Woods Task Force on Labour Relations noted that many Canadian unions in fact permit their members to opt out of the obligation to contribute to political action, in which event the equivalent sum is sometimes given to charity. However, the Task Force thought that this did not go far enough to protect the individual and that there was a 'need for a public policy with respect to the use of union funds for political purposes'.[82] With this in mind the Task Force was attracted to the British Act of 1913 and recommended that similar measures should be adopted in Canada, with an additional safeguard to protect the anonymity of dissenting members who might wish to avoid any possibility of retaliation. Thus it was suggested that dissenting members should be able to opt out either by notifying the union or by stating their desire to do so in a signed letter to the Canada Labour Relations Board. The Board would then check the authenticity of the request against the employer's personnel records and inform the union of the number of members opting out. The union would then be obliged to revert these members' shares of the union's political contributions to its general operating fund. The Task Force stopped short of recommending any further controls, expressing the view that 'There is no case for placing any more stringent constraints upon unions in this area unless other institutions are brought under similar controls'.[83] These recommendations have never been implemented.

The law in Australia is governed by the decision of the High Court in *Williams* v. *Hursey*[84] which affirmed the legality of compulsory political levies. Before that decision, the position was very unclear and was complicated by the plethora of legislation which dominates Australian labour law. In Australia it is perfectly possible for a union to register under three different sets of statutes, and each was a potential source of limitation of political expenditure. First, trade unions may register under the State Trade Union Acts. Most Australian States have enacted legislation which is identical in terms to the British Trade Union Acts 1871–6. It was on the basis of such legislation, it will be recalled, that the House of Lords held in *Osborne* that a registered union could not lawfully impose a compulsory political levy of its members. Secondly, many States have enacted industrial conciliation and arbitration laws, registration under which confers a number of advantages on the organisations concerned. These include the assumption of corporate status, a legal obligation on employers to apply awards issued under the Acts, and protection from the emergence of rival unions. However, the absence of express language permitting such expenditure raised the question of whether it was consistent with registration under statutes concerned with conciliation and arbitration that a union should spend money for political purposes. The third potential area of difficulty was the Commonwealth Conciliation and Arbitration Act. The federal system operates in circumstances involving employers and employees in more than one State and covers about 4 out of every 10 Australian employees, with the State systems together mopping up much of the rest.[85] The federal system offers the same facilities to unions as the State systems and presents similar problems of *vires*, and raises the further difficulty that the Australian Constitution only confers upon the federal legislature the power to make provision for conciliation and arbitration.[86] Can federal law still confer by implication a power to engage in political action? If so, what is the effect of State law which expressly denies trade unions that power?

The *Osborne* judgment was a bombshell as much in Australia as it had been in Britain. In *Attorney-General for New South Wales* v. *Brewery Employés Union of NSW*,[87] the High Court of Australia cited *Steele* v. *SWMF*[88] with approval and the prevailing English view about the purpose of the Trade Union Acts was echoed by Isaacs J. when he said:

> a trade union is an unincorporated association of individuals with certain objects specified in the Act, which were once illegal but are so no longer; and that, unless forbidden by Statute, they may, like any other association of individuals, have any other objects not unlawful.[89]

But after *Osborne* such views were discarded. In *O'Sullivan* v. *Finch*[90] it was held that a union registered under the NSW Trade Union Act 1881 could not levy its members to raise money to run a political newspaper. Also in NSW, it was held in *Allen* v. *Gorten*[91] that a union could not use its funds to support an anti-conscription campaign during the First World War. In delivering judgment, Harvey J. said, in expressly following *Osborne*, that the grant of a donation to a purpose which could not be brought within the statutory definition was *ultra vires* and that the anti-conscription campaign was not a matter which affected trade unions as such, but was a political matter which affected all the lieges of the Crown in exactly the same way. The *Osborne* judgment was also followed in Western Australia where in *True*'s case the Supreme Court held that a union could not lawfully levy its members to help an Australian Labor Party election campaign.[92] Of crucial importance was the decision in that case that registration under the State arbitration system did not affect the powers of trade unions as governed by the Trade Union Acts. In delivering judgment Dwyer C.J. said that registration under the arbitration system did not alter the character of the organisation which was subject to all the limitations previously applicable.[92] And he continued by saying that the 'inclusion of a power to make a levy for conducting a political campaign appears foreign to the principle of operating a system of industrial arbitration'.[93]

Yet notwithstanding the obvious application of *Osborne* throughout Australia, only two States legislated to deal with the problem. The first was Queensland which, in its Trade Union Act 1915, defined a trade union as 'any combination, whether temporary or permanent, the principal objects of which are under its constitution statutory objects'.[94] Statutory objects included the pursuit of political objects which were defined in almost identical terms to the objects listed in the British Act of 1913. The 1915 Act was repealed by the Industrial Conciliation and Arbitration Act 1961, but that Act adopted similar provisions relating to political objects.[95] Neither statute, it may be noted, embraced any safeguards for individuals. In contrast, the Industrial Arbitration Act 1940 of New South Wales included measures on political objects which in all respects were very similar to British law.[96] Thus, a trade union was given the power 'to apply and use the moneys and other property of the union for or in connection with any lawful object or purpose for the time being authorised by its rules'.[97] The Act then provided that without limiting the generality of these provisions, a union could apply its money and property in the furtherance of political objects which were also defined in almost identical terms to those adopted in the British Act, save that the NSW statute included the following additional political object, 'the maintenance and publication of a newspaper other than a non-political trade journal'.[98] The Act further provided that the promotion of political objects was conditional on the union adopting rules that required payments in furtherance of the political objects to be made from a separate political fund; that contribution to the fund was not to be made a condition of membership of or admission to the union; and that non-contributors to the fund were not to be excluded from any benefit of the union or placed under any disability or at any disadvantage as compared with other members of the union because of their exemption.[99] The individual rights provisions were repealed by the Industrial Arbitration (Amendment) Act 1959 with the result that like Queensland, NSW permits unions to engage in political action without constraint and without being troubled by the need to permit exemption from the common obligation. But Queensland and New South Wales are alone in making such provision.

The federal courts initially responded in a rather ambivalent manner to the question of union political spending. On the one hand, the Commonwealth Arbitration Court recognised the inclusion of political objects in the rules of registered unions. In *Australian Railways Union* v. *National Union of Railwaymen*,[100] Dethridge C.J. said:

> The Legislature has recognized that registered organizations may, in addition to their activities within the purview of the Act or the Court, have political objects or policies. This is shown by the proviso which appeared in the original Section 55 prohibiting preference to organizations if they showed political activities.[101]

Five years later, in *O'Carroll* v. *Australian Journalists' Association*[102] a

case concerned with the cancellation of the registration of the defendant union, Dethridge C.J. said:

> An organization registered in this Court may be formed for the
> purpose of achieving, in addition to objects connected with in-
> dustrial relations such as this Court deals with, other extraneous
> objects with which this Court has no concern – those objects may,
> for instance, be political, social, artistic, or in the nature of insur-
> ance benefit. The Statutory Regulations made under the Act,
> while requiring that an association applying to be registered shall
> have rules relating to certain prescribed matters so as to make it
> proper to be registered as an organization whose existence facili-
> tates the functions of the Court, further expressly provides that
> the rules of such an association 'may also provide for any other
> matters not contrary to law'.[103]

But although it was thus not unlawful for unions registered under
federal law to engage in political action, the Commonwealth Arbitration Court nevertheless kept a tight reign on such activity. Federal
arbitration law provided that union rules should neither be contrary to
law, nor impose on members requirements which were tyrannical or
oppressive, or conditions of membership which were unreasonable.[104]
In *Little* v. *Flockhart*[105] a union rule, which required candidates for
office to sign a declaration that they were in no manner identified with
any political body which was opposed to the ALP, was challenged as
being unlawful in contravention of the aforementioned provisions of
federal law. The union justified the declaration on the ground that it
was lawfully affiliated to the ALP under its rules and that the practice
was necessary to ensure that the affairs of branches should not fall
under the control of persons who may be identified with an opposing
political party. Kelly C.J. held that such considerations did not justify
the rule and said:

> In judging whether a rule imposes an unreasonable condition
> upon membership of a registered organization the Court must
> bear in mind the purposes of the registration, which are the
> purposes of the Act, as they lie within the power of the Parlia-
> ment to legislate upon matters incidental to the specific power
> conferred by . . . the Constitution . . . a prohibition against . . .
> adherence to or identification with any political body which may
> be opposed to the platform of the party to which the organization
> has chosen to affiliate itself cannot but be regarded as a restriction
> upon the fulfilment of the purposes of the Act and in particular of
> the purposes of the registration of the organization thereunder.[106]

It will be noted that this decision went much further than *Birch* v.
NUR[107] which had been decided in the English High Court in the
previous year. Although Danckwerts J. had held that non-political

levy-paying members could not be excluded from branch office, there was nothing in English law to exclude people from office on political grounds alone. As we have seen, several British unions have rules comparable to the type struck down in *Little*'s case.

Such then was the position before the High Court of Australia was given the opportunity to consider the question in *Williams* v. *Hursey*. Trade Unions in all but two States had no power under the Trade Union Acts to engage in political action. State arbitration statutes provided no basis for such action and although unions registered under the federal statute could engage in politics, it was still far from clear what limits or controls the courts might impose on such action. And it had still to be decided precisely what was the effect on federally registered unions of State laws under which political action was prohibited. These questions were definitively settled in the *Hursey* case where the Hobart Branch of the Waterside Workers' Federation of Australia, with a view to aiding an ALP election campaign, imposed a compulsory political levy on its members. The Federation was registered as an organisation under the Commonwealth Conciliation and Arbitration Act, but was not registered as a trade union under the Tasmanian Trade Union Act 1889. The Hurseys (father and son) refused to pay the levy, and after a number of unpleasant incidents involving members of their branch they sought a declaration that the levy was *ultra vires*. By the time the matter reached the High Court, three issues arose for consideration. The first was whether the union's rules permitted the raising of a compulsory political levy: there was no express term authorising such a course, the rules simply providing that one of the Federation's objects was 'by all lawful means' to 'foster the best interests of the members of the organisation' and that levies could be imposed for this purpose. Fullagar J. held that this was sufficient for the Federation to require compulsory political levies, taking the view that it could embark on any activity which could fairly and reasonably be regarded as likely to further the interests of its members. A similar conclusion was reached by both Taylor and Menzies JJ. with the former saying that assistance to one political party or another may reasonably be thought to be a legitimate method of serving the industrial interests of the members of a trade union.

The second issue was whether the political levy was authorised by law. As we have seen, federal legislation prohibits registered organisations from having rules which are 'contrary to law'. It was argued before the Court, on the basis of the *Osborne* judgment, that as it was illegal for a trade union to engage in political action, rules permitting such action could not form part of the constitution of a registered organisation under federal law. In dealing with this argument Fullagar J. was prepared to dismiss it on the simple constitutional ground that it was not possible for a State statute to prescribe what shall or shall not be the powers of a corporation which is created and empowered by a law of the Commonwealth. However, he did proceed to discuss some of the wider issues and in so doing held that *Osborne* did not apply to the present case, departing from *Wilson* v. *Scottish Typographical Association*[108] by holding that the Lords' decision had no application to unregistered unions:

> The objects to which an unincorporated society may devote its funds may be limited by the contract which constitutes it, and it may be possible to restrain by injunction a breach of that contract. But breach of contract is one thing, and *ultra vires* or incapacity is another and quite different thing. The capacity of an unincorporated society can depend on nothing but the capacity of its individual members. Their capacity, or the capacity of some of them, may be affected by such matters as infancy or lunacy, but otherwise it is unlimited. The whole basis of the reasoning of Lords Halsbury, Macnaghten and Atkinson lies in a region completely alien to natural persons – a region inhabited only by corporations.[109]

Menzies J. disagreed with Fullagar J. on the application of *Osborne* to unregistered unions but nevertheless held that registration under the federal statute made political action lawful. Upon registration, he held, an organisation has all the power which springs from its rules and State law cannot add to or detract from these powers. There was no limit in the federal Act on political activity, and although it did not permit the registration of rules which were contrary to law, a rule permitting a political levy did not fall into this category because rules made or levies imposed in contravention of State legislation were nugatory but not illegal. Such rules were merely unenforceable in some States but enforceable in others (NSW and Queensland) and on registration as an organisation the rules became enforceable in all States as part of the constitution of the organisation. Taylor J. proceeded on grounds similar to Menzies J., holding that the term contrary to law in the federal legislation did not mean unenforceable at law but illegal and that a registered organisation could have political levy rules because they were not contrary to law in this narrow sense.

The third question was whether the political levy requirements were tyrannical or oppressive, or imposed unreasonable conditions on the membership of the union. This was a potentially difficult issue for the defendants. In *re Federated Ironworkers' Association*,[110] in what appears to have been a policy of grudging acceptance of union political action, the Commonwealth Arbitration Court had held as unlawful under these provisions a rule which provided for the exemption of dissenters from the payment of the political levy! The Court gave two reasons for its decision: first, the rules did not specify the party to which the funds would be given; and secondly, and perhaps more ominously, Kirby J. held it unreasonable to compel a member to pay a political levy or otherwise proclaim his objection to making such a payment. He continued by saying that he saw no reason for opposition to a rule providing for a voluntary political levy and he thought it perhaps possible that satisfactory safeguards could make a compulsory political levy acceptable. Although he did not say what safeguards he had in mind, he indicated that the British Act of 1913 would 'repay study'. Yet notwithstanding this decision, Fullagar J., the only member of the High Court to tackle this question, held that a rule could not be tyrannical or oppressive merely because it required members against their will to contribute money for a purpose which is relevant to their group interests, and is reasonably and in good faith believed by a majority of the members to be for the benefit of the group. He distinguished *Ironworkers* on the ground that the proposed rule in that case did not deal with the imposition of a levy in aid of a specified political party.

So upon registration under federal law, Australian unions acquire the power to engage in political action and to exact levies from all their members for this purpose. In practice this means that most union members may be lawfully required to pay political levies. A recent survey has shown that federally registered unions account for well over 80 per cent of the country's total union membership.[111] In this light, it is not surprising that the decision in *Hursey* should have caused concern and disquiet in Australia. The Democratic Labor Party, of which the Hurseys were members, unsuccessfully sought to present a private members Bill in the Commonwealth Parliament designed to prohibit compulsory political levies. It also proposed to bring the question before the United Nations Committee on Human Rights, the ILO and the International Confederation of Free Trade Unions.[112] And in order to avert federal legislation aimed at safeguarding individual freedom, the Australian Council on Trade Unions declared against compulsory levies in 1960.[113] However, there is no legal protection against compulsion and it seems that only a small number of unions give their members the opportunity to contract out.[114] Yet few members of these unions bother to take advantage of this facility, despite the fact that a recent survey of Australian trade unionists found that only 17 per cent of ALP affiliated union members involved in the survey said that they approved of union affiliation to the party.[115] It seems that some if not all of the unions which offer this facility do so for reasons of security. One such union is the Federated Clerks' Union which 'is affiliated to the ALP in New South Wales and to the Democratic Labor Party in Victoria, though it is quite possible that a majority of members in both states usually vote for the Liberal Party'.[116] It has since been claimed that there is now no union affiliation with any party other than the ALP, though the Victoria branch of the Clerks' union still maintains close links with the DLP.[117]

BRITISH LAW IN CONTEXT

The four jurisdictions examined in this chapter display two fundamentally different approaches to the question of trade union political spending. In all these jurisdictions, however, the balance is tilted much more firmly in favour of the union than in this country where the statutory rights for dissenters appear rather sophisticated, detailed and refined in contrast. This is manifestly so when British law is compared with Canadian law where there is no legal protection of dissenters' rights. The same is true of Australia where only exceptionally the law prohibits trade union political spending, as in the case of unions registered under State arbitration laws only (outside NSW and Queensland), or under State trade union legislation only, or not registered at all. In the other jurisdictions, New Zealand and the United States, it may be questioned whether the legal controls adequately protect individual conscience. New Zealand unions can easily evade the controls by using general funds with impunity. In the United States, the federal election laws were openly flouted for a long time;[118] it is unclear whether a private legal remedy lies in non-union shop situations;[119] the plans giving effect to the *Allen* decision have not been adopted by anything like all the unions; and the plans which have been adopted are controlled and managed to an unacceptable extent by union officials.

It would be difficult to believe that Britain has much to learn in this area from any of these jurisdictions. The Australian and Canadian approach would serve little purpose for as we have seen, the unions which would be most tempted to take advantage of any removal of legal controls would be the very ones which would be compelled by internal pressures to retain the status quo. In any event, the political levy is much too sensitive an issue in this country even to begin to contemplate any such possibility. The question apparently induces a much more muted response in Australia where no serious attempt has been made to restrict the unions' power to use their funds for any purpose they think fit to include in their rules, despite the fact that so few unionists appear to support affiliation with the ALP. Rawson has suggested that 'lack of information, and probably lack of interest, is one explanation of why the widespread opposition to Labor affiliation has had so few destructive consequences for the ALP'.[120] And if the Australian approach would have little to commend it in this country, though in theory the case for its adoption may be a good one, there is equally little to be said for diluting members' rights along the lines of New Zealand and United States law. If dissenters are to have a right of exemption, it should be effective and fair in its administration. New Zealand potentially fails at the first hurdle while American law clearly stumbles at the second. This is not to say, however, that comparisons with these four jurisdictions is uninformative. The value of the exercise lies in highlighting the detailed and comprehensive nature of individual protection in this country which is without parallel in any of the major labour law systems of the world. Nor is this to say that our own system is beyond reform. However, developments and protections in other jurisdictions are factors which might usefully be borne in mind when considering whether there is a need to further tighten up the individual protections in the 1913 Act.

ISSUES FOR REFORM

In Part 3 we have explored the role of the 1913 Act as an instrument for controlling trade union political expenditure. We have seen that little would be gained by repealing the Act for unions seem unlikely to raise the levels of their political spending if legal restraints were lifted. Although none of the jurisdictions examined in the last chapter offer quite the same degree of protection for individuals as Britain, the experience of these jurisdictions reinforces the argument against repeal by showing the extent, whether conscious or otherwise, to which the principles underlying the British Act of 1913 have been accepted by western democracies. They have been followed by courts and parliaments in several countries, and have been adopted as a blueprint for reform in another. However, the success of the 1913 Act as a reasonable compromise should not induce complacency. Although the principles it embraces are widely accepted, this is not to deny that the Act could be improved in any way. After all, it has never been substantially reformed in almost seventy years existence, with the exception of the period 1927–46 when a radically different method of collecting political fund dues was in force.

THE POLITICAL OBJECTS

So far as the scope of the Act is concerned, it is not unreasonable to suggest that the political objects should be redrawn, though it is true that no important problems yet appear to have arisen in practice. Perhaps the most serious difficulty is that the Act does not apply to European Assembly elections; another is that it is uncertain whether it applies to expenditure such as that incurred in supporting newspapers, in promoting candidates for the Labour Party leadership election, in holding ballots in connection with such an election, and in supporting groups within a party. Otherwise the problems are cosmetic, though the Act could probably do with a face-lift. There is no reason why it should apply to the registration of electors and representation on boards of guardians. Equally it might appear that the Act is anachronistic in making no reference to political parties, and clinging to an 'outdated individualistic ideology'[1] according to which general elections are fought by individual candidates rather than by representatives of political parties. Many of these problems could be resolved by replacing the present political objects in s.3(3) of the 1913 Act with the following much simpler formula:

> The political objects to which this section applies are the expend-iture of money in order to support or promote the interests of a political party (whether nationally or locally), or in connection with the activities of a political party, or in connection with the election of a candidate for Parliament, the European Assembly or any local authority which has power to raise money by means of a rate.[2]

A similar suggestion was originally made by the author to the Hansard Society's inquiry on the financing of political parties and was endorsed by it. It is consistent with the principles of the 1913 Act, realistically takes account of the modern function of trade union political funds and would seem to provide a solution to most of the outstanding problems under the present law. Moreover, it is couched in sufficient-ly flexible terms to permit the Certification Officer to respond to any new or unforeseen contingencies which may arise in the future.

The only difficulty which might arise is that this definition excludes the maintenance of members of Parliament as presently provided by section 3(3)(c) of the 1913 Act. However, as construed, that measure is now a dead letter and in fact it is not unknown for unions which have a political fund to make payments to members of Parliament who have assisted them, from their general funds. In 1975, ASLEF made a payment of £500 to Mr Leslie Huckfield MP from its general fund. If paragraph (c) was to be construed in a manner which did not deny it any effect, then there are several unions which do not have political funds which might have to reconsider their position with regard to parliamentary representation. It is difficult to believe however that members of Parliament would not look after the interests of unions without the modest financial payment which they presently receive for this purpose. A more convincing argument against retaining this measure is that it has outlived the function for which it was conceived. The government in 1912 had not intended to include this measure in the Act, taking the view that the introduction of a State payment of £400 to members of Parliament in 1911 had thereby relieved the unions of the need to maintain parliamentary representatives. The measure was adopted in Standing Committtee only after Ramsay MacDonald had pressed for its inclusion on the ground that 'it was not impossible that some succeeding Government, should a majority of the voters ever be so wrong-headed as to revert to Toryism, might reverse payment of Members'.[3] In fact there have been several sub-sequent Conservative administrations but it is now inconceivable that members of Parliament should not be paid for their services.

CONTRACTING IN

The enactment of the Trade Disputes and Trade Unions Act 1946 was met by ritual resistance by the Opposition. However, although the Conservative Party pledged itself to restore contracting in, this never materialised and subsequent Conservative governments seemed content to let the matter lie.[4] A number of motions on this subject have been submitted to the annual conference of the party but have never been called for debate, and CTU appears to accept that the present system is not inappropriate. Until the late 1970s it was left to Conservative backbenchers to keep faint interest in this issue barely alive, and a private member's Bill was introduced in 1966.[5] More recently, however, the Conservative Party has taken active steps to encourage trade union members to contract out,[6] and has flirted with the idea of restoring contracting in. Other organisations have begun to question whether the safeguards embraced in the Act are adequate. A pamphlet published by *Aims,* the Free Enterprise group, claimed that 'In Britain today we have the shameful situation of millions of workers who vote Conservative, Liberal and Nationalist or not at all contributing through the trade unions to the Labour Party. They do this because of fear, pressures, the desire for a quiet life, apathy, or sheer ignorance'.[7] In a similar vein, Mr William Rodgers wrote in a feature in *The Times* in January 1982 that the 'process of "contracting-out" is laborious. It can be delayed and frustrated by recalcitrant trade union officials and is a semi-public act which can lead to victimisation'. However, such comments should be treated with caution. They are made by or on behalf of organisations which are regarded by trade unions as being hostile to their interests; and no evidence is provided to support the allegations. In fact they are not unlike the claims made by Mr Robert Carr to the Donovan Royal Commission that contracting out was indefensible and created pressures and iniquities which should be removed. Mr Carr was then asked to provide details of such abuses, and in the words of the Commission: 'He thought . . . that he might be able to supply details of specific cases if given the time – an expectation apparently not fulfilled'.[8]

The solution to these alleged problems is thought by some to be the reintroduction of a system of contracting in, as operated between 1927 and 1946. There can be no doubt that for some reason, the reintroduction of contracting out in 1946 led to a significant rise in the number of trade unionists paying the political levy, as is demonstrated in table 13. The number of people contributing to trade union political funds thus rose from 38 per cent of the total membership of the TUC in 1945 to 60 per cent in 1948. More specifically, in NUR during the same period the numbers rose from 60 per cent of the total member-

Table 13. Trade union affiliations 1945–48

Year	No. affiliated to	
	Labour Party	TUC
1945	2,510,369	6,575,654
1946	2,635,346	6,671,120
1947	4,386,074	7,540,397
1948	4,751,030	7,791,470

SOURCE: Labour Party Report 1978
and TUC Annual Report 1978.

ship contributing to 81 per cent, while in ISTC the jump was from 39
per cent to 84 per cent. Yet as we saw in chapter 3, the experience of
1927 to 1946 did not seriously affect the health of the Labour Party.
Although it had a short-term impact on the finances of the party, in
the long term its effect was mitigated, with many unions collecting
more money from political-levy-paying members than they might
otherwise have done. But there can be little doubt that the measure
added to the administrative burdens of trade union officials by making
it more difficult for them to collect the levy. And more importantly, it
reduced the income *potential* of the party by leading to a considerable reduction in levy-paying members. The finances of the modern
Labour Party are such that it needs to develop alternative sources of
finance as well as rely on trade union funds. As we have already seen,
these funds have reached the limits of what they can do for the party
and in very many cases they almost certainly could not be significantly
increased to compensate for a declining number of contributors
caused by a system of contracting in.

Yet these considerations would be less persuasive if there was any
reason to believe that the present legal protection was ineffective or
that the reason why people pay under contracting out but not contracting in is because of force or fear. But quite simply there is no
evidence that this happens on any significant scale. The Donovan
Royal Commission was unable to find any such evidence and there
appear to be no other studies which establish its existence. This led
the Donovan Commission to argue:

in the continued absence of such evidence we are unable to say
that the case for substituting 'contracting-in' for 'contracting-
out' has been established. Considerations which tell the other
way are that a very considerable number of trade unionists do in
fact contract out. The Chief Registrar of Friendly Societies has

reported that 113 trade unions with a total membership of 7,997,000 had political funds in 1966, but the total number of members contributing was over 1½ million less, namely 6,423,000. The Act of 1913 requires that it shall be a rule of any trade union setting up a political fund that no member who is exempt from the liability to contribute should be discriminated against in any way (except in relation to the control or management of the political fund itself). The Act further provides that, if any member considers himself aggrieved by any breach of the rule, he may complain to the Registrar of Friendly Societies. We understand that there are very few such complaints.[9]

and to conclude:

> When 'contracting-in' was substituted in 1927 for 'contracting-out' the result was to diminish very considerably the amount of money received by the trade unions' political funds; whereas when 'contracting-out' was restored in 1946 the contributions rose again. We have no doubt that this is due very largely to the innate reluctance of people to take positive steps involving the filling up and despatch of a form when only a very small sum is involved: and that the problem of 'contracting-in' or 'contracting-out' is not so much a question of industrial relations as a political question, namely whether the Labour Party shall get the benefit of this reluctance or not. Parliament in 1913 enacted provisions (which were restored in 1946) in favour of members of trade unions who object to paying a political levy, enabling them to 'contract-out' if they wished, and we have no evidence to show that these are ineffective, and that the protection conferred by the Act of 1913 is illusory. In the circumstances, we do not recommend any change.[10]

The case against these conclusions has yet to be convincingly made.

INDIVIDUAL SAFEGUARDS

The only evidence of any difficulty in the operation of the individual rights is that not all trade unionists are fully aware that they pay a political levy and that they may claim exemption. Evidence of this problem was first brought to light by Goldthorpe *et al.*, in their study of the 'affluent worker' in Luton in the years 1962–4, in which it was found that large numbers of trade union members were making a political contribution 'without realising this; that is to say, either they do not think that they pay the levy but have not contracted out or they admit to having no knowledge of the levy at all . . . it is in fact only amongst the craftsmen that a majority of the unionists pay the political levy and know that they do; in the other groups this proportion averages out . . . in the region of only two-fifths'.[11] This problem was also identified in a study by Moran of a UPW branch in Colchester, Essex.[12] When he asked the members of the branch whether they paid the political levy, 51 per cent claimed that they did, 39 per cent said that they did not, and 10 per cent did not know one way or the other. However, the author was able to establish that everybody in the sample was paying the levy and he observed: 'The most common immediate response was bafflement. Members were often simply unaware of what the question was about, and many of the "correct" answers came in the form of statement like "I suppose I must", which almost constituted straightforward confessions of ignorance.'[13] His conclusion was that: 'The answers to this question clearly show the important role played by ignorance in allowing the U.P.W. to pursue without difficulty a policy which is supported by only a small minority of members'.[14]

This evidence suggests that there is a measure of misunderstanding among trade union members. Yet as the Hansard Society has pointed out 'far more systematic and extensive evidence than is contained in these . . . restricted case studies would be required before any safe *generalisation* could be made about the awareness amongst trade unionists of political levy payments'.[15] And if lack of awareness is an extensive problem, then that is hardly something which can be attributed to the present law. The political fund rules already provide: 'The Secretary of each branch, shall take steps to secure that every member of the branch, so far as practicable, receives a copy of these rules, and shall supply a copy to any member at his request. A copy thereof shall also be supplied forthwith to every new member following his admission to the organisation.'[16] And in some cases add: 'No levy shall come into force as respects a new member until the expiration of one month from his being supplied with a copy of [the] rules . . . . following admission to the organisation'.[17] Union members cannot be compelled to read the rules, though it could be argued that trade unions could do more to publicise the right of exemption. An interesting proposal was contained in a private member's Bill introduced in the Commons in 1967 by Mr A. Grant.[18] This provided that every trade union application form should contain details of the right to be exempt from making a political contribution. But although several unions already contain this information on their application forms, it would be difficult to justify a legal obligation to this effect. There is no reason to suppose that lack of awareness of members of their rights is limited to political fund questions and there seems no reason in principle why this matter should be singled out for special treatment on the application form. And indeed it is a curious request to ask a union to take further steps to publicise a right which they may believe to be damaging to their interests. Surely, if a trade unionist is concerned for his conscience it is up to him to take steps to protect it. It is simply unreasonable to ask unions to induce the creation of such objections.

This is not to say that the political fund rules ought not to be changed in any way. If evidence can be provided to substantiate Rodgers' allegations then the method of contracting out could be altered. Rather than being controlled by branch officials, there seems no reason in principle why it could not be done direct by the member through head office which would then be required to notify the employer, or itself accept responsibility for paying a rebate of the political levy to the member at the end of each year. If this was not thought to provide sufficient privacy for the individual then an adaptation of the Woods Task Force proposals could be implemented in this country.[19] Thus, individuals could register their objection with the Certification Officer who could keep a list of all exempt members in all unions. A union could then be required to refund annually the total amount of the exempt members' political levies to the Certification Officer who would be responsible for repayment of the levy to individual members. Such a proposal would clearly be fraught with administrative inconvenience. It would also involve the inevitable consequence of all members being permitted to vote on political fund questions, regardless of whether or not they paid the levy. Otherwise, exempt members would need to be known to branch officials and would thus be exposed to the coercion to which Rodgers refers. However, this is not a likely proposal, but it does indicate that even if the present safeguards are inadequate, there are options available which do not fundamentally alter the way in which the political levy is collected. Such a solution would be a far better means of responding to the alleged problems of unlawful pressure being exerted on members. For it is only in this way that the member will be above pressure and will remain anonymous. This is not guaranteed by contracting in. Such a method of collection does not contain any magic ingredient: people who fail to contract in are known to union officials just as are those who contract out.

THE POLITICAL LEVY,
THE CONSERVATIVES AND THE SDP

Political parties other than the Labour Party have increasingly been looking to trade union funds for support. CTU have argued that trade union branches should be encouraged to make donations from their political funds to Conservative meetings or to help with the expenses of CTU.[20] This suggestion gave rise to the litigation in *Parkin* v. *ASTMS*[21] where a branch of the Association proposed to donate money to the Conservative Party 'for the purpose of promoting a better understanding of the policies and aims of Conservative trade unionists within the union, and ensuring the co-operation and help of Conservative trade union M.P.s . . .' Under the rules of the Association, branches are entitled, on request to the NEC, to have one-third of the political levies collected by them returned to be used for local purposes. In this case the request was refused, being contrary to the rules and objects of the Association on the ground that branches may only use their funds to support the Labour Party. Two questions arose for consideration. The first was whether the branch was entitled to receive the money for payment to the Conservative Party, and the second was whether the intended use of the money was in furtherance of the political objects.

The first question was answered in the affirmative, despite the fact that the Association is affiliated to the Labour Party. Although the rules of the Association did not expressly state that the political fund could only be used to finance the Labour Party, it had agreed at its annual delegate conference in 1970 to affiliate to the party. Nevertheless, Woolf J. was unable 'to say that a branch is debarred from using its portion of the political fund in the way it chooses because that is contrary to the general policy of the union as manifest by decision of conference to join a particular political party'. This is a conclusion that is rather difficult to follow, for although there was no express prohibition in the rules on the use of branch funds for Conservative Party purposes, the arguments against any such power seem compelling. First, it led to what counsel for the union described as the ridiculous situation of a branch using funds for a purpose which was wholly inconsistent with the policy of the union. Secondly, it is no answer to the union's refusal to hand over the money that it had no express power to withhold the money because it was being used to finance the Conservatives. The rules are not a statutory code but are a contract which has to be fleshed out with regard to circumstances and implied terms which develop over time. On any appropriate ground of implication, whether by custom and practice or by adopting the officious bystander test, there is no reasonable basis for denying that the union had acted perfectly lawfully. Finally, under the rules of the union a branch can be disbanded if it acts contrary to the Association's rules or policy. Surely this implies that the branch must always act in a manner consistent with the rules and policy, and that the Association can take preventative steps to avoid any conflict?

However the plaintiff won a Pyrrhic victory, for the second issue for consideration was answered in the negative. Although Woolf J. assumed that a payment to a political party was in furtherance of the political objects and that the rules made in pursuance of section 3 should be liberally construed, he was nevertheless unconvinced that one of the purposes for which the branch sought the money was in furtherance of the political objects:

The first purpose is specified as 'promoting a better understanding of the policies and aims of Conservative trade unionists within the union', and, with some hesitation, I would be prepared to hold that that is a political object within section 3 and rule 36, because it is a method of improving knowledge of Conservative policy at, what may be described as, the grass roots, and therefore an indirect method of assisting the election of Conservative candidates. However, the second purpose is described as 'ensuring the co-operation and help of Conservative trade union M.Ps. who are not at present allowed to be represented on the [union's] parliamentary committee'. So far as that second purpose is concerned, I consider that the union is right in saying that that does not fall within the limited political objects specified in section 3 and rule 36.[22]

Consequently, the NEC was right to refuse the application because it was about to be used for an improper purpose. Nevertheless, an important principle has been established by *Parkin*, namely, that branch funds may be used to support the Conservatives, the SDP, or any other party, even where the union is affiliated to the Labour Party. The problem may well give rise to some controversy within other unions for there are only a handful which by their rules specifically provide that political funds may only be used to support the Labour Party. ASTMS hastily changed its rules to ensure that union money could not be used to support any party but the Labour Party. Other unions would be well advised to do the same, for CTU seems to be engaged in a determined campaign to recruit members and mobilise support within a number of different trade unions.

The SDP has also set its sights on union money. However, early overtures by some party officials for financial assistance to union leaders have been resisted and the party has turned its attention to other devices to tap union funds. One suggestion which is a repeat of an unsuccessful amendment by Conservative backbenchers argued in Standing Committee in 1912 is that trade union members should be free to determine which party is to receive their political levy.[23] Under the SDP proposals, trade union members would contract in, and those contracting in would be free to earmark their contribution for a particular political party. The union would then be required to aggregate the contributions and transfer the totals to the respective party annually.[24] This would obviously benefit a number of parties, for Conservatives, Liberals, Nationalists, and Communists as well as the SDP all presumably have support in the unions. Yet while it is easy to understand the need of the SDP to explore all possible avenues of support, being denied as yet any major institutional financing, it is difficult to see this suggestion as being otherwise than profoundly silly. Trade unions are first and foremost in the business of protecting and promoting the interests of their members. They are not and should never be asked to become agents for the collection of dues for all the political parties of the State. It would be absurd if unions were required to pledge administrative resources and time to collect money for political parties which may be out seriously to weaken or conceivably perhaps even destroy them. Freedom of association implies the freedom of the group to judge how its interests will best be satisfied. If a member disapproves of the manner in which the majority or the accountable officers of the association exercise that judgment on political matters, then he does not have to pay the levy. It is well to remember that this is a privilege which is not available to the members of other institutions. Equally, it is worth bearing in mind that if an individual wishes to give money to the SDP he is free to do so. Trade unions are not the only vehicles through which individuals may make political contributions.

ADJUDICATION

One final question for reform relates to the machinery for the adjudication of complaints under the 1913 Act. The Donovan Royal Commission suggested that all trade union rule-book disputes, including those occurring under political fund rules, should be heard by a review body of three members, one of whom would be a lawyer, with the other two being chosen from a panel of trade unionists which would be appointed by the Secretary of State for Employment after consultation with the TUC.[25] More recently, it has been advocated that jurisdiction over political fund disputes and all other rule-book questions should be referred directly to the Employment Appeal Tribunal, though the Certification Officer should continue to perform a conciliatory function.[26] This last suggestion suffers from a number of difficulties, though they are not necessarily insuperable. First, there seems no reason why industrial tribunals should be by-passed in these disputes, but not in employer-worker cases; and secondly, it is difficult to see why a body on which employers are represented should be involved in adjudicating on a dispute that will normally relate almost exclusively to the internal government of the union.

But even if a review body on the Donovan model was established by statute, there is no reason why the Certification Officer should lose his jurisdiction in political fund matters. This has been a model specialist jurisdiction in almost every sense. First, the Certification Officer and his predecessors have built up considerable expertise in this field. This arises not only from their handling of complaints and adjudicating on disputes, but also from the administrative responsibilities that they bear. The Officer is responsible for supervising ballots on the adoption of political fund rules; he is responsible for issuing the model rules; and he receives trade union political fund accounts annually. Secondly, there is an element of predictability and certainty built into the system. Complaints are all dealt with by a single individual and the period of tenure is generally for a fairly lengthy period. If complaints were dealt with by a review body or by the EAT this feature would be lost, with different personnel dealing with different complaints. So it might be difficult to build up a corpus of mutually consistent decisions. Thirdly, the jurisdiction is clearly as accessible for the individual as any other tribunal in the labour law field. Certainly, the EAT would be no advantage in this respect. The procedure and adjudication would tend to be much more formal and less flexible and the complainant might find that legal representation would be inevitable. This is not to say that the Certification Officer procedures could not be improved. There seems no reason why he should not be given the power to award reasonable expenses, failing which it might be an issue for reflection whether he should adopt the approach of his predecessors and travel to areas where the complainant resides. There is no obvious reason why the complainant should bear the expense of travelling to London. Finally, the Certification Officer is efficient in the sense that his decisions seem to be generally accepted by the parties. They are lucid, well written and well argued and generally far superior to most industrial tribunal decisions. It is not insignificant that the right of appeal from a decision of the Certification Officer has been used on only one occasion.

APPENDIX

The Trade Union Act 1913
(2 & 3 Geo. 5 c.30)

1. Amendment of law as to objects and powers of trade unions
    (2) For the purposes of this Act, the expression 'statutory objects' means . . . the regulation of the relations between workmen and masters, or between workmen and workmen, or between masters and masters, or the imposing of restrictive conditions on the conduct of any trade or business, and also the provision of benefits to members.
2. Definition of trade union
    [(1) In this Act, except so far as the context otherwise requires, 'trade union' means an organisation (whether permanent or temporary) which either –
    a) consists wholly or mainly of workers of one or more descriptions and is an organisation whose principal purposes include the regulation of relations between workers of that description or those descriptions and employers or employers' associations; or
    b) consists wholly or mainly of –
    i) constituent or affiliated organisations which fulfil the conditions specified in paragraph (a) above (or themselves consist wholly or mainly of constituent or affiliated organisations which fulfil those conditions), or
    ii) representatives of such constituent or affiliated organisations; and in either case is an organisation whose principal purposes include the regulation of relations between workers and employers or between workers and employers' associations, or include the regulation of relations between its constituent or affiliated organisations.]
    [(1A) In this Act, except so far as the context otherwise requires, 'employers' association' means an organisation (whether permanent or temporary) which is unincorporated and either –
    a) consists wholly or mainly of employers or individual proprietors of one or more descriptions and is an organisation

whose principal purposes include the regulation of relations
between employers of that description or those descriptions
and workers or trade unions; or
b) consists wholly or mainly of –
  i) constituent or affiliated organisations which fulfil the
  conditions specified in paragraph (a) above (or themselves
  consist wholly or mainly of constituent or affiliated organisations which fulfil those conditions), or
  ii) representatives of such constituent or affiliated organisations;
and in either case is an organisation whose principal purposes
include the regulation of relations between employers and
workers or between employers and trade unions, or include
the regulation of relations between its constituent of affiliated
organisations.]

3. Restriction on application of funds for certain political purposes
  (1) The funds of a trade union shall not be applied, either directly
or in conjunction with any other trade union, association, or
body, or otherwise indirectly, in the furtherance of the political
objects to which this section applies (without prejudice to the
furtherance of any other political objects), unless the furtherance
of those objects has been approved as an object of the union by a
resolution for the time being in force passed on a ballot of the
members of the union taken in accordance with this Act for the
purpose by a majority of the members voting; and where such a
resolution is in force, unless rules, to be approved, . . . by the
[Certification Officer], are in force providing –
  a) That any payments in the furtherance of those objects are to
  be made out of a separate fund (in this Act referred to as the
  political fund of the union) and for the exemption in accordance with this Act of any member of the union from any obligation to contribute to such a fund if he gives notice in accordance with this Act that he objects to contribute; and
  b) That a member who is exempt from the obligation to contribute to the political fund of the union shall not be excluded
  from any benefits of the union, or placed in any respect either
  directly or indirectly under any disability or at any disadvantage as compared with other members of the union (except in
  relation to the control or management of the political fund) by
  reason of his being so exempt, and that contribution to the
  political fund of the union shall not be made a condition for
  admission to the union.
  (2) If any member of a trade union alleges that he is aggrieved by
a breach of any rule made in pursuance of this section, he may

complain to the [Certification Officer], and the [Certification Officer], after giving the complainant and any representative of the union an opportunity of being heard, may, if he considers that such a breach has been committed, make such order for remedying the breach as he thinks just under the circumstances; and any such order of the [Certification Officer] . . . on being recorded in the county court, may be enforced as if it had been an order of the county court. In the application of this provision to Scotland the sheriff court shall be substituted for the county court . . .

(3) The political objects to which this section applies are the expenditure of money –

a) on the payment of any expenses incurred either directly or indirectly by a candidate or prospective candidate for election to Parliament or to any public office, before, during, or after the election in connection with his candidature or election; or

b) on the holding of any meeting or the distribution of any literature or documents in support of any such candidate or prospective candidate; or

c) on the maintenance of any person who is a member of Parliament or who holds a public office; or

d) in connection with the registration of electors or the selection of a candidate for Parliament or any public office; or

e) on the holding of political meetings of any kind, or on the distribution of political literature or political documents of any kind, unless the main purpose of the meetings or of the distribution of the literature or documents is the furtherance of statutory objects within the meaning of this Act.

The expression 'public office' in this section means the office of member of any county, county borough, district, or parish council, or board of guardians, or of any public body who have power to raise money, either directly or indirectly, by means of a rate.

(4) A resolution under this section approving political objects as an object of the union shall take effect as if it were a rule of the union and may be rescinded in the same manner and subject to the same provisions as such a rule.

(5) The provisions of this Act as to the application of the funds of a union for political purposes shall apply to a union which is in whole or in part an association or combination of other unions as if the individual members of the component unions were the members of that union and not the unions; but nothing in this Act shall prevent any such component union from collecting from any of their members who are not exempt on behalf of the association or combination any contributions to the political fund

of the association or combination.

4. Approval of rules

(1) A ballot for the purposes of this Act shall be taken in accordance with rules of the union to be approved for the purpose, . . . by the [Certification Officer], but the [Certification Officer] shall not approve any such rules unless he is satisfied that every member has an equal right, and, if reasonably possible, a fair opportunity of voting, and that the secrecy of the ballot is properly secured.

(2) If the [Certification Officer] is satisfied, and certifies, that rules for the purpose of a ballot under this Act or rules made for other purposes of this Act which require approval by the [Certification Officer], have been approved by a majority of members of a trade union . . . voting for the purpose, or by a majority of delegates of such a trade union voting at a meeting called for the purpose, those rules shall have effect as rules of the union, notwithstanding that the provisions of the rules of the union as to the alteration of rules or the making of new rules have not been complied with.]

5. Notice of objection to contribute towards political objects

(1) A member of a trade union may at any time give notice, in the form set out in the Schedule to this Act or in a form to the like effect, that he objects to contribute to the political fund of the union, and, on the adoption of a resolution of the union approving the furtherance of political objects as an object of the union, notice shall be given to the members of the union acquainting them that each member has a right to be exempt from contributing to the political fund of the union, and that a form of exemption notice can be obtained by or on behalf of a member either by application at or by post from the head office or any branch office of the union or the office of the [Certification Officer].

Any such notice to members of the union shall be given in accordance with rules of the union approved for the purpose by the [Certification Officer], having regard in each case to the existing practice and to the character of the union.

(2) On giving notice in accordance with this Act of his objection to contribute, a member of the union shall be exempt, so long as his notice is not withdrawn, from contributing to the political fund of the union as from the first day of January next after the notice is given, or in the case of a notice given within one month after the notice given to members under this section on the adoption of a resolution approving the furtherance of political objects, as from the date on which the member's notice is given.

[5A. Appeals

An appeal shall lie, in accordance with section 136(2) of the Employment Protection (Consolidation) Act 1978, to the Employment Appeal Tribunal on any question of law arising in any proceedings before or arising from any decision of the Certification Officer under section 3, 4 or 5 of this Act.]

6. Mode of giving effect to exemption from
contributions to political fund

Effect may be given to the exemption of members to contribute to the political fund of a union either by a separate levy of contributions to that fund from the members of the union who are not exempt, and in that case the rules shall provide that no moneys of the union other than the amount raised by such separate levy shall be carried to that fund, or by relieving any members who are exempt from the payment of the whole or any part of any periodical contributions required from the members of the union towards the expenses of the union, and in that case the rules shall provide that the relief shall be given as far as possible to all members who are exempt on the occasion of the same periodical payment and for enabling each member of the union to know as respects any such periodical contribution, what portion, if any, of the sum payable by him is a contribution to the political fund of the union.

[6A. Application of sections 3 to 6 to employers' associations

Sections 3 to 6 of, and the Schedule to, this Act shall apply, with the necessary modifications, in relation to unincorporated employers' associations as they apply in relation to trade unions.]

[7. Definition of Certification Officer

In this Act references to the 'Certification Officer' are references to the officer appointed under section 7 of the Employment Protection Act 1975.]

8. Short title and construction

This Act may be cited as the Trade Union Act 1913, and shall be construed as one with the Trade Union Acts 1871 and 1876; and this Act and the Trade Union Acts 1871 to 1906 may be cited together as the Trade Union Acts 1871 to 1913.

SCHEDULE
Section 5   FORM OF EXEMPTION NOTICE
Name of Trade Union

POLITICAL FUND (EXEMPTION NOTICE)

I hereby give notice that I object to contribute to the Political Fund of the ....
Trade Union, and am in consequence exempt, in manner provided by the Trade Union Act 1913, from contributing to that fund.

A.B.

Address ....

..... day of .... 19....

NOTES AND REFERENCES

The place of publication is London unless otherwise stated

CHAPTER ONE
The Emergence of the Labour Party

1. S. and B. Webb, *Industrial Democracy* (1902) p.247.
2. Although there were pockets of artisans who enjoyed the franchise, this was exceptional. See H. M. Pelling, *A History of British Trade Unionism*, 3rd ed. (Harmondsworth 1976) p.61.
3. S. and B. Webb, op.cit., p.248.
4. C. F. Brand, 'The Conversion of British Trade Unions to Political Action' (1925) 30 *Am. Hist. Rev.* 251.
5. S. and B. Webb, op.cit., p.248.
6. It may also be that the Seditious Meetings Act 1817 operated as a restraint. This provided that no meetings exceeding 50 persons were to be held for the purpose of considering or preparing any petition, complaint, declaration or address to the King or Parliament for alteration of matters of State, unless five days notice of the meeting was given in the press.
7. For an analysis of the development of GNCTU, see W. H. Oliver, 'The Consolidated Trades' Union of '34' (1964) 17 *Econ. Hist. Rev.* 1.
8. G. D. H. Cole, *British Working Class Politics 1832-1914* (1941) p.11.
9. D. Simon, 'Master and Servant', in J. Saville (ed.) *Democracy and the Labour Movement* (1954) pp.160-200.
10. See F. E. Gillespie, *Labor and Politics in England 1850-1867* (Durham, North Carolina 1927) p.228.
11. See S. and B. Webb, *The History of British Trade Unionism* (1920) p.253.
12. Pelling, op.cit., p.61.
13. A. E. Musson, *British Trade Unions 1800-1875* (1976) p.37.
14. S. and B. Webb, *History*, pp.175-7.
15. ibid., p.177.
16. See, for example, Pelling, op.cit., p.43.
17. Including F. C. Mather, *Chartism* (1965) p.33.
18. Musson, op.cit., p.45.
19. See W. H. Fraser, *Trade Unions and Society: the Struggle for Acceptance 1850-1880* (1974) pp.120-45 and Gillespie, op.cit., pp.197-234.
20. See Pelling, op.cit., pp.64-5.
21. (1867) 2 Q.B. 153.
22. S. and B. Webb, *History*, p.263.
23. Cole, op.cit., p.29.
24. See S. and B. Webb, *History*, p.274.
25. *R.* v. *Druitt* (1867) 10 Cox C.C. 592.
26. See H. W. McCready, 'British Labour and the Royal Commission on Trade Unions 1867-1869' (1955) 24 *Univ. of Toronto Q.* 390.
27. Pelling, op.cit., p.69.
28. S. and B. Webb, *History*, p.270.
29. F. Harrison, 'The Trades Union Bill' (1869) 6 *Fort. Rev.* 30.
30. S. and B. Webb, *History*, p.271.
31. On the origins of the TUC, see A. E. Musson, *Trade Union and Social History* (1974) p.23.
32. ibid., p.40.
33. ibid., p.37.

34. S. and B. Webb, *History*, p.281.

35. TUC Parliamentary Committee Standing Orders 1873, quoted by B. C. Roberts, *The Trades Union Congress 1868-1921* (1958) p.74.

36. (1872) 12 Cox C.C. 316.

37. S. and B. Webb, *History*, p.284.

38. This section has drawn heavily on the following works: F. Bealey and H. Pelling, *Labour and Politics 1900-1906; A History of the Labour Representation Committee* (1958); J. Clayton, *The Rise and Decline of Socialism in Great Britain 1884-1924* (1926); W. B. Gwyn, *Democracy and the Cost of Politics* (1962); H. M. Pelling, *Origins of the Labour Party 1880-1900*, 2nd ed. (Oxford 1965); H. M. Pelling, *A History of British Trade Unionism*; H. M. Pelling, *A Short History of the Labour Party*, 5th ed. (1976); D. F. Macdonald, *The State and the Trade Unions*, 2nd ed. (1976).

39. For details, see M. Beer, *A History of British Socialism* (1921) pp.222-5; and A. W. Humphrey, *A History of Labour Representation* (1912) pp.1-104.

40. Pelling, *Origins*, p.2.

41. S. and B. Webb, *History*, p.369.

42. Quoted by A. E. P. Duffy, 'New Unionism in Britain, 1889-1890: A Reappraisal' (1961) 14 *Econ. Hist. Rev.* 306 at p.314.

43. See E. J. Hobsbawm, *Labouring Men* (1968) p.184.

44. Pelling, *Origins*, p.84.

45. Pelling, *History*, p.114.

46. ibid.

47. See also J. Saville, 'Trade Unions and Free Labour: The background to the Taff Vale decision', in A. Briggs and J. Saville (eds), *Essays in Labour History* (1960) p.317 where it is recorded that employers began to employ non-union labour on a 'large scale' and that there rose a veritable crescendo of demands that the freedom of non-unionists be protected by the State against the tyranny of the New Unions.

48. *Temperton* v. *Russell* [1893] 1 Q.B. 715.

49. *Trollope* v. *London Building Trades' Federation* (1895) 72 L.T. 342.

50. [1896] 1 Ch. 811.

51. Pelling, *Origins*, p.222.

52. [1901] A.C. 426.

53. See esp. *Quinn* v. *Leatham* [1901] A.C. 495 where a secondary boycott was held to be an unlawful conspiracy even though the acts, if done by an individual, were not actionable, and even though the conspirators had acted in furtherance of their own interests.

54. [1910] A.C. 87.

CHAPTER TWO
The Osborne Judgment

1. See e.g., the Royal Commission on Labour, Fifth and Final Report, Cd.7421 (1894) where it was noted at para.70 that a trade society of the strongest, best established and wealthiest kind might probably, after meeting its working expenses, apply its income to parliamentary representation, among other things.

2. 1876 Act, s.16.

3. Report of the Chief Registrar of Friendly Societies 1876, p.41.

4. Report of the Chief Registrar of Friendly Societies 1904, p.4.

5. Labour Party Archives, LRC 26/215/1.

6. See e.g. *The Times*, 12 January 1907 where it is reported that a circular was issued by the Lancashire and Cheshire Conservative Working Men's Federation protesting about compulsory political levies. See further H. A. Clegg, A. Fox and A. F. Thompson, *A History of British Trade Unionism since 1889* (Oxford 1964) p.417.

7. See P. P. Poirier, *The Advent of the Labour Party* (1958) pp.214-15.

8. LRC Circular 'Labour Representation and Trade Unionism' dated 27 November 1905. Labour Party

Archives, LRC 28/317. For further details of the background to this case, see J. O. French, *Plumbers in Unity* (1965) pp.79-81.

9. Labour Party Archives, LRC 26/216 i-iv.
10. See W. B. Gwyn, *Democracy and the Cost of Politics* (1962) p.180.
11. Labour Party Archives, LRC 28/317.
12. ibid.
13. ibid.
14. See Minutes of the Triennial Delegate Meeting of the Dock, Wharf, Riverside and General Workers' Union of Great Britain and Ireland 1914, p.51.
15. Labour Party Report 1906, p.13.
16. Labour Party Archives, LRC 28/348/2. Undated correspondence from the Registry of Friendly Societies.
17. Labour Party Archives, LPGC 2/138/1-3 ; 2/139 ; 2/166/2.
18. 159 Parl. Debs. 778.
19. Labour Party Report 1906, pp.44-6.
20. ibid., p.55.
21. The text of the opinion may be found at 26 H.C. Debs. 982-3.
22. [1907] 1 K.B. 361.
23. ibid. at 369.
24. ibid. at 367.
25. ibid.
26. [1910] A.C. 87.
27. H. M. Pelling, *A History of British Trade Unionism*, 3rd ed. (Harmondsworth 1976) p.130.
28. (1908) 77 L.J. Ch.763.
29. ibid. at 765.
30. [1909] 1 Ch.163.
31. ibid. at 184 (Fletcher Moulton L.J.).
32. ibid. at 175 (Cozens Hardy M.R.).
33. ibid. at 184 (Fletcher Moulton L.J.).
34. ibid. at 175.
35. ibid. at 102 (Lord Atkinson).
36. (1875) L.R. 7 H.L. 653.
37. (1880) 5 App. Cas. 473.
38. (1885) 10 App. Cas. 354.

39. ibid. at 362-3.
40. [1910] A.C. at 96 (Lord Macnaghten).
41. ibid. at 103 (Lord Atkinson).
42. ibid. at 97.
43. ibid. at 112.
44. ibid. at 113-14.
45. ibid. at 115.
46. ibid. at 111-12.
47. ibid. at 111.
48. S. and B. Webb, *The History of Trade Unionism* (1920) p.615.
49. F. W. Maitland, Introduction to Gierke, *Political Theories of the Middle Ages* (Cambridge 1900) pp.29-38.
50. A. V. Dicey, 'The Combination Laws' (1904) 17 *Harv. L. Rev.* 511.
51. W. M. Geldart, 'Legal Personality' (1911) 27 L.Q.R. 90.
52. H. J. Laski, 'The Personality of Associations' (1916) 29 *Harv. L. Rev.* 404.
53. Maitland, op.cit., p.38.
54. Geldart, op.cit., pp.94-5.
55. F. W. Maitland, 'Moral Personality and Legal Personality' in *Selected Essays* edited by H. D. Hazeltine, G. Sapsley and P. H. Winfield (Cambridge 1936) p.237. See also W. M. Geldart, op.cit. and 'The Status of Trade Unions in England' (1912) 25 *Harv. L. Rev.* 579.
56. [1910] A.C. at 107-8.
57. (1885) 12 R. 1206 at 1211.
58. (1901) 70 L.J. K.B. 396.
59. [1901] A.C. 426.
60. ibid. at 442.
61. [1905] A.C. 256 at 279-80.
62. [1901] A.C. at 437.
63. *Parl. Papers* 1868-9, vol.XXXI.
64. ibid., p.14.
65. ibid., p.43.
66. ibid., p.59.
67. (1867) 2 Q.B. 153.
68. [1910] A.C. at 98-9.
69. P.R.O., CAB 37/103/50.
70. Namely Burt and MacDonald, union sponsored members elected in 1874.
71. [1956] A.C. 104.

72. ibid. at 144.

73. 1876 Act, s.16.

74. [1910] A.C. at 111.

75. See H. J. Hanham, *The Nineteenth Century Constitution 1815-1914* (1969) p.300; and J. P. Mackintosh, *The British Cabinet*, 3rd ed. (1977) ch.6.

76. M. Ostrogorski, *Democracy and the Organisation of Political Parties* (1902) p.591.

77. See R. K. Alderman, 'The Conscience Clause of the Parliamentary Labour Party' (1966) 19 *Parl. Aff.* 22.

78. Quoted by P. G. Richards, *Parliament and Conscience* (1970) p.24.

79. P. S. Snowden, *An Autobiography* (1934) p.224.

80. See Alderman, op.cit. Cf. H. M. Pelling, *A Short History of the Labour Party*, 5th ed. (1976) p.21.

81. See R. T. McKenzie, *British Political Parties*, 2nd ed. (1964) pp.473-5.

82. (1851) 13 D. 1243.

83. ibid. at 1252.

84. (1918) S.R. (N.S.W.) 202. It may also be noted that shortly after the Osborne Judgment was delivered, the Lord Chancellor advised the Prime Minister that a trade union would not be allowed to subscribe to a Free Trade Campaign or one for registration reform, or to spend money on a Hyde Park demonstration, unless it was a demonstration which fell within the statutory objects. However, he thought that unions could join trades councils as these dealt with industrial matters as well as political ones. P.R.O., CAB 37/104/57.

85. [1910] A.C. at 104-5.

86. On municipal representation, see *Wilson v. Amalgamated Society of Engineers* [1911] 2 Ch.324.

87. *The Times*, 9 July 1910. See also *Thurloway v. Am. Union of Shop Assistants*, *The Times*, 9 Dec. 1910.

88. (1911) 2 S.L.T. 478.

89. *The Times*, 19 October 1910. See also *Muirhead v. Fife and Kinross Miners' Association*, *The Times*, 5 October 1910.

90. [1910] A.C. at 102.

91. ibid. at 93.

92. ibid. at 94-5.

93. [1912] A.C. 421 at 429.

94. 1912 S.C. 534.

95. ibid. at 541.

96. L.J.C. MacDonald, Lord Salvesen and Lord Guthrie concurred on this point.

97. (1959) 103 C.L.R. 30.

CHAPTER THREE
The Trade Union Act 1913

1. The account in this introduction is drawn mainly from Labour Party Reports 1909-12; TUC Reports 1910-12; and Reports of Special Conferences of the Joint Board, 10 November 1910 and 20/21 June 1911.

2. TUC Report 1910, p.148.

3. 21 H.C. Debs. 103.

4. W. B. Gwyn, *Democracy and the Cost of Politics* (1962) p.193.

5. ibid., p.195. He also notes that some unions simply gave up collecting money for political purposes. Cf. A. E. Musson, *The Typographical Association* (1954) pp.356-7 where it is claimed that after *Buck*'s case, very few members of the Association refused to contribute to a voluntary fund.

6. [1911] 2 Ch.324. See also *Furner v. London Soc. of Compositors* (1909) 17 Board of Trade Labour Gazette 101 where it was held that a political levy exacted from all the members of the society was unlawful, even though there was no provision in the rules to expel recalcitrant members.

7. 16 H.C. Debs. 1321-63.

8. See TUC Report 1911, p.72.

9. See R. Page Arnot, *The Miners: Years of Struggle* (1953) pp.155-6. Cf. Gwyn, op.cit., pp.197-8.

10. H. M. Pelling, *A Short History of the Labour Party*, 5th ed. (1976) p.27.

11. See G. D. H. Cole, *A Short History of the British Working Class Movement*, vol.3 (1948) pp.57-8. See also Pelling, *Short History*, pp.27, 30.

12. The responses of individual Cabinet Ministers are taken from P.R.O., CAB 37/103/42-7.

13. 20 H.C. Debs. 275-6.

14. P.R.O., CAB 37/105/33.

15. ibid.

16. 26 H.C. Debs. 1015-16.

17. ibid., col.1017.

18. TUC Parliamentary Committee, Quarterly Report, March 1912, p.17.

19. 41 H.C. Debs. 3017 (J.R.Clynes). See also J. R. Clynes, *Laws to Smash the Labour Party* (Manchester, n.d.).

20. 41 H.C. Debs. 3068 (J. Ramsay MacDonald).

21. ibid., col.3020 (J. R. Clynes).

22. 47 H.C. Debs. 1738.

23. TUC Parliamentary Committee, Report of Proceedings in Standing Committee C (1913) pp.5-6.

24. See Labour Party Reports 1911-13.

25. Report of a Special Conference of the Joint Board (1913) p.2.

26. B. C. Roberts, *The Trades Union Congress 1868-1921* (1958) p.258.

27. See TUC Parliamentary Committee, Report of Proceedings in Standing Committee C (1913) p.37; and 47 H.C. Debs. 1092-1136.

28. 26 H.C. Debs. 934.

29. ibid., col.990.

30. ibid., col.936.

31. ibid., cols 932-3.

32. See TUC Parliamentary Committee, Report of Proceedings in Standing Committee C (1913) p.15; and 47 H.C. Debs. 1357-92.

33. See 47 H.C. Debs. 1395-9.

34. See TUC Parliamentary Committee, Report of Proceedings in Standing Committee C (1913) p.21.

35. 47 H.C. Debs. 1395-9.

36. 26 H.C. Debs. 999.

37. 41 H.C. Debs. 2983.

38. TUC Parliamentary Committee, Report of Proceedings in Standing Committee C (1913) pp.12-13.

39. 47 H.C. Debs. 1423-50.

40. ibid., col.1424.

41. 47 H.C. Debs. 1683.

42. P.R.O., CAB 24/182.

43. Labour Party Archives, L.P./T.U.A./11.

44. 'Trade Union Extravagance', Reprint from *Morning Post* [N.D.] TUC Library, Box H.D. 6495.

45. 181 H.C. Debs. 858.

46. 'Trade Union Extravagance'.

47. P.R.O., CAB 27/269.

48. ibid.

49. P.R.O., CAB 24/138.

50. P.R.O., CAB 24/158.

51. P.R.O., CAB 23/45/16.

52. 162 H.C. Debs. 2239.

53. P.R.O., CAB 23/49/11.

54. 181 H.C. Debs. 833-41.

55. P.R.O., CAB 24/182.

56. P.R.O., CAB 27/236.

57. ibid.

58. P.R.O., CAB 24/181, and CAB 24/180.

59. P.R.O., CAB 24/188.

60. P.R.O., CAB 24/181.

61. P.R.O., CAB 27/327.

62. P.R.O., CAB 24/182.

63. P.R.O., CAB 24/180.

64. P.R.O., CAB 23/53/65.

65. 1927 Act, s.4(2).

66. P.R.O., CAB 24/180.

67. 205 H.C. Debs. 1332-97.

68. ibid.

69. ibid.

70. TUC Report 1927, p.418.

71. 205 H.C. Debs. 1305 *et seq.*

72. A not unreasonable belief. See A. Duff Cooper, *Old Men Forget* (1953) p.413; and G. M. Young, *Stanley Baldwin* (1952) p.124.

73. *Warner and TGWU*, Registrar's Report 1932, p.6.

74. Labour Party Archives, Box, Trade Disputes Act Correspondence 1934-1945.

75. *Warner and TGWU*, Registrar's Report 1932, p.6.
76. *Griffiths and GMWU*, Registrar's Report 1928, p.4.
77. See respectively, Registrar's Report 1936, p.6, and Labour Party Archives, File L.P./U.N./18.
78. The following pages are based on material found in the Annual Reports of the unions concerned, and in Labour Party Reports 1926-46.
79. TUC Report 1929, p.420.
80. TUC Report 1939, p.243.
81. P.R.O., CAB 16/30/7.
82. P.R.O., CAB 23/66.
83. TUC Report 1931, pp.253-5.
84. TUC Report 1936, p.205.
85. TUC Report 1939, p.243.
86. TUC Report 1940, p.207.
87. TUC Report 1941, p.180 and TUC Report 1943, p.25.
88. 419 H.C. Debs. 192 *et seq.*
89. P.R.O., CAB 16/71.
90. P.R.O., CAB 16/170.
91. 419 H.C. Debs. 233, 456.

CHAPTER FOUR
Trade Union Political Objects
1. Statutory objects are defined in s.1(2) as being 'the regulation of the relations between workmen and masters, or between workmen and workmen, or between masters and masters, or the imposing of restrictive conditions on the conduct of any trade or business, and also the provision of benefits to members'.
2. 1913 Act s.3(3).
3. The Certification Officer has inherited this work, which was originally performed by the Chief Registrar of Friendly Societies. See chapter 6.
4. 1974 Act, Sch.3. See also Industrial Relations Act 1971, s.61 and Sch.8.
5. For details, see R. D. Coates, *Teachers' Unions and Interest Group Politics* (Cambridge 1972) ch.2. It may also be noted that NALGO postponed its decision to be certified as a trade union under the Trade

Union Act 1913, s.2(2) (which would have been conclusive evidence that the organisation was a trade union within the meaning of the Act (s.2(5))) because to be so certified, and concede that it was a trade union, would curtail its freedom to spend money on political objects. NALGO has never had a political fund. See A. Spoor, *White Collar Union: Sixty Years of N.A.L.G.O.* (1967) pp.69-70.
6. Royal Commission on Trade Unions and Employers' Associations, Minutes of Evidence 36, para.203.
7. Royal Commission on Trade Unions and Employers' Associations, Minutes of Evidence 8, para.1416.
8. C. Grunfeld, *Modern Trade Union Law* (1966) goes further by suggesting at p.10 that constitutional objects should be ignored if they conflict with the practice of the union for it is the *real* constitution which should be considered. However, it is not altogether clear why the Chief Registrar embarked upon this exercise. Under the 1913 Act he only had jurisdiction to deal with a breach of the political fund rules of unions which had adopted such rules. He had no jurisdiction to deal with a complaint that a union with no political fund rules was using money in breach of the 1913 Act.
9. Registrar's Report 1925, p.3.
10. *Rothwell* v. *APEX* [1976] I.C.R. 211.
11. See TUC Report 1924, p.273.
12. STUC Annual Report 1974, p.149.
13. As was recognised in *Hardie & Lane Ltd* v. *Chiltern* [1928] 1 K.B. 663, 667, the test of a trade union was its objects, not its personnel.
14. See J. D. Stewart, *British Pressure Groups: Their Role in Relation to the House of Commons* (Oxford 1958) pp.171-6.

15. 1913 Act, s.3(1).
16. Donovan Report, Cmnd. 3623, Appendix 7, para.4.
17. ibid.
18. [1980] I.C.R. 662 at 670.
19. [1981] I.R.L.R. 247, noted by K. Ewing (1981) 10 I.L.J. 190.
20. [1980] A.C. 672.
21. [1981] I.R.L.R. at 250.
22. ibid. at 257.
23. *The Sunday Times*, 24 May 1981.
24. Annual Report of the Certification Officer 1980, p.55.
25. ibid.
26. Though in practice it seems that unions use their political funds for this purpose.
27. M. Rush, *The Selection of Parliamentary Candidates* (1969) pp.291-4.
28. ibid., p.293. This was two more than A. Ranney, *Pathways to Parliament* (1965) p.263, was able to detect.
29. J. Ellis and R. W. Johnson, *Members from the Unions* (1974) p.6.
30. [1980] I.R.L.R. 335. See also *Forster*'s complaint, Registrar's Report 1925, p.3.
31. *The Times*, 16 August 1978. On expenditure in the 1979 election see M. Pinto-Duschinsky, 'Financing the British General Election of 1979' in H. R. Penniman (ed.), *Britain at the Polls, 1979* (Washington 1981).
32. *The Financial Times*, 11 April 1979, and *The Guardian*, 16 April 1979.
33. [1952] 1 All E.R. 697.
34. ibid. at 699.
35. Cd. 8463 (1917).
36. [1952] 1 All E.R. at 700.
37. *The Financial Times*, 11 April 1979.
38. *PO* v. *UPW* [1974] I.C.R. 378.
39. cf. *The Marley Tile Co. Ltd* v. *Shaw* [1980] I.R.L.R. 25.
40. [1976] I.R.L.R. 215.
41. I. Richter, *Political Purpose in Trade Unions* (1973) p.52.
42. Very often, these maxima are not reached by unions. See W. D. Muller, *The Kept Men?* (Hassocks 1977) p.55.
43. Registrar's Report 1957, pp.3-4.
44. P.R.O., CAB 37/105/33.
45. *Forster*'s complaint, Registrar's Report 1925 at 4.
46. [1981] I.R.L.R. 427.
47. ibid. at 430.
48. [1981] I.R.L.R. 247.
49. *The Glasgow Herald*, 27 March 1965.
50. *McCarthy* v. *APEX* [1980] I.R.L.R. 335.
51. ibid. at 339. See also *Forster*'s complaint, Registrar's Report 1925, p.3.
52. *Citrine's Trade Union Law* (1967) 3rd ed. by M. A. Hickling, p.440.
53. 13 H.L. Debs. 1389.
54. (1915) 113 L.T. 808 at 811.
55. [1980] I.R.L.R. 335.
56. [1981] I.R.L.R. at 253.
57. Registrar's Report 1925 at 7.
58. [1980] I.R.L.R. at 339.
59. ibid. at 338.
60. Registrar's Report 1966, p.8.
61. Registrar's Report 1957, p.4.
62. ibid. at 5.
63. (1920) 36 T.L.R. 666. See also *Williams* v. *Cotter, The Times*, 8 May 1925.
64. (1915) 113 L.T. 808. See also *Carter* v. *United Society of Boilermakers* (1915) 113 L.T. 1152; *McArdle* v. *United Society of Boilermakers* (1915) 1 S.L.T. 437; and *Lund* v. *Am. Soc. of Dyers, Bleachers, Finishers and Kindred Trades, The Times*, 18 October 1913.
65. (1937) 81 *Sol. J.* 179. See also *Wilson* v. *NUS* [1929] 1 Ch.216.
66. *The Durham Chronicle*, 3 July 1942.

CHAPTER FIVE
Trade Union Political Action

1. See also A. J. M. Sykes, 'Attitudes to Political Affiliation in a Printing Trade Union' (1965) 12 *Sc. J. Pol. Econ.* 161.
2. *Brodie* v. *Bevan* (1921) 38 T.L.R. 172.

3. These rules were formulated in 1913 because the Chief Registrar had not seen a single set of rules which satisfied the requirements of the 1913 Act.

4. Model Rule 7.

5. Model Rule 6.

6. Model Rule 4.

7. Labour Party Archives, Box, Trade Disputes Act Correspondence 1934-1945.

8. See M. Harrison, *Trade Unions and the Labour Party since 1945* (1960) p.23.

9. And see The Funds for Trade Union Ballots Regulations, S.I. 1252/1980.

10. 409 H.L. Debs. 1291.

11. P.R.O., CAB 27/269.

12. But see NUM Rules, r.44 which provides that the political fund rules can only be altered with the approval of a two-thirds majority vote taken at the union conference. So the procedure for revocation may well be more onerous than the statutory procedure for the introduction of such rules.

13. Harrison, op.cit., pp.24-5.

14. ibid., p.21.

15. See J. D. Stewart, *British Pressure Groups: Their Role in Relation to the House of Commons* (Oxford 1958) pp.168-9.

16. RSD 1949, p.241. See also Registrar's Report 1924, p.5 where it is noted that the Musicians' Union collected the political levy from the members of only seven branches. Cf. *Sharpe and AEU*, Registrar's Report 1967, p.17.

17. *Newman and BISAKTA*, RSD 1948, p.257.

18. *The Times*, 5 September 1978.

19. Registrar's Report 1931, p.5.

20. Unions which have been running deficits in recent years include ACTT and NUTGW.

21. Registrar's Report 1953, p.4.

22. Model Rule 4.

23. Model Rule 3.

24. Registrar's Report 1965, p.13.

25. Donovan Report, Cmnd. 3623, para.926.

26. S. and B. Webb, *The History of Trade Unionism* (1920) p.687.

27. *The Times*, 6 March 1978.

28. *The Times*, 13 March 1978.

29. RSD 1947, p.221. See also Registrar's Report 1963 where it is noted that 'from time to time' complaints were made that a member has sought exemption from the political contribution by means of a form which is not supplied from union sources and that branch officials declined to act on such notice. See further *Gasson and NACODS* Registrar's Report 1969, p.21.

30. *Valentine and ETU*, Registrar's Report 1957, p.3.

31. *Templeman and AUEFW*, Registrar's Report 1969, p.22.

32. *McCarthy v. APEX* [1979] I.R.L.R. 255.

33. *Nutter and AEU*, RSD 1948, p.240.

34. See 194 H.C. Debs. 1025-6.

35. Donovan Report, Cmnd. 3623, para.719.

36. Quoted by Marsh and Staples, 'Check-Off Agreements in Britain: A Study of their Growth and Functions', Royal Commission on Trade Unions and Employers' Associations Research Paper 8 (1968).

37. [1981] I.R.L.R. 307.

38. *Robinson and NACODS, Durham Area*, Registrar's Report 1966, p.9. This decision gave effect to the practice followed by the Chief Registrar at least since 1951. See J. E. Mortimer, *A History of the Association of Engineering and Ship-building Draughtsmen* (1960) p.317.

39. *McCarthy v. APEX* [1979] I.R.L.R. 255; and *Reeves v. TGWU* [1979] I.R.L.R. 290.

40. See also *Cleminson v. POEU* [1980] I.R.L.R. 1.

41. [1980] I.R.L.R. at 312.

42. ibid. at 313. It may also be noted that another, much different point was raised before the EAT which had not arisen before the Certification Officer. This was the argument that the practice of rebates contravened the Truck Act 1831, ss.2, 3. The EAT concluded that this was a matter for the courts, not for it. However, it is difficult to see how any action on this ground would succeed. See *Hewlett* v. *Allen* [1894] A.C. 383 and *Williams* v. *Butlers Ltd* [1975] I.C.R. 208.

43. Some agreements already provide that the check-off will not apply to a new employee until the beginning of the first quarter from the commencement of employment. See e.g. AUEW (Eng. Sect.) Model Agreement on the Deduction of Trade Union Contributions.

44. This is already provided for in some unions, including GMWU, NATSOPA, and NUR.

45. A similar ban is imposed by the rules of MNAOA and REOU.

46. Directly by NUR Rules, r.5(1); indirectly by a host of other unions which insist that the General Secretary be a delegate to the Labour Party conference. Such unions include NATSOPA, ASLEF, NUTGW, EETPU, and UCATT. The Standing Orders of the party require all delegates to be individual members of the party.

47. GMWU Rules, r.48.

48. Registrar's Report 1935, p.4.

49. *Reeves* v. *TGWU* [1980] I.R.L.R. 307.

50. RSD 1948, p.234.

51. [1979] I.C.R. 554.

52. [1980] I.R.L.R. at 313.

53. [1981] I.R.L.R. 247.

54. ibid. at 254.

55. Registrar's Report 1956, p.2.

56. [1981] I.R.L.R. at 254.

57. (1979 Unreported) but noted in Annual Report of Certification Officer 1979, p.24.

58. [1950] Ch.602.

59. Registrar's Report 1932, p.9.

60. RSD 1948, p.229.

61. [1950] Ch. at 613.

62. NUR Rules, r.10.

63. cf. C. Grunfeld, *Modern Trade Union Law* (1966) pp.299-307.

64. One of the private member's bills which had been sponsored before the passing of the 1913 Act had provided that any member of a trade union who objected to paying the political levy could give written notice requiring the union to use a proportionate part of his dues to augment the fund from which either sick benefit or unemployment benefit was paid.

65. Registrar's Report 1928, p.4. See also *McCafferty and Irish TGWU*, Registrar's Report 1952, p.36 (Eire).

66. *Cleminson* v. *POEU* [1980] I.R.L.R. 1.

67. ibid.

68. Registrar's Report 1933, p.4.

69. See, e.g. *First Edinburgh and Leith Building Society* v. *Munro* (1883) 21 S.L.R. 291.

70. (1979 Unreported).

71. Labour Party Constitution, cl.VII(1). See Labour Party Report 1962, p.222; see also Labour Party Report 1974, p.168.

72. Labour Party Rules for Constituency Labour Parties, cl.IV(4). The Labour Party constitution no longer expressly requires delegates to be contributors to the political fund of their respective trade unions. However, this is secured by the fact that all delegates (with the exception of those from Northern Ireland) must be members of the party and by the fact that contribution to the political fund of a member's trade union is a condition of membership.

73. Registrar's Report 1932, p.9.

CHAPTER SIX
Political Fund Complaints

1. Trade Union Act 1913, s.3(2).

2. Industrial Relations Act 1971, ss.81-3.

3. Employment Protection Act 1975, s.7.

4. See chapter 3. The following account is drawn from 47 H.C. Debs. 1423-50.

5. 13 H.L. Debs. 862. It is perhaps worth noting that the right to complain to the Chief Registrar was not universally acclaimed on the Labour side. It was argued by Mr Stephen Walsh, e.g., that easy access to the Registrar would simply stimulate complaints. See 47 H.C. Debs. 1428-30.

6. Friendly Societies Act 1896, s.1(3). He still is: see now Friendly Societies Act 1974, s.2(5).

7. That amendment is considered at 13 H.L. Debs. 1409-14 from which the following account is drawn.

8. Friendly Societies Act 1974, s.2(1). See now Friendly Societies Act 1981.

9. Since 1912, only six men have held this post. They are as follows: Sir George Stuart Robertson K.C. (1912-1937); Sir John Fox O.B.E. (1937-1947); Sir Bernard Kerr White K.B.E. (1947-1954); Sir Cecil Brookesby Crabbe (1954-1963); Samuel Dixon Musson C.B., M.B.E. (1963-1972); Keith Brading C.B., M.B.E. (1972-   ).

10. Employment Protection Act 1975, s.7.

11. ibid., s.7(1).

12. ibid., sch.1(11).

13. Official Report, Standing Committee F, col.325 (10 June 1975).

14. See *Parkin* v. *ASTMS* (1979, Unreported).

15. Donovan Report, Cmnd. 3623, para.584.

16. See, e.g., P. Davies and M. Freedland, *Labour Law Text and Materials* (1979) pp.734-7.

17. TUC Report 1976, p.94.

18. TUC Report 1978, p.391. See further, K. D. Ewing and W. M. Rees, 'The TUC Independent Review Committee and the Closed Shop' (1981) 10 I.L.J. 84.

19. Royal Commission on Trade Unions and Employer's Associations 1965-1968, Minutes of Evidence 8, para.1369.

20. ibid., para.1371. But compare J. Rear (1976) 5 I.L.J. 261 where it is noted that in the complaint of *Coleman and POEU*, Registrar's Report 1974, p.26, the matter was dealt with by means of a round the table discussion.

21. Trade Union Act 1913, s.3(2).

22. RSD 1948, p.257.

23. Mr Jack Cleminson, a recent complainant, wrote that as a life-long Conservative, he objected to supporting the Labour Party and was concerned to ensure that the party did not receive money under 'false pretences'. *News for Trade Unionists*, January 1979.

24. Registrar's Report 1969, p.21.

25. 47 H.C. Debs. 1444.

26. D. Newell (1980) 9 I.L.J. 122. See also Annual Report of the Certification Officer 1977, p.24.

27. The complaint was resolved without the need for a formal order.

28. Registrar's Report 1921, Part A.

29. Annual Report of the Certification Officer 1979, p.23.

30. Annual Report of the Certification Officer 1977, p.24.

31. *Sharpe and AEU*, Registrar's Report 1967, p.17.

32. *Flexton and AEU*, Registrar's Report 1965, p.13.

33. Registrar's Report 1912, Part A.

34. The Certification Office issues Notes on Procedure which make provision for procedure of this kind. The Notes also 'request' each party to prepare a statement of their case for circulation before the hearing.

35. The Chief Registrar said in evidence to the Donovan Commission that he always tried to keep the procedure simple so that people were

not frightened and that it was designed to be an easy and cheap form of jurisdiction (loc.cit. (see note 19), para.1371).

36. This is not to deny that there may be a certain tension in trying to adopt informal proceedings within the confines of an accusatorial structure. In *Richards* v. *NUM* [1981] I.R.L.R. 247 counsel for the union complained that he had great difficulty in distinguishing argument from evidence. The complainant did not give evidence from the witness table and did not call any witnesses. Counsel argued that cross-examination was therefore virtually impossible.

37. ibid.

38. 47 H.C. Debs. 1427.

39. *Forster and National Amal. Union of Shop Assistants, Warehousemen and Clerks*, Registrar's Report 1925, p.3 and *Griffiths and GMWU*, Registrar's Report 1928, p.4.

40. See *Now!*, 26 October 1979.

41. This distrust was not without foundation. The unions had suffered from the courts in a long line of cases, including *J. Lyons and Sons* v. *Wilkins* [1896] 1 Ch.811; *Taff Vale Railway Co. Ltd* v. *ASRS* [1901] A.C. 426; *Quinn* v. *Leatham* [1901] A.C. 495; and the *Osborne* judgment.

42. See K. Ewing, 'Trade Union Political Fund Rules: A Note on Adjudication' (1980) 9 I.L.J. 137.

43. *Vaughan and National Association of Operative Plasterers*, Registrar's Report 1932, p.9.

44. *Robinson and NACODS, Durham Area*, Registrar's Report 1966, p.9.

45. *Templeman and AUEFW*, Registrar's Report 1969, p.22.

46. *Richards* v. *NUM* [1981] I.R.L.R. 247; and *McCarthy* v. *APEX* [1980] I.R.L.R. 335 respectively.

47. *McCarthy* v. *APEX* [1979] I.R.L.R. 255 and *Reeves* v. *TGWU* [1979] I.R.L.R. 290. The latter decision was overturned by the EAT. See [1980] I.R.L.R. 307.

48. See *Cleminson* v. *POEU* [1980] I.R.L.R. 1 and also *Reeves* v. *TGWU* [1979] I.R.L.R. 290.

49. See *Parkin* v. *ASTMS* (1979, Unreported).

50. Trade Union Act 1913, s.3(2).

51. 47 H.C. Debs. 1444.

52. See *Bond and Parker and TGWU*, Registrar's Report 1933, p.4.

53. 47 H.C. Debs. 1444.

54. There are no reported decisions of the Chief Registrar of Trade Unions.

55. It is not clear how many of these orders were registered in the County Court.

56. See e.g., the complaints by *Richards* v. *NUM* [1981] I.R.L.R. 247 and *McCarthy* v. *APEX* [1980] I.R.L.R. 335.

57. See *Griffiths and GMWU*, Registrar's Report 1928, p.4.

58. See e.g., *Robinson and NACODS, Durham Area*, Registrar's Report 1966, p.9.

59. See e.g., *Valentine and ETU*, Registrar's Report 1957, p.3.

60. See *Cleminson* v. *POEU* [1980] I.R.L.R. 1.

61. *Parkin* v. *ASTMS* (1979, Unreported).

62. *Newman and BISAKTA*, RSD 1948, p.257.

63. Registrar's Report 1969, p.21.

64. See Notes on Procedure, op.cit. (see note 34), para.6.

65. 47 H.C. Debs. 1444-5.

66. [1927] 1 Ch.539. Forster brought this action after having failed before the Chief Registrar (see above). His claim that the union had acted in breach of the 1913 Act was dismissed on the ground that there was no such cause of action. It was held that an action would only lie for a breach of the rules.

67. ibid. at 546.

68. *Andrews* v. *Mitchell* [1905] A.C. 78.

69. 1958 Act, s.11. See now Tribunals and Inquiries Act 1971, s.14. It may be noted, however, that neither the

Chief Registrar nor the Certification Officer come under the jurisdiction of the Council on Tribunals.

70. 1971 Act, s.115. An appeal lay on fact and law.

71. 1975 Act, s.88(2)(a). See now Employment Protection (Consolidation) Act 1978, s.136. So far there has been only one appeal to the EAT. See *Reeves* v. *TGWU* [1980] I.R.L.R. 307.

72. 1975 Act, s.88(4). See now EPCA 1978, s.136(4).

73. This point was raised in the EAT, though not before the Certification Officer. The EAT dismissed the point for want of jurisdiction.

74. [1897] A.C. 615.

75. *De Smith's Judicial Review of Administrative Action*, 4th ed. J. M. Evans (1980) pp.358-9.

76. 47 H.C. Debs. 1444.

77. ibid., cols 1449-50.

78. [1950] Ch.602.

79. A point which arose in *Coleman and POEU*, Registrar's Report 1974, p.26 and in *McCarthy* v. *APEX* [1979] I.R.L.R. 255.

80. See *Corrigan and USDAW*, Registrar's Report 1957, p.4.

81. *Williams* v. *Cotter, The Times*, 8 May 1925.

82. *Parkin* v. *ASTMS* [1980] I.C.R. 662.

83. Report of the Committee on Administrative Tribunals and Enquiries, Cmnd. 218 (1957).

CHAPTER SEVEN
The Function of Political Action

1. Houghton Report, Cmnd. 6601 (1976), para.9.1.

2. Labour Party Report 1980.

3. Labour Party Report 1975.

4. S. Perlman, *A Theory of the Labor Movement* (Reprinted New York 1970) p.144.

5. ibid., p.149. See also I. Richter, *Political Purpose in Trade Unions* (1973).

6. 'Trade Unions and Politics' in A.

Flanders, *Management and Unions* (1975) p.24. See also H. A. Clegg, *Trade Unionism under Collective Bargaining* (Oxford 1976) pp.100-5.

7. Flanders, op.cit., p.30.

8. ibid., p.31.

9. S. H. Beer, *Modern British Politics* (1969) p.329.

10. See E. H. Phelps Brown, *The Growth of British Industrial Relations* (1960) p.307.

11. B. C. Roberts, *The Trades Union Congress 1868-1921* (1958) p.310.

12. Cd. 9230 (1918) para.34.

13. W. M. C. Citrine, *Two Careers* (1967) p.215.

14. H. M. Pelling, *A History of British Trade Unionism*, 3rd ed. (Harmondsworth 1976) p.215.

15. Royal Commission on Trade Unions and Employers' Associations, Selected Written Evidence 4, para.168.

16. See R. D. Coates, *Teachers' Unions and Interest Group Politics* (Cambridge 1972) p.104 and D. Volker 'N.A.L.G.O.'s Affiliation to the T.U.C.' (1966) 4 B.J.I.R. 59.

17. V. L. Allen, *Trade Union Leadership* (1957) p.150.

18. National Union of Wallcovering, Decorative and Allied Trades, Annual Report 1977, p.2.

19. BIFU Rules, r.B5. Emphasis added.

20. See also G. Cyriax 'Labour and the Unions' (1960) 31 P.Q. 324; M. Harrison, *Trade Unions and the Labour Party since 1945* (1960) p.349; and Richter, op.cit., pp.137-8.

21. Unpublished evidence submitted to the Houghton Committee on Financial Aid to Political Parties, p.10.

22. Unpublished evidence submitted to the Labour Party Commission of Enquiry (1980) Appendix C.

23. Unpublished evidence submitted to the Labour Party Commission of Enquiry (1980) para.1.4.

24. Affiliation to the Labour Party: Discussion Paper (1980) Unpublished, para.9.

25. TUC, SWE 4, op.cit. (see note 15) para.152.

26. See J. D. Stewart, *British Pressure Groups: Their Role in Relation to the House of Commons* (Oxford 1958) p.177; J. Blondel, *Voters, Parties and Leaders* (revised ed., Harmondsworth 1967) p.215; and W. D. Muller, *The Kept Men?* (Hassocks 1977) p.72.

27. See J. Ellis and R. W. Johnson, *Members from the Unions* (1974) p.15; and Harrison, op.cit., p.298.

28. ASTMS, Unpublished evidence submitted to the Houghton Committee on Financial Aid to Political Parties, p.7.

29. Cmnd. 3888 (1969).

30. On this, see E. S. Heffer, *The Class Struggle in Parliament* (1973) pp.105-41.

31. A. J. P. Taylor, *English History 1914-1945* (Harmondsworth 1970) p.157.

32. Richter, op.cit., p.70.

33. ibid., p.168.

34. Harrison, op.cit., pp.101-2.

35. M. Rush, *The Selection of Parliamentary Candidates* (1969) p.168.

36. ibid.

37. The permitted expenditure is slightly higher for county constituencies.

38. Richter, op.cit., p.183.

39. ibid.

40. R. Rose, *The Problem of Party Government* (Harmondsworth 1976) p.237.

41. Annual Report of the Certification Officer 1980, p.55.

42. Unpublished Evidence to the Labour Party Commission of Enquiry (1980) para.6.1.

43. See Sir O. Kahn-Freund, *Labour and the Law*, 2nd ed. (1977) p.202.

44. W. E. J. McCarthy, *The Closed Shop in Britain* (Oxford 1964) p.3.

45. See A. Rowe, 'Conservatives and Trade Unionists', in Z. Layton-Henry, *Conservative Party Politics* (1980) p.210.

46. Report of the Labour Party Commission of Enquiry (1980) para.7.1.

47. P. Wintour, 'Basnett takes the Lead', *New Statesman*, 23 November 1979, p.801.

48. ibid.

49. Unpublished evidence to the Labour Party Commission of Enquiry (1980).

50. Excluding donations to the General Election Fund.

51. L. Minkin, *The Labour Party Conference* (1978) p.12.

52. Hansard Society, *Paying for Politics: The Report of the Commission upon the Financing of Political Parties* (1981) p.24.

53. ibid.

54. See M. Pinto-Duschinsky, *British Political Finance 1830-1980* (Washington 1981) ch.9.

55. Report of the Labour Party Commission of Enquiry (1980) para.8.1.

56. Houghton Report, Cmnd. 6601 (1976), Appendix J.

57. ibid., para.9.30.

58. See Pinto-Duschinsky, op.cit., p.297.

59. 171 Parl. Debs. 756-78.

60. ibid., col.759.

61. ibid., col.760.

62. Hansard Society, op.cit., pp.17-20.

63. See L. C. B. Gower, *The Principles of Modern Company Law*, 4th ed. (1979) pp.170-1.

64. 725 H.C. Debs. 46.

65. 278 H.L. Debs. 146.

66. ibid., col.212.

67. Hansard Society, op.cit., p.29.

68. 952 H.C. Debs. 215. The question of company political donations was briefly referred to in the Report of the Jenkins Committee on Company Law, Cmnd. 1749 (1962) para.50 where the Committee referred to evidence which it had received to the effect that companies should be

prohibited from making political donations. The Committee refused to comment on the evidence, taking the view that the issues involved did not raise questions of company law.

69. See Report of the Committee of Inquiry on Industrial Democracy, Cmnd. 6706 (1977).

70. ibid., p.22.

CHAPTER EIGHT
Comparative Approaches and Solutions

1. On the relationship between trade unions and the Australian Labor Party, see D. W. Rawson, 'Unions and Politics' in P. W. D. Matthews and G. W. Ford (eds), *Australian Trade Unions* (Melbourne 1968) pp.165-89 and D. W. Rawson, *Unions and Unionists in Australia* (Sydney 1978) pp.80-100.

2. On the financing of the NDP, see K. Z. Paltiel, *Political Party Financing in Canada* (Toronto 1970) pp.56-61.

3. See J. D. Greenstone, *Labor in American Politics* (Chicago 1977). See also C. H. Rehmus and D. B. McLaughlin, *Labor and American Politics* (Ann Arbor 1967).

4. R. K. Scott and R. J. Hrebenar, *Parties in Crisis: Party Politics in America* (New York 1979) p.194.

5. See 2 U.S.C. c.14; for Canadian developments, see for example, Election Finances Reform Act 1975 (Ontario); Election Finances and Contributions Disclosure Act 1977 (Alberta); Financing of Political Parties Act 1977 (Quebec); and Political Process financing Act 1978 (New Brunswick).

6. 1975 Act, s.19.

7. By s.62, the Quebec Act in contrast prohibits donations from any source other than an individual elector.

8. 2 U.S.C. s.441a.

9. 424 U.S. 1 (1976).

10. ibid. at 46.

11. See *McDougall* v. *Wellington Typographical I U W* (1913) 16 G.L.R. 309;

Ohinemuri and Batteries Employees' I U W v. *Registrar of Industrial Unions* [1917] N.Z.L.R. 829; and *Gould* v. *Wellington Waterside Workers' I U W* [1924] N.Z.L.R. 1025.

12. See 246 *N.Z. Parl. Debs.* 301.

13. 1936 Act, s.4(1).

14. ibid.

15. 246 *N.Z. Parl. Debs.* 301.

16. Statutes Amendment Act 1948, s.40(2).

17. Political Disabilities Removal Amendment Act 1950, s.2(1)(a).

18. Political Disabilities Removal Act 1960, s.2(2).

19. 1973 Act, s.182(2)(a).

20. D. L. Mathieson, *Industrial Law in New Zealand* (Wellington 1970) p.233.

21. 1960 Act, s.3(2).

22. ibid., s.3(3).

23. Mathieson, op.cit., p.234.

24. ibid., p.233.

25. 1960 Act, s.3(4).

26. See H. H. Wellington, *Labor and the Legal Process* (New Haven 1968) pp.218-19.

27. S. E. Morrison and H. S. Commager, *The Growth of the American Republic 1865-1950* (New York 1950) p.217, quoted in Wellington, op.cit., p.219.

28. Wellington, op.cit., p.219.

29. J. Tanenhaus, 'Organised Labor's Political Spending: The Law and its Consequences' (1954) 16 *J. Politics* 441.

30. This provision, amending the Federal Corrupt Practices Act of 1925, lasted only for the duration of the War.

31. See Rehmus and McLaughlin, op.cit., pp.160-84.

32. 352 U.S. 567 at 580.

33. s.304, amending s.313 of the Federal Corrupt Practices Act of 1925.

34. ibid.

35. 93 Cong. Rec. 6439 (1947), quoted in *Pipefitters Local Union No.562* v. *United States*, 407 U.S. 385 (1972).

36. 93 Cong. Rec. 6440 (1947), quoted in *Pipefitters*, ibid.
37. 335 U.S. 106 (1948).
38. ibid. at 115.
39. 352 U.S. 567 (1957).
40. 407 U.S. 385 (1972).
41. ibid. at 406.
42. See Rehmus and McLaughlin, op.cit., pp.202-22.
43. See Scott and Hrebenar, op.cit., p.191. Between 1972 and 1976, for example, the Auto Workers donated over $2m for election purposes. Maritime unions, the steelworkers, and the machinists also made substantial direct contributions.
44. 335 U.S. at 121.
45. 352 U.S. at 589.
46. ibid. at 591-2.
47. Quoted in Wellington, op.cit., p.231.
48. R. M. Cohen, 'Of Politics, Pipefitters and Section 610: Union Political Contributions in Modern Context' (1973) 51 *Texas Law Rev.* 936 at p.947.
49. *United States* v. *Painters Local 481*, 172 F. 2d 854 (1949).
50. *United States* v. *Construction and General Laborers Local 264*, 101 F. Supp. 869 (1951).
51. 367 U.S. 740 (1961).
52. 351 U.S. 225 (1956).
53. 367 U.S. at 776.
54. ibid. at 771.
55. ibid. at 774-5.
56. ibid. at 775.
57. 373 U.S. 113 (1963).
58. ibid. at 123-4.
59. ibid. at 123.
60. 431 U.S. 209 (1977).
61. ibid. at 234-5.
62. ibid. at 235-6.
63. ibid. at 237.
64. 371 F. Supp. 754 (1973).
65. 323 U.S. 192 (1944).
66. These plans are fully discussed in N. E. Nelson, 'Union Dues and Political Spending' (1977) 28 *Labor Law J.* 109.
67. ibid., pp.115-16.
68. It appears however that the State, County and Municipal Employees provide for independent review in the case of non-member agency fee payers. See Nelson, op.cit., p.114.
69. See *Reid* v. *UAW* 479 F. 2d 517 (1973) and *Seay* v. *McDonnell Douglas Corporation* 371 F. Supp. 754 (1973).
70. *Seay* v. *McDonnell Douglas*.
71. 407 U.S. 385 at 414-15.
72. 2 U.S.C. s.441b(b)(2).
73. ibid.
74. 457 F. Supp. 1102 (1978). At the 1976 federal election the National Education Association P.A.C. donated $752,272.
75. [1980] I.R.L.R. 307.
76. 457 F. Supp. 1102 at 1109-10.
77. (1964) 41 D.L.R. (2d) 1.
78. [1925] A.C. 396.
79. (1964) 41 D.L.R. (2d) at 12.
80. ibid.
81. ibid., esp. per Judson J. at 18-19.
82. *Canadian Industrial Relations*. The Report of the Task Force on Labour Relations (Ottawa 1968) para.516.
83. ibid., para.518. See also E. E. Palmer, *Responsible Decision-Making in Democratic Trade Unions*, Task Force on Labour Relations Study No.11 (Ottawa 1968) pp.120-4.
84. (1959) 103 C.L.R. 30.
85. R. M. Martin, *Trade Unions in Australia* (Victoria 1975) pp.28-9.
86. Australian Constitution, s.51 (xxxv).
87. (1908) 6 C.L.R. 469.
88. [1907] 1 K.B. 361.
89. (1908) 6 C.L.R. at 589.
90. (1914) 13 A.R. 279.
91. (1918) 18 S.R. (N.S.W.) 202.
92. *True* v. *Australian Coal and Shale Employees Federation Union of Workers, W.A. Branch* (1949) 51 W.A.L.R. 73.
93. ibid. at 76.
94. 1915 Act, s.4.
95. 1961 Act, s.5.
96. 1940 Act, s.107. Similar provisions were originally enacted in

Industrial Arbitration (Amendment) Act 1918, s.52A. However, that measure was repealed in 1926 but re-enacted in 1940.

97. ibid., s.107(1).
98. ibid., s.107(2).
99. ibid., s.107(1)(c).
100. (1933) 32 C.A.R. 443.
101. ibid. at 450.
102. (1938) 39 C.A.R. 319.
103. ibid. at 319.
104. The present law, to be found in s.140 of the Conciliation and Arbitration Act 1904, provides that the rules of a registered organisation should not be contrary to law or impose conditions, obligations or restrictions which are oppressive, unreasonable or unjust.
105. (1951) 73 C.A.R. 18.
106. ibid. at 21.
107. [1950] Ch.602.
108. 1912 S.C. 534.
109. (1959) 103 C.L.R. at 66.
110. (1948) 61 C.A.R. 726.
111. See the discussion in Martin, op.cit., p.28.
112. See R. C. Tadgell, (1960) 2 M.U.L.R. 405 at p.412.
113. Martin, op.cit., p.54.
114. See D. W. Rawson, 'Unions and Politics', loc.cit., p.181.
115. D. W. Rawson, *Unions and Unionists in Australia*, pp.91-4.
116. D. W. Rawson, 'Unions and Politics', loc.cit., pp.180-1.
117. D. Plowman, S. Deery and C. Fisher, *Australian Industrial Relations* (Sydney 1980) pp.209-10.
118. See Scott and Hrebenar, op.cit., p.199.
119. On this, see Cohen, op.cit., p.956.
120. D. W. Rawson, *Unions and Unionists in Australia*, p.94.

CHAPTER NINE
Issues for Reform

1. The phrase is used by K. Z. Paltiel, *Political Party Financing in Canada* (Toronto 1970) p.257 in a critique of Canadian electoral law.
2. Hansard Society, *Paying for Politics: The Report of the Commission upon the Financing of Political Parties* (1981) p.64.
3. TUC Parliamentary Committee, Report of Proceedings in Standing Committee C (1913) p.26.
4. See M. Harrison, *Trade Unions and the Labour Party since 1945* (1960) pp.29-30.
5. 737 H.C. Debs. 1361-6.
6. See chapter five, *supra*.
7. Aims, *Trade Union Political Funds* (1978).
8. Donovan Royal Commission, Cmnd. 3623, paras 922-3.
9. ibid., para.923.
10. ibid., para.924.
11. Goldthorpe *et al.*, *The Affluent Worker: Industrial Attitudes and Behaviour* (Cambridge 1970) p.111.
12. Moran, *The Union of Post Office Workers* (1974).
13. ibid., p.91.
14. ibid.
15. Hansard Society, op.cit., p.26.
16. Model Rule 12.
17. Model Rule 7.
18. 746 H.C. Debs. 1-4.
19. *Canadian Industrial Relations.* The Report of the Task Force on Industrial Relations (Ottawa 1968). See chapter 8, *supra*.
20. See A. Rowe, 'Conservatives and Trade Unionists' in Z. Layton-Henry, *Conservative Party Politics* (1980) p.210.
21. [1980] I.C.R. 662.
22. ibid. at 670-1.
23. TUC Parliamentary Committee, Report of Proceedings in Standing Committee C (1913) pp.22-3.
24. See *The Times*, 7 January 1982. See also 949 H.C. Debs. 986-94.
25. Donovan Royal Commission, paras 658-69.
26. R. Kidner, 'Trade Union Political Fund Rules' (1980) 31 N.I.L.Q. 3.

TABLE OF CASES

TABLE OF STATUTES
AND REGULATIONS

TABLE OF DECISIONS

INDEX